PSYCHOLOGY SORTED BOOK 1 – CORE APPROACHES

Key research for students and teachers

Second edition

Laura Swash & Claire Neeson

PSYCHOLOGY SORTED - BOOK 1
SECOND EDITION

However, this book is primarily written for IB Diploma psychology students and their teachers. The layout is organised around the IB Diploma psychology guide, and the topics and content are specially chosen to be relevant to the curriculum. Nonetheless, other psychology students and teachers will also benefit from the breadth and depth of the clear layout, cross-topic links and detailed key studies.

This second edition of Book 1 is updated to include material added by the IB in December 2019

Dedications:

To Max, Louis and Joseph, my three fantastic boys. Claire

With thanks to all those who have bought our books. Laura

PSYCHOLOGY SORTED - BOOK 1
SECOND EDITION

CONTENTS

Page

INTRODUCTION 1

BIOLOGICAL APPROACH 3

Overview 3

1. Relationship between the brain and behaviour 4

2. Hormones and pheromones and their effects on behaviour 12

3. Relationship between genetics and behaviour 15

4. Role of animal research in understanding human behaviour 19

KEY STUDIES 27

1. Relationship between brain and behaviour 27

   Techniques used to study the brain in relation to behaviour 27

   Localization of function 33

   Neuroplasticity 38

   Neurotransmitters and their effects on behaviour 45

2. Hormones and pheromones and their effects on behaviour 61

   Hormones and their effects on behaviour 61

   Pheromones and their effects on behaviour 72

3. Relationship between genetics and behaviour 79

   Genes and their effects on behaviour 79

   Genetic similarity 85

   Evolutionary explanation for behaviour 90

4. Role of animal research in understanding human behaviour 97

i

Page

Value of animal models in research to provide insight into human behaviour — 97

Ethical considerations in animal research — 114

COGNITIVE APPROACH — 123

Overview — 123

1. Cognitive processing — 124

2. Reliability of cognitive processes — 128

3. Emotion and cognition — 131

4. Cognitive processing in a technological world — 133

KEY STUDIES — 139

1. Cognitive processing — 139

  Models of memory — 139

  Schema theory — 148

  Thinking and decision-making — 154

2. Reliability of cognitive processes — 168

  Reconstructive memory — 168

  Biases in thinking and decision-making — 174

3. Emotion and cognition — 178

  The influence of emotion on cognitive processes — 178

4. Cognitive processing in a technological (digital/modern) world — 190

  The influence of technologies on cognitive processes — 190

  Methods used to study the interaction between technologies and cognitive Processes — 203

Page

SOCIOCULTURAL APPROACH 207

Overview 207

1. The individual and the group 208

2. Cultural origins of behaviour and cognition 212

3. Cultural influences on individual behaviour 214

4. The influence of globalization on individual behaviour 218

KEY STUDIES 223

1. The individual and the group 223

Social identity theory 223

Social cognitive theory 228

Formation of stereotypes and their effects on behaviour 235

2. Cultural origins of behaviour and cognition 248

Culture and its influence on behaviour and cognition 248

Cultural dimensions 260

3. Cultural influences on individual behaviour 268

Enculturation 268

Acculturation 274

4. The influence of globalization on individual behaviour 283

The effect of the interaction of local and global influences on behaviour 283

Methods used to study the influence of globalization on behaviour 283

BIBLIOGRAPHY 291

BOOK 1 – CORE APPROACHES
Key research to support students and teachers

INTRODUCTION

This is Edition 2 of *Psychology Sorted.* It has been updated to include material added by the IB since our first edition was published. The changes are very few, and it remains a book for teachers and students that is structured to help you use examples of the wealth of psychological research that is relevant to the IB Diploma Psychology syllabus. These are just recommendations based on the knowledge of two highly experienced IB Diploma Psychology teachers, who know how teachers and students struggle to find, understand and summarise original research so it may be used to answer questions. The IB always takes the approach that any relevant research is acceptable, but this freedom also leads to anxiety regarding which to choose as 'most relevant' and how to not become swamped by all the research that is available.

It has been presumed by some that to produce a list of studies that others have used successfully over the years in their psychology courses is somehow to be unnecessarily restrictive. On the contrary, it releases teachers' time for creative use of these resources; it also encourages students to look at the background to the theories and explore the philosophical differences between the different approaches.

HOW TO USE THIS BOOK

Each chapter in the book comprises a one-page overview of each core psychological approach followed by a structured layout of topics, content and author-recommended studies, in a table format, that also includes links to other areas of the psychology curriculum. Use the tables to identify studies that are relevant to the approaches and option(s) and use them to structure learning. This linked approach reduces the content and allows it to be used to meet different learning outcomes. The studies are split into *classic, critique/extension* and *recent* categories, to give a feel for how thinking is debated and has progressed on the key issues. You do not have to use all of the studies recommended; you can dip in and out as you please. Further resources that are easily accessible for reading/watching at home come after every table, with QR codes to enable easy access by mobile devices.

Each chapter ends with key study summaries of every study in the tables, organised by their main content use and links to other areas. This allows for advance curriculum planning that exploits the overlaps between the core approaches and the options. Each study is summarised clearly, with the aim of the study, participants, procedure, results and conclusion, reducing teacher workload considerably. A brief summary, evaluation of the study and an example of critical thinking for each topic area are also given. Again, the evaluation and critical thinking is only an example, and students should be encouraged to develop their own.

PSYCHOLOGY SORTED - BOOK 1
SECOND EDITION

Book 1 is devoted to the core approaches – biological, cognitive and sociocultural.

Book 2 comprises the options – abnormal psychology, development, health and human relationships.

When planning a topic using the books look at the content areas and the recommended studies, check the relevance to your option(s) and use what suits you best. For example, if you are studying the abnormal psychology and human relationships options, then go through the last 'links to' column in each overview grid, to see what is relevant from other parts of the psychology curriculum. For example, from the biological overview grid you will be reminded to use Fisher et al.'s research when studying or teaching the human relationships option.

Content	Research	Use in Biological Approach	Links to
Techniques used to study the brain in relation to behaviour.	Classic **Fisher et al. (2005)** – fMRI **Maguire (2000)** – MRI scan. (Also see localization and neuroplasticity).	Draw out the differences between the MRI scans of brain structure and the fMRI scans of brain activity.	**Human Relationships:** Fisher et al. used fMRI scanning in a small-scale study to investigate brain regions associated with 'being in love'.

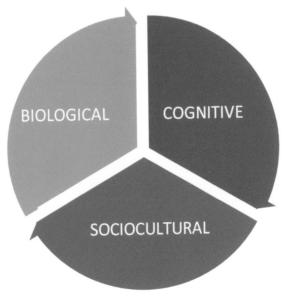

The Core Approaches

Biological Approach

 Ethics

 Methods

Relationship between brain and behaviour	Hormones and pheromones and their effects on behaviour	Relationship between genetics and behaviour	Role of animal research in understanding human behaviour

Techniques used to study the brain in relation to behaviour

Hormones and their effects on behaviour

Genes and their effects on behaviour

Value of animal models in research to provide insight into human behaviour

Localization of function

Pheromones and their effects on behaviour

Genetic similarity

Neuroplasticity

Contrast

Outline

Evolutionary explanation for behaviour

Ethical **consider-** ations in animal research

Neuro-transmitters and their effects on behaviour

Describe

Discuss

To what extent?

Evaluate

Explain

BIOLOGICAL APPROACH

Topic 1: Relationship between the brain and behaviour

Key idea: There is a correlation between brain structure/activity and human behaviour. A change in one will lead us to expect a change in the other.

Content	Research	Use in Biological Approach	Links to
Techniques used to study the brain in relation to behaviour	Classic **Fisher et al. (2005)** – fMRI **Maguire (2000)** – MRI scan. (Also see localization and neuroplasticity).	Draw out the differences between the MRI scans of brain structure and the fMRI scans of brain activity.	**Human Relationships.** Fisher et al. used fMRI scanning in a small-scale study to investigate brain regions associated with 'being in love'.
	Critique/Extension **Bennett and Miller (2010)** – investigation into reliability of fMRI findings	Challenges of reliable fMRI scanning and number of 'false positives'. Interpretation of scans takes experience and skill.	
	Recent **Thomas & Baker (2012)** challenges results of MRI studies of training-dependent neuroplasticity.	Use of MRI in training-dependent neuroplasticity research has some problems based mainly on specificity of task, replicability and robustness of design and statistics.	**Neuroplasticity.** Can training in one specific task show in structural changes in brain regions?

Further resources

BBC Radio Discovery series (2007). Interesting summary of brain scanning and ethics of its use. http://www.bbc.co.uk/programmes/b007mhxl

Sample, I. (21 Nov 2016). Tests raise hopes for radical new therapy for phobias and PTSD. (Article on fMRI decoded neural feedback as treatment for phobias and PTSD.) *The Guardian* https://tinyurl.com/ja342e7

BBC Radio Discovery.
Brain Scanning

BIOLOGICAL APPROACH

Topic 1: Relationship between the brain and behaviour

Key idea: There is a correlation between brain structure/activity and human behaviour. A change in one will lead us to expect a change in the other.

Content	Research	Use in Biological Approach	Links to
Localization of function	Classic **Maguire (2000)** also see techniques used to study the brain and neuroplasticity.	Correlation between spatial memory (learning of routes) and size of the posterior right hippocampus suggests localization of this function.	**Human Relationships**: Fisher et al. used fMRI scanning in a small-scale study to investigate brain regions associated with 'being in love'.
	Critique/Extension **Tremblay, Dick & Small (2013)**	Language function is distributed in the brain. Contradicts the theories of Broca and Wernicke that language comprehension and production are localized in two designated areas of the brain. Theory of distribution of function can be traced back to Lashley (1930). The modern Human Connectome Project (2010) is based on this theory.	**Techniques used to study the brain.** The use of the fMRI method.
	Recent **Schmaal et al. (2016)** – correlation between changes in hippocampus and amygdala and major depressive disorder.	Suggests localization of MDD in limbic system, though does not rule out effects elsewhere in brain.	**Abnormal Psychology**: Huge meta-analysis of MRI data showed that MDD in some cases, but not all, is correlated with a decrease in size in the hippocampus and amygdala.

Further resources *(both of these are also relevant for neuroplasticity)*
BBC Radio All in the Mind series (2017). Adolescent brain.
http://www.bbc.co.uk/programmes/b0832fq5

TED talk by Sarah-Jayne Blakemore (2012). The mysterious workings of the
adolescent brain. https://tinyurl.com/pab6vub

BBC All in the Mind

All in in the brain or all in the mind?
Cc.image adapted from pixabay.com

Topic 1: Relationship between the brain and behaviour
Key idea: There is a correlation between brain structure/activity and human behaviour. A change in one will lead us to expect a change in the other.

Content	Research	Use in Biological Approach	Links to
Neuroplasticity	Classic **Gotgay et al. (2004)**	**Research which covered neural pruning (the process whereby neurons and synaptic connections that are no longer used are eliminated) and neural networks (the map of synaptic connections, including neural branching).**	**Biological approach:** Neural networks and neural pruning. **Development: Developing as a learner** - brain development.
	Classic **Maguire (2000) –** also see techniques used to study the brain and localization.	Correlation between spatial memory (learning of routes) and changes in the posterior hippocampi suggest neuroplasticity in response to learning.	**Biological approach:** Neural networks and neural pruning.
	Critique/Extension **HM (Milner & Corkin, 1968; Corkin, 1997) -** could also be used for localization of brain function.	There is no counter-argument to the *existence* of neuroplasticity. However, this case study and the reported findings show the limits of it: a severely damaged hippocampus does not regrow and therefore cannot be used to organise short-term memories.	

Content	Research	Use in Biological Approach	Links to
	Recent **Luby et al. (2013)**	Exposure to poverty in early childhood impacts cognitive development by school age, showing neuroplasticity of the brain. These effects are mediated positively by good caregiving and negatively by stressful life events.	**Development:** The influence of poverty/socio-economic status on cognitive and social development. How resilience can be developed through good caregiving.

Further resources

BBC *All in the Mind* series (2017). New brain cells and depression. http://www.bbc.co.uk/programmes/b08v09y4

TED talk by Jocelyne Bloch (2015). The brain may be able to repair itself – with help.   https://tinyurl.com/zoztysv

TED talk by Sandrine Thuret

TED talk by Sandrine Thuret (2015). 'You can grow new brain cells. Here's how.' https://tinyurl.com/q2k3cnj

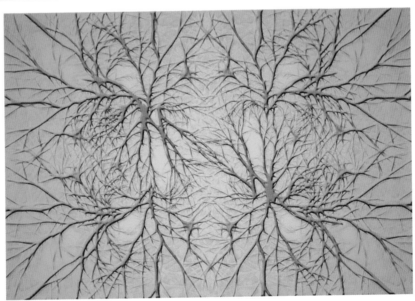

Neural networks and dendritic branching
Cc. image from pixabay.com

BIOLOGICAL APPROACH

Topic 1: Relationship between the brain and behaviour

Key idea: There is a correlation between brain structure/activity and human behaviour. A change in one will lead us to expect a change in the other.

Content	Research	Use in Biological Approach	Links to
Neurotransmitters and their effects on behaviour. **A. Dopamine - role in motivation**	Classic **Fisher et al. (2005)**	Early stage, intense romantic love is associated with activity in subcortical dopamine-rich regions associated with motivation.	**Biological Approach:** Techniques used to study the brain - Fisher et al. used fMRI scanning. **Human Relationships:** Fisher et al. used fMRI scanning in a small-scale study to investigate brain regions associated with 'being in love'. Found dopamine to be associated with the motivation that drives us towards another.
	Critique/Extension **Volkow et al. (2004)**	Drug addiction results in a large and fast increase of dopamine that exceeds the increase produced by other pleasures. This works through the mesolimbic (reward) pathway and results in *incentive salience* (motivation to repeat the act).	**Health:** Part of biological argument for addiction. Could be used to critique cognitive and sociocultural research and to help create a biopsychosocial argument.

Content	Research	Use in Biological Approach	Links to
A. Dopamine (cont'd) - role in motivation	Recent **Guo et al. (2014)**	Opportunistic eating behaviour and BMI were both positively associated with dopamine in the dorsal and lateral striatum, whereas BMI was negatively associated with dopamine in the ventromedial striatum. These results suggest that obese people have alterations in dopamine neuro- circuits that may increase their motivation to overeat while at the same time making food intake less rewarding, less goal-directed, and more habitual.	**Excitatory synapse:** the agonist dopamine binds to the receptor neurons and creates a action potential. **Health:** Part of biological argument for obesity. Could be used to critique cognitive and sociocultural research and to help create a biopsychosocial argument.
	Extension **Romach et al. (1999)**	Looks at the link between dopamine and addiction to cocaine, particularly in the ways that dopamine may reinforce (strengthen) the craving for the drug and how the dopamine antagonist ecopipam might be used to treat dependence on cocaine.	**The effect of an antagonist on human behaviour**
B. Serotonin	Classic **Crockett et al. (2010)**	High levels of serotonin promote prosocial behaviour. Tested by using SSRI agonist citalopram.	**The effect of an agonist on behaviour.** **Human Relationships**: Biological explanation for prosocial behaviour.

Content	Research	Use in Biological Approach	Links to
B. Serotonin (cont'd)	Critique **Chan & Harris (2011)**	Effect of serotonin was to make participants more *emotionally* engaged with a dilemma, short- circuiting what Crockett claims is moral and prosocial behaviour.	**Human Relationships:** Argument that serotonin *reduces* attention to fairness - focusing attention on the desire to do no direct personal harm.
	Recent **Young (2013)**	Accepts that serotonin results in prosocial behaviour and suggests that positive feedback from this encourages more prosocial behaviour and improves mood and subsequent social interactions.	**Abnormal Psychology**: Diathesis-stress model of interaction between biology, cognition and environment.
C. GABA (Gamma-aminobutyric acid)	Extension **Streeter et al (2010)**	GABA is the main inhibitory neurotransmitter, which means it decreases the receptor neuron's action potential, and therefore makes the synapse inhibitory, and the neurons nearby will not act. It has been associated with relieving anxiety, improving sleep and helping with ADHD. Found that yoga increased GABA levels	**Inhibitory synapse:** the neurotransmitter GABA binds to the receptor neurons and decreases their action potential.

Further resources

Guardian newspaper article (03 Feb 2013). The unsexy truth about dopamine. https://www.theguardian.com/science/2013/feb/03/dopamine-the-unsexy-truth

TED talk by Molly Crockett (2012). Beware of neurobunk. https://www.ted.com/talks/molly_crockett_beware_neuro_bunk

Guardian. Dopamine - the unsexy truth

BIOLOGICAL APPROACH

Topic 2: Hormones and pheromones and their effects on behaviour

Key idea: There is a correlation between hormonal and pheromonal activity and human behaviour.

Content	Research	Use in Biological Approach	Links to
Hormones and their effects on behaviour **A. Cortisol**	Classic **Fernald & Gunnar (2009)**	A poverty-alleviation programme lowered levels of the stress hormone cortisol in poor children aged 2-6 years old, especially in those whose mothers also had depression.	**Development:** The effect of poverty/SES on cognitive development.
	Critique/Extension **Miller et al. (2007)**	Meta-analysis of research into the link between stress and cortisol showed a complex picture of lowered cortisol in relation to chronic stress, as higher cortisol levels fall over time. This suggests an interaction between time and environment and cortisol secretion.	**Health:** Part of the biological argument for stress.
	Recent **Beesley et al. (2018)**	Elevated cortisol levels upon awakening were a reliable predictor of subsequent anxiety in family members of adult ICU patients.	**Health:** Elevated cortisol levels associated with stress and later anxiety.
B. Testosterone	Classic **Zak et al. (2009)**	In the behavioural economics' Ultimatum Game, men with artificially raised testosterone, when compared to themselves on placebo, were 27% less generous towards strangers with money they controlled.	**Development:** Role of testosterone in puberty.
	Critique/Extension **Inoue et al. (2017)**	Testosterone has a variable effect, depending on a man's social status: it may enhance socially dominant behaviour among high-status males, but lead to strategic submission to seniority among lower status males.	

Content	Research	Use in Biological Approach	Links to
	Recent **Nave et al. (2017)**	One-off doses of testosterone lead to an increase in impulsivity and a reduction in cognitive reflection. These effects could underlie the already-documented rise in dominance or aggression.	**Human relationships:** Biological explanation for origins of conflict amongst male groups.

Further resources

BBC news article (2009). Testosterone link to aggression 'all in the mind.'
http://news.bbc.co.uk/1/hi/health/8400172.stm

TED talk by Nadine Burke Harris (2014). How childhood trauma affects health across a lifetime. https://tinyurl.com/op5odrb

*TED Talk.
Childhood trauma
and health*

Trauma can last a lifetime
(Image a composite of two CC licensed images from Pixabay.com)

BIOLOGICAL APPROACH
Topic 2: Hormones and pheromones and their effects on behaviour
Key idea: There is a correlation between hormonal and pheromonal activity and human behaviour.

Content	Research	Use in Biological Approach	Links to
Pheromones and their effects on behaviour	Classic **Zhou et al. (2014)**	Investigated the effect of AND on women and estratetraenol (EST, signalling femaleness) on men and found human visual gender perception was affected by these 'putative' (possible) pheromones.	**Human Relationships**: Biological argument regarding choice of mate.
	Critique/Extension **Wedekind (1995)**	MHC (major histocompatability complex) is a group of genes that, while possibly not pheromones, can be smelt in sweat. If attraction to those with a different MHC from our own is followed by mating (a big 'if'), this maximises the immune responses in offspring, making them stronger.	**Human Relationships**: Biological argument regarding choice of mate.
	Recent **Hare et al. (2017)**	Found that exposure to androstadienone (AND) or estratetraenol (EST) had no effect on gender perception.	

Further resources
TED talk by Tristram D. Wyatt (2013). The smelly mystery of the human pheromone. https://tinyurl.com/jwdlzsj

Wyatt, T.D. (2015). The search for human pheromones: the lost decades and the necessity of returning to first principles. *Proceedings of the Royal Society of Biology,* Vol. 282 http://dx.doi.org/10.1098/rspb.2014.2994

TED talk by Tristram Wyatt

BIOLOGICAL APPROACH

Topic 3: Relationship between genetics and behaviour

Key Idea: It is an interaction between genes and environment that affects human behaviour.

Content	Research	Use in Biological Approach	Links to
Genes and behaviour	Classic **Caspi et al. (2003)**	Looked at the relation between inherited short alleles on the 5HTT serotonin transporter gene and incidences of stress and subsequent depression.	**Abnormal Psychology:** Genetic explanation for inherited predisposition to depression as a response to environmental stressors.
	Critique/Extension **Risch et al. (2009)**	Meta-analysis of 14 research studies into effects on depression of the interaction between the serotonin transporter genotype and stressful life events. Found no relationship between depression and the genotype or stress and the genotype, although there was a relationship between stress and depression.	**Abnormal Psychology:** Critique of genetic argument for depression.
	Recent **Yehuda et al. (2016)**	Demonstrated an epigenetic association between parental trauma of Holocaust survivors' preconception with epigenetic alterations that are evident in both exposed parent and children, providing insight into how severe trauma can have intergenerational effects.	**Health:** Trauma suffered by parents' can result in epigenetic changes that predispose children to a stress response in their own lives

	OR Tobi et al. (2018)	Epigenetic mechanism of DNA methylation in babies born to mothers who were starving during the Dutch Hunger Winter affected their later health and life expectancy.	**Health:** Genetic inheritance explanation for health problems – obesity, diabetes and schizophrenia.

Further resources

New York Times article explaining Tobi et al.'s research findings.
https://www.nytimes.com/2018/01/31/science/dutch-famine-genes.html

NYT article on Tobi et al.

TED talk by Sebastian Seung (2010). I am my connectome.
https://www.ted.com/talks/sebastian_seung

The *University of Utah* has an excellent genetics website. Explore it at
http://learn.genetics.utah.edu/content/epigenetics/

University of Utah genetics website

DNA and depression
(Image a composite of two CC licensed images from Pixabay.com)

BIOLOGICAL APPROACH

Topic 3: Relationship between genetics and behaviour.

Key Idea: It is an interaction between genes and environment that affects human behaviour.

Content	Research	Use in Biological Approach	Links to
Genetic similaritiy	Classic **McGue et al. (2000)**	MZ and DZ male and female twin study into adolescents and the gene- environment interaction in drug addiction.	**Twin study**
	Critique/Extension **Lynskey et al. (2010)**	Review of research using genetic similarities as the basis for investigation into adolescent substance abuse.	**Twin and kinship (family) studies**
	Recent **Christakis & Fowler (2014)**	Friends' genotypes are positively correlated: therefore friends are genetically similar.	

Further resources

A link to one of the world's largest ongoing studies into the interaction between genes and environment. https://www.teds.ac.uk/

Link to largest G x E study

Baggini, J. (19 March 2015). Do your genes determine your entire life? *The Guardian.* https://tinyurl.com/ybu8se7y

Do your genes determine your life?

BIOLOGICAL APPROACH

Topic 3: Relationship between genetics and behaviour

Key Idea: It is an interaction between genes and environment that affects human behaviour.

Content	Research	Use in Biological Approach	Links to
Evolutionary explanation for behaviour	Classic **Singh (1993)**	Males choose female partners whose small (0.7) waist-to-hip ratio suggests fertility.	**Human Relationships**: Evolution and long-term mate choice. Males prefer young, healthy and fertile females; females prefer older and financially stable men.
	Critique/Extension **Dixson (2016)**	Review of research suggests preferred waist-to-hip ratio varies cross- culturally.	
	Recent **Conroy-Beam & Buss (2016)**	Stated mate preferences have a causal role in real-life mate choices.	

Further resources

TED talk by Denis Dutton (2010). A Darwinian theory of beauty.
https://www.ted.com/talks/denis_dutton_a_darwinian_theory_of_beauty

TED talk by Anjan Chatterjee (2016). How your brain decides what is beautiful.
https://tinyurl.com/y8j3wa6y

Youtube talk by David Buss. The evolution of human mating.
https://www.youtube.com/watch?v=3aJoxZD-6Z0

TED talk by Denis Dutton

Buss. The evolution of human mating

BIOLOGICAL APPROACH
Topic 4 (HL extension): The role of animal research in understanding human behaviour.
Key Idea: To what extent the results of animal research can be generalised to give insight into human behaviour.

Content	Research	Use in Biological Approach	Links to
The value of animal models in research to provide insight into human behaviour. **A. The relationship between the brain and behaviour.** *Example:* **neuroplasticity.**	Classic **Rosenzweig *et al*. (1972)**	Study into neuroplasticity of rats' brain in response to environmental stimuli.	**Development:** the influence of poverty/socio-economic status on cognitive development. See Luby et al. (2013).
	Critique/Extension **Wexler (2010)**	Main difference between animals and humans is the *extent* to which neuroplasticity occurs in humans. It is far greater than in animals.	
	Recent **Murphy et al. (2014)**	Diet also changes the brain in animals and humans.	**Development** (as above). **Health -** Determinants of health and protective factors.

Content	Research	Use in Biological Approach	Links to
B. Hormones and pheromones and their effects on behaviour. *Example:* ***cortisol***	Classic **Barr et al. (2004)**	ACTH and cortisol levels of infant macaque monkeys rose when initially separated from their mother soon after birth, and fell after chronic separation. This effect was intensified by a short allele on the serotonin-transporter gene, showing an interaction between genetic inheritance, stress and hormone effect.	**Health:** Health problems. Biological correlation with separation leading to stress, which raised and then lowered cortisol levels and damaged health, as chronic/repeated stress is associated with a number of disorders.
	Critique/Extension **Shively et al. (2009)**	Review of research into elevated cortisol in monkeys. Concluded that elevated cortisol due to stress resulted in weight gain.	
	Recent **Jackson et al. (2017)**	Long-term stress in humans is related to weight gain around the middle. (Confirming results of animal studies.)	**Health:** Determinants of health, risk factors; health problems, explanations of health problems.

C. Genes and their effects on behaviour.
 	
Examples:
  stress
  genetic
  disease
	Classic
	Weaver et al. (2004)
		Behavioural epigenetics: rat pups raised by nurturing mothers were less sensitive to stress as adults. Deprived pups showed epigenetic changes and later went on to become worse mothers. Acquired epigenetic modifications can be inherited and passed on to offspring; behaviour is not just learnt.	**Development:** Influences on cognitive and social development, the role of nurturing in resilience.

Content	Research	Use in Biological Approach	Links to
C. Genes and their effects on behaviour. (cont'd) *Examples:* **stress** **genetic** **disease** **(cont'd)**	Critique/Extension **Nithianantharajah & Hannan (2006)**	Interaction of genes and environment – environmental enrichment improves outcome in genetic diseases, such as Huntington's in mice.	**Development**: Developing identity-attachment styles affected by genes.
	Recent **Lassi & Tucci (2017)**	Gene-environment interaction influences attachment in mice.	

Further resources

BBC article reporting success of a drug to slow the progress of Huntington's Disease in humans (developed after 30 years of research using animals). http://www.bbc.com/news/health-42308341

See this page on the *University of Utah* website
http://learn.genetics.utah.edu/content/epigenetics/rats/

BBC article on Huntington's Disease

BIOLOGICAL APPROACH

Topic 4 (HL extension): The role of animal research in understanding human behaviour.

Key Idea: To what extent the results of animal research can be generalised to give insight into human behaviour.

Content	Research	Use in Biological Approach	Links to
Ethical considerations in animal research. **A. The relationship between the brain and behaviour.**	Classic **Rosenzweig et al. (1972)**	The rats were killed after the experiment, in order to weigh the cerebral cortex.	**The value of animal models in research to provide insight into human behaviour.** **Development:** The influence of poverty/socio-economic status on cognitive development.
	Critique/Extension **BPS (2012)**	Guidelines for working with animals: **Replace** animals with alternatives. **Reduce** the number of animals used. **Refine** procedures to minimise suffering.	
	Recent **Xu et al. (2015)**	**Refine procedures:** Not only is breeding and keeping animals in cages for research purposes unethical, it means that the results lack ecological validity. Xu et al. used macaque monkeys to investigate the natural occurrence of depression in socially stable groups under natural conditions.	

Content	Research	Use in Biological Approach	Links to
B. Hormones and pheromones and their effects on behaviour.	Classic **Barr et al. (2004)**	Monkeys were forcibly held down to have blood taken to measure ACTH and cortisol levels. Baby monkeys were separated from their mothers after birth.	**The value of animal models in research to provide insight into human behaviour.**
	Critique/Extension **BPS (2012)**	**Refine procedures** to minimise suffering. Use saliva swabs for short-term measurement of cortisol levels, and hair concentration measurement for longer-term measures.	
	Recent **Stanton et al. (2015)**	Investigated the effect of maternal stress on the glucocorticoid levels of infant chimpanzees by examining and measuring fecal glucocorticoid metabolite concentrations of mothers and babies in the wild.	**Health:** Determinants of health – risk factors.
C. Genes and their effects on behaviour.	Classic **Weaver et al. (2004)**	Some new-born rat pups were removed from their birth mothers and 'adopted' by other mothers. Rats were anaesthetised for removal of hippocampal material and for infusions into the brain, and had blood taken regularly and were restrained to induce stress.	**The value of animal models in research to provide insight into human behaviour.**

Content	Research	Use in Biological Approach	Links to
C. Genes and their effects on behaviour (cont'd)	Critique/Extension **BPS (2012)**	**Replace** animals by studies of humans. Instead of stressing animals, choose humans already being treated for stress or depression and investigate heritability in children at time of birth.	
	Recent **Scheinost et al. (2017)**	Summary of human studies into correlation between pre-natal maternal stress and epigenetic changes in the infant. Can be used to demonstrate that mouse studies into maternal stress are no longer necessary.	

Further resources

Graham et al. (1994). Sniffy the virtual rat: simulated operant conditioning. *Behavior Research Methods, Instruments, & Computers* 26 (2), pp. 134-141
https://tinyurl.com/y9d9bc92

Article on Sniffy the Virtual Rat

Nuffield Council on Bioethics (2014). *Genetics and Human Behaviour: the ethical context*, p.63. Excellent summary of issues surrounding research that uses animals. https://tinyurl.com/y9zqsquz

TED talk by Paul Wolpe (2010). It's time to question bio-engineering.
https://tinyurl.com/h5bwe7h

TED talk by Paul Wolpe

Genetically modified sheep help develop treatment for Huntington's disease
(Image a composite of two CC licensed images from Pixabay.com)

Key Studies

The studies in the rest of this chapter are all summaries, in order, of the biological studies named in the overview above, with the Edition 2 updates that extend the biological approach to an understanding of neurons, neural networks and neural pruning. Agonists, antagonists, and their role in excitatory and inhibitory action in the synapses are also introduced, to support students in a deeper understaning of neurotransmitter action.

It is not suggested that you use all of these, but it is a comprehensive and inclusive list that would allow you to teach and study biological psychology at pre-university and year 1 university level. The full reference is given underneath each summary, and virtually all of these are available freely online. Happy reading!

* *

BIOLOGICAL APPROACH KEY STUDIES

TOPIC 1: RELATIONSHIP BETWEEN THE BRAIN AND BEHAVIOUR

Key Idea: There is a correlation between brain structure/activity and human behaviour. A change in one will lead us to expect a change in the other.

Content 1: Techniques used to study the brain in relation to behaviour.

KEY STUDY: *Fisher et al. (2005). Reward, motivation, and emotion systems associated with early-stage intense romantic love.*

Links to
- **Neurotransmitters and their effect on behaviour.** Dopamine contributes to the arousal of being in love.
- **Human Relationships.** Fisher et al. used fMRI scanning in a small-scale study to investigate brain regions associated with 'being in love'.

Brief Summary
An approach to explaining attraction which focuses on the workings of those neurotransmitters, the chemical messengers in the brain, which are responsible for emotional responses to a range of stimuli.

Aim
To investigate the brain systems involved in early-stage intense romantic love.

Participants
10 females and 7 males, who were students at New York State University via a self-selecting sampling method, aged from 18-26 years old (mean age 20). All participants reported being 'in love' (a range of 1-17 months with a mean of 7 months).

Procedure
Participants were placed in an fMRI scanner and shown a photograph of their loved one followed by a distraction task and then a 'neutral' photograph of an acquaintance with whom they had a non-emotional relationship.

Results

Brain area	Associated with specific neurotransmitter	Associated behaviour
Right ventral tegmental areas (midbrain)	Dopamine	Reward and motivation
Right caudate nucleus (midbrain)	Dopamine	Reward and motivation

Conclusion

The results suggest that people in the early, intense stages of romantic love access the areas of the brain most associated with motivation and reward, giving rise to the idea that people become 'addicted to love'. Fisher et al (2005) suggest that dopaminergic reward pathways contribute to the 'general arousal' component of romantic love and that romantic love is primarily a motivation system, rather than an emotion, making it a biological process rather than a cognitive one.

Evaluation of Fisher et al. (2005)

Strengths

✓ This is a highly controlled clinical method of obtaining data and Fisher and her colleagues checked objectivity at every stage of the procedure. This standardised procedure means that the study is replicable, which increases its reliability.

✓ Identification of the reward centre of the brain as being active during the fMRI gives support to the idea that human beings may have evolved a brain system which ensures that they become 'hooked' on an individual, which increases the possibility of them reproducing. This gives Fisher et al.'s theory of love being addictive some validity.

Limitations

X The small sample size of 17 participants means that the results are not very meaningful and may not be robust in terms of statistical analysis. The size of the sample also limits generalisability of the findings.

X It is overly reductionist to use brain scans to determine how romantic love is experienced: there may be a range of other factors involved, such as similarity, same upbringing, shared ideals, cultural influences.

Reference

Fisher, H., Aron, A., Mashek, D. J., Strong, G., Li, H., & Brown, L. L. (2005). Reward, motivation, and emotion systems associated with early-stage intense romantic love. *Journal of Neurophysiology, 94*(1), pp. 327-337.

KEY STUDY: *Bennett & Miller (2010) How reliable are the results from functional magnetic resonance imaging?*

Brief Summary

This study challenges the extent to which fMRI scanning is reliable, citing the number of 'false positives' some research has produced. Interpretation of scans takes experience and skill.

Aim

To investigate the extent to which fMRI scanning is a reliable method for researchers to use when investigating the link between brain and behaviour.

Procedure

This research is in the form of a review article in which the technique of fMRI scanning is assessed in terms of its reliability. The researchers used a range of published psychological literature in order to gain an overview of the state of research using this technology, with the emphasis being on the extent to which the procedures and results of the studies could be said to be reliable.

Main Findings/Comments

Bennett & Miller (2010) point out that there is very little agreement among researchers concerning the precision and accuracy of fMRI scans in relation to behaviour. They argue that this is a huge oversight in terms of conducting research as reliability is the foundation on which scientific knowledge is based. fMRI scans are increasingly being used in therapeutic settings (such as when investigating epilepsy) so their reliability is paramount to successful medical outcomes. However, there may be a range of extraneous factors that could influence the accuracy and precision of the fMRI process.

For example:

- Some machines appear to function better than others given the variety of potential errors in calibration or in response to external factors, such as the light level in the room, which may affect the precision of the measurement. The scanner is a precise device designed to operate within a narrow set of well-defined circumstances. Any deviation from these circumstances will increase interference and decrease the reliability of the measurements.

- Researchers themselves can be a source of error/interference depending on how well they handle the equipment and how knowledgeable they are in their understanding of the findings.

- Participants may introduce a source of error too: their cognitive state will vary over time, with differences in attention and arousal. This means that using the test-retest method for checking reliability may produce different results each time of testing.

- The reliability of fMRI scans has been investigated using correlational analyses which is also not a good test-retest method as it determines the relationship between two variables but not the stability of a single variable over time.

- Sample sizes in fMRI studies have generally been small which reduces the robustness of the data and therefore the reliability of the findings.

Conclusion

Bennett & Miller (2010) argue that sources of error in fMRI scanning should be minimised by the collecting of more data (longer and more complex testing of participants), by increasing sample size and by ensuring that operators have in-depth expertise in using an fMRI scanner.

Evaluation of Bennett & Miller (2010)
Strengths

✓ A review article takes secondary data (previously published research) and provides a general
✓ overview of it, highlighting the most pertinent findings and pointing out the areas in need of attention: this means the researchers have access to a wide range of studies and their accompanying data which is time and cost-effective.
✓ The researchers used a number of studies in their review, increasing the robustness of the quantitative data.

Limitations

X The use of secondary data means that the researchers cannot know the extent of the control involved in the original studies which could limit the reliability of their findings and conclusion.
X It is possible that the researchers may have been affected by confirmation bias when conducting the review of the literature, looking for examples that support their idea that fMRI scans are unreliable. If so, this would affect the credibility of their report.

Reference

Bennett, C. M., & Miller, M. B. (2010). How reliable are the results from functional magnetic resonance imaging? *Annals of the New York Academy of Sciences, 1191*(1), pp. 133-155.

****

KEY STUDY: *Thomas & Baker (2012). Teaching an adult brain new tricks: a critical review of evidence for training-dependent structural plasticity in humans.*

Links to
- **Neuroplasticity.** Can training in one specific task show in structural changes in brain regions?

Brief Summary

Use of MRI in training-dependent neuroplasticity research has some problems based mainly on specificity of task, replicability and robustness of design and statistics.

Aim

To challenge the procedure, findings and statistical analyses of research into training-dependent neuroplasticity.

Participants

The article is a critical review of 20 studies of MRI research that had investigated training-dependent (i.e. participants who learned to juggle; participants who took part in an aerobics programme) changes in brain structure (neuroplasticity). The 20 pieces of research all used healthy adults; they were all longitudinal (from three days up to one year in duration of training) and used participants primarily under the age of 30.

Main findings and comments

- Some of the studies in the sample used hypotheses based on animal studies of training-dependent neuroplasticity which is problematic because: i) human brains are more complex and so require finer detail in the way they are analysed; ii) animal research has used more invasive methods and procedures which could not, ethically, be carried out on human participants, making generalisability an issue.

- Effect size in the studies is very small, particularly when compared to the animal studies, meaning that the evidence they provide is not particularly robust or compelling.

- The authors point out that research in this field must focus on the *specificity* of the task that the participants are being trained in so that when the MRI scans are analysed there can be no doubt that it is *the training itself* that has brought about region-specific plasticity. They argue that 15 of the 16 studies using a control group were not scrupulous in ensuring that the difference between the training group and the control group were controlled sufficiently to justify the claims made by the researchers. Four of the 20 studies did not even use a control group, making comparisons impossible.

▪ Data, according to this review, are not always handled in objective ways: they argue that the split-half method should be used on VBM (voxel-based morphometry) analyses to check for consistency across the scans. They claim that statistical analyses are not applied rigorously enough to the scans, meaning that reliability is compromised.

▪ Studies that have been replicated in terms of their procedure (e.g. Draganski et al., 2004) have not found the same results in terms of which specific brain regions have undergone changes that can be linked to training. This finding means that the 20 studies in the sample are not reliable, as reliability is based on replicating a procedure and finding similar results.

▪ Only half of the 20 studies sampled used a correlational measure as well as MRI analysis. The authors point out that this is a definite oversight as it means that it is difficult for the researchers to claim validity as the neuroplasticity could be as a result of something other than the training.

Conclusion

Research into neuroplasticity does not provide wholly convincing evidence that training can produce changes in specific brain regions. Better experimental design and more rigorous statistical methods are needed.

Evaluation of Thomas & Baker (2012)

Strengths

✓ The article takes a critical and detached view of 20 studies of MRI methodology linked to neuroplasticity, giving the authors a clear and objective overview of the available literature, meaning that they were able to look for common flaws in the studies.

✓ It is important to highlight possible flaws with MRI as it is a costly, time-consuming procedure that must be used by skilled clinicians, both in the operation of the equipment and the subsequent analysis of the scans.

Limitations

X The studies used in the review vary widely: some documented the effects of three days training, some 120 days (the highest being 365 days); some training involved juggling, some involved learning Morse code; some used a sample of 11, some 60 (the highest); some had a mean age of 22, some 66. Using such a disparate set of studies means that it is difficult to find any commonality between studies, which could affect the credibility of the authors' argument.

X The article may suffer from confirmation bias, in which only negative aspects of MRI studies of neuroplasticity are given prominence.

Reference

Thomas, C., & Baker, C. I. (2013). Teaching an adult brain new tricks: a critical review of evidence for training-dependent structural plasticity in humans. *NeuroImage*, *73*, pp. 225-236.

****

Content 2: Localization of function

KEY STUDY: Maguire et al. (2000). Navigation-related structural change in the hippocampi of taxi drivers.

Links to

- **Localization of brain function; neuroplasticity; techniques used to study the brain.** There may be specific brain areas linked to specific functions, which change in response to cognition and the environment.
- **Neural networks and neural pruning.**

Brief Summary

Correlation between spatial memory (learning of routes) and size of the posterior right hippocampus suggests localization of this function.

Aim

To investigate neuroplasticity: the ability of the brain to change in terms of volume of grey matter dependent on learning and experience.

Participants

16 healthy, right-handed male licensed London taxi drivers who had passed 'The Knowledge', a test of spatial memory. The age of the sample ranged from 32-62 years with a mean age of 44. They had all been taxi drivers for at least 18 months, with the longest period of experience being 42 years.

The taxi drivers' MRIs were compared with the pre-existing MRI scans of 50 healthy right-handed males who were not taxi drivers.

Procedure

The participants were placed in an MRI scanner and their brains were scanned. The focus of the scan was to measure the volume of grey matter in the hippocampus of each participant and then to compare it to the scans of the control group. The grey matter was measured using voxel-based morphometry (VBM) that focuses on the density of grey matter and pixel counting (on both the taxi drivers and the control group scans).

Results

The posterior hippocampi, especially in the right hippocampus, of the taxi drivers showed a greater volume of grey matter than that of the controls, who had increased grey matter in their anterior hippocampi compared to the taxi drivers.

Maguire also carried out a correlational analysis and she found that right posterior hippocampal grey matter showed a positive correlation to length of time spent as a taxi driver.

Evaluation of Maguire et al. (2000)

Strengths

✓ This is a highly controlled clinical method of obtaining a good amount of objective data that can then be easily compared and analysed (which Maguire did via three different methods).
✓ The correlational analysis of time spent as a taxi driver linked to increased volume of hippocampal grey matter lends validity to the idea of neuroplasticity due to learning and experience.

Limitations

X Because a correlation cannot show cause-and-effect it is impossible to know whether the taxi drivers already had naturally high levels of hippocampal grey matter. (This may have actually led to them becoming taxi drivers in the first place).
X The results are only generalisable to male, right-handed London taxi drivers: other workers who use spatial navigation on a daily basis should also be tested for similar neuroplasticity.

Reference

Maguire, E. A., Gadian, D. G., Johnsrude, I. S., Good, C. D., Ashburner, J., Frackowiak, R. S., & Frith, C.D. (2000). Navigation-related structural change in the hippocampi of taxi drivers. *Proceedings of the National Academy of Sciences*, *97*(8), pp. 4398-4403.

****

KEY STUDY: *Tremblay, Dick & Small (2013). Functional and structural aging of the speech sensorimotor neural system: functional magnetic resonance imaging evidence.*

Links to
- **Techniques used to study the brain.** The use of the fMRI method.

Brief Summary
This is part of a series of studies looking at how language is distributed through the brain. This contradicts the theories of Broca and Wernicke that language comprehension and production are localized in two specialised areas of the brain. Therefore it contradicts theory of localization.
Theory of distribution of function can be traced back to Lashley (1930) and his unsuccessful search for the engram (a specific part of the brain where learning and memory were localized). The modern Human Connectome Project (2010) is focusing on mapping neural pathways and connectomes (neural networks).

Aim
To investigate aging related to speech perception and production using fMRI scanning to highlight the functional and structural changes in the associated brain areas.

Participants
Younger: 20 healthy, right-handed Americans aged 18-38 years old; 11 female, 9 male.
Older: 19 healthy, right-handed Americans aged 57-70 years old; 11 female, 8 male.

Procedure
The participants were placed into an fMRI scanner and while in the scanner they were each individually shown 120 short video clips of a native English-speaking woman articulating bisyllabic words (nouns). These words were either simple or complex, as measured in terms of whether or not they included a consonant cluster.

Results
From a total of 960 trials the young participants made 15 errors and the old participants made 14 errors (possibly suggesting that for this study the researchers should have used participants older than those aged 57-70 years old). The researchers found that age does not necessarily bring with it changes in the brain areas associated with perception and production of speech. For example, there was no difference in the volume of grey matter seen in the parts of both hemispheres of the young and the old participants. Age-related changes were seen in areas

including the auditory cortex which is linked to hearing. Most age-related changes were localised to specific areas of the brain and are linked to specific tasks. The findings revealed a host of intricate and complex relationships between the structure of the brain and its related functions, some of which contradict earlier neurobiological research.

Conclusion

There may be more to discover in the investigation of ageing and verbal communication regarding structural and functional neural networks.

Evaluation of Tremblay, Dick & Small (2013)

Strengths

- ✓ The study directly compares young participants with older participants, thus providing clear and objective evidence as to which brain regions associated with speech are affected by the aging process.
- ✓ The researchers screened their participants for depression, language and neurological disorders and cognitive functioning: by doing so they were able to reduce the possibility of these factors acting as confounding variables.

Limitations

- X The sample is small and is limited to Americans, thus it is not easy to generalise to a wider demographic.
- X This was a snapshot study, carried out in one testing session: a longitudinal study would provide the researchers with increased data, showing changes over time that would give their findings increased validity.

Reference

Tremblay, P., Dick, A. S., & Small, S. L. (2013). Functional and structural aging of the speech sensorimotor neural system: functional magnetic resonance imaging evidence. *Neurobiology of aging, 34*(8), pp. 1935-1951.

****

KEY STUDY: *Schmaal et al. (2016). Subcortical brain alterations in major depressive disorder: findings from the ENIGMA Major Depressive Disorder working group.*

Links to
- **Techniques used to study the brain.** The use of the fMRI method; localization of brain function.
- **Abnormal Psychology.** Huge meta-analysis of MRI data showed that Major Depressive Disorder (MDD) in some cases, but not all, is correlated with a decrease in size in the hippocampus and amygdala.

Brief Summary

Suggests that MDD may be localised in the limbic system, though it does not rule out effects elsewhere in brain.

Aim

To investigate structural alterations in the brain associated with MDD.

Participants

The researchers used the existing MRI scans of a total of 8,927 participants: 1,728 of whom were suffering from MDD and 7,199 of whom were non-depressed, healthy controls.

Procedure

The researchers used statistical tests (e.g. multiple linear regression) and MRI-specific software to analyse and measure the grey matter in seven different areas of the brain including the amygdala, nucleus accumbens and hippocampus.

Results

The participants with MDD showed 1.24% reduction in their hippocampal grey matter compared to the controls. This was particularly prevalent in participants with early-onset MDD (i.e. MDD which started before the age of 21). The early-onset MDD participants also had less grey matter in the amygdala.

Conclusion

Early-onset MDD may be localised to the hippocampus and amygdala.

Evaluation of Schmaal et al. (2016)

Strengths

✓ This meta-analysis used a huge sample comprising a total of 8,927 individual MRI scans which means that the resulting quantitative data is robust and reliable. Using statistical analyses means that the measure is free of bias and objective which also increases reliability.

✓ The researchers obtained written informed consent from each participant which means that they followed ethical guidelines and did not compromise the privacy of the participants.

Limitations

X The conclusions reached by the researchers are based to some extent on correlations between brain regions and MDD: they cannot provide a cause-and-effect explanation of where MDD may be localised.

X The use of a meta-analysis involves analysing secondary data over which the researchers have had no control: they have no way of ensuring that the MRI scans were carried out properly, with accurately calibrated equipment. This could mean that reliability is compromised somewhat.

Reference

Schmaal, L., Veltman, D. J., van Erp, T. G., Sämann, P. G., Frodl, T., Jahanshad, N., ... & Vernooij, M.W. (2016). Subcortical brain alterations in major depressive disorder: findings from the ENIGMA Major Depressive Disorder working group. *Molecular Psychiatry*, *21*(6), p. 806.

****

Content 3: Neuroplasticity.

KEY STUDY: Gotgay et al. (2004). Dynamic Mapping of Human Cortical Development During Childhood Through Early Adulthood.

Links to

- **Neural networks and neural pruning.**
- **Development. Developing as a learner** - theories of brain development.

Background

Research which covered neural pruning, the process whereby neural networks (neurons and synaptic connections) that are no longer used are eliminated, and neural branching -which extends the network of synapses within the brain.

Aim
To chart brain development using MRI scans in children from age the age of 4 to 21 years.

Participants
13 children and teenagers from the USA. Every two years of the study's duration (10 years per child) the children were scanned using MRI technology, enabling the researchers to amass a large amount of data spanning years of brain development.

Procedure
MRI scans were used to highlight the ways in which the grey matter of the cortex had been affected due to neural pruning, which showed up on the scans as diminished areas (synapses that were no longer used were visible on the scans). Neural branching was evident in the volume of grey matter observed as increasing with age in areas that are linked to cognitive and functional milestones in human development.

Results
The first areas of the brain to mature were those associated with the most basic of functions, such as the motor cortex in the frontal lobe of the brain which controls voluntary movements. Areas that involve spatial orientation and language were the next to develop in the parietal lobes. Areas with more advanced and sophisticated cognitive functioning in the prefrontal cortex develop last (at some point in a person's early 20s).

Conclusion
The brain only reaches full maturity in adulthood, with more emotional and impulsive behaviour (of the type seen in young children) being largely due to the lack of development in the prefrontal cortex, the area of the brain that is in charge of executive functioning (e.g. impulse control, inhibiting of emotional responses). The brain undergoes a systematic process of neural pruning whereby the neural networks which are no longer used are eliminated to make way for the more advanced and sophisticated networks to develop.

Evaluation of Gotgay et al. (2004)

Strengths
- ✓ The use of a longitudinal design in this study means that the researchers were able to track changes over time which increases the internal validity of the research.
- ✓ Using MRI scans to measure brain development is a reliable way of analysing volume of grey matter in the brain as it eliminates researcher bias in the process of obtaining the data and it is a precise and clinical method.

Limitations
- X The use of such objective, clinical methodology means that the study lacks ecological validity and explanatory power: it is not clear as to *why* brain areas develop according to the study's findings,

only that they appear to follow the same pattern.

X   The ways in which the participants of the study functioned as learners was not measured so it is unclear as to how able they were cognitively when compared to their brain development.

Reference
Gotgay, G., Giedd, J., Lusk, L., Hayashi, K., Greenstein, D., Vaituzis, A., Nugent III, T., Herman, D., Clasen, L., Toga, A., Rapoport, J., Thompson, P. (2004). Dynamic Mapping of Human Cortical Development During Childhood Through Early Adulthood. *Proceedings of the National Academy of Sciences, 101*(21), pp. 8174-8179.

****

KEY STUDY: *Maguire et al. (2000). Navigation-related structural change in the hippocampi of taxi drivers.*

See Maguire et al.'s study (above), which looks at the change in the hippocampi of the taxi drivers, with the grey matter in the posterior hippocampus increasing in density through the expansion of neural networks and increase in synapses, and a corresponding atrophy in the anterior hippocampus, presumably due to neural pruning, though Maguire does not explain why this happens.

****

KEY STUDY: *Corkin, (1997). HM's Media Temporal Lobe Lesion: Findings from Magnetic Resonance Imaging.*

Links to
- **Localization of brain function.** Memory appears to be localised to the hippocampus.

Brief Summary
There is no counter-argument to the *existence* of neuroplasticity. However, this case study and the reported findings show the limits of it: a severely damaged hippocampus does not seem to regrow and therefore cannot be used to organise short-term memories. Milner & Scoville (1957) had carried out a case study of HM, employing a range of measures made possible by the longitudinal and in-depth nature of this case study. He was assessed using psychiatric measures such as personality, mood and depression questionnaires as well as interviews with psychiatrists. His scores did not indicate depression, anxiety or psychosis and he communicated a good awareness of his condition (i.e. he did not 'forget' that he was suffering from anterograde amnesia). He completed a standard IQ test on which his score was normal, however his scores on the Wechsler Memory Scale test demonstrated his severe memory

impairment.

Aim
To investigate the case of a brain-damaged patient with reference to the impact such damage had on the patient's memory using MRI scanning.

Participants
This study was carried out over several years and involved just one participant, 'HM' (Henry Molaison), born in 1926 in Connecticut, USA. Having been run over by a bicycle at the age of nine, HM began to experience epileptic fits which became so severe that eventually surgery was the only option left to the doctors as a means of controlling his epilepsy. At the age of 27 HM underwent a bilateral medial temporal lobe re-section, a procedure which involved the removal of about two thirds of his hippocampus. HM's epilepsy improved but a side-effect of the operation was that he suffered extreme anterograde amnesia and partial retrograde amnesia: he totally lost the ability to form new memories while long-term memories from the past remained fairly intact.

Procedure
In 1992 and 1993, when HM was 66 and 67 years old, he underwent MRI scanning.

Results
Corkin (1997) found via her MRI scans of HM that the early surgery carried out on HM as a child had damaged key areas of the brain associated with memory such as the hippocampus and the amygdala in the temporal lobe.

Both scans showed that the lesioning (also called ablation or cutting) of H.M.'s brain was 3cm less than Scoville had estimated. It therefore did not extend as far into the posterior hippocampal region as he thought, although there was surrounding damage, as stated, in the medial temporal lobe. Approximately 50% of the posterior hippocampus on each side remained, but this had shrunk considerably on the right side. Corkin et al. believe this could be due to both the removal of the rest
of the hippocampus, and also to the drugs and continuing (though reduced) epileptic seizures.

Conclusion
Damage to the hippocampus and surrounding areas may be linked to long-term anterograde amnesia.

Evaluation of Milner & Corkin (1968); Corkin (1997)

Strengths

✓ The documenting of this research as a case study involved over 50 years of investigation using both qualitative and quantitative methods (triangulation), generating both reliable and rich data.

✓ HM provided researchers with a unique and extreme case of amnesia which has been used over the years as the yardstick by which to measure and compare other cases of memory loss: much was learnt about the brain and its link to cognition over the course of the study's duration.

Limitations

X The use of a case study does bring with it some possibility of extraneous variables confounding results: it could be that HM's brain was already damaged by his epilepsy; his life in a care home brought him some degree of stress which could also be a source of interference. He was also still on medication, which itself could have caused some brain damage.

X It is possible that continued focus on his condition might have brought HM some distress, which is an ethical consideration the researchers should have kept in mind; as also should the issue of his being fit and able enough to give fully informed consent to being studied.

References

Corkin, S., Amaral, D. G., González, R. G., Johnson, K. A., & Hyman, B. T. (1997). HM's medial temporal lobe lesion: findings from magnetic resonance imaging. *Journal of Neuroscience*, *17*(10), 3964-3979.

Milner, B., Corkin, S., & Teuber, H. L. (1968). Further analysis of the hippocampal amnesic syndrome: 14-year follow-up study of HM. *Neuropsychologia*, *6*(3), pp. 215-234.

****

KEY STUDY: *Luby et al. (2013) The effects of poverty on childhood brain development: the mediating effect of caregiving and stressful life events.*

Links to

- **Neuroplasticity.** The effects of caregiving on brain development.
- **Development.** The influence of poverty/socio-economic status on cognitive and social development. How resilience can be developed through good caregiving.

Brief Summary

Exposure to poverty in early childhood impacts cognitive development by school age, showing neuroplasticity of the brain. These effects are mediated positively by good caregiving and negatively by stressful life events.

Aim

To investigate whether poverty experienced in childhood is shown in delayed brain development and to investigate the extent to which mediating factors may influence early deprivation.

Participants

Children who were already enrolled on a 10-year longitudinal study of Preschool Depression comprised the target population for this study: a sample of 145 children (right-handed) was drawn from this population. The children were from the USA.

Procedure

Prior to being scanned via MRI, the children had undergone regular testing: once a year (for a duration of 3-6 years) the children had taken part in a series of tests aimed at measuring their cognitive, emotional and social aptitudes. The involvement of significant adults in their lives was also recorded (e.g. how close they were to their caregivers) as well as the occurrence of any negative and stressful events in their lives. Once this collection of information had been amassed per child, each one underwent two MRI scans. The whole brain was scanned on one of the MRI sessions and the other MRI session looked only at the hippocampus and the amygdala.

Results

Both the hippocampus and the amygdala showed less white and grey matter in the MRI scans of the children in this study. While both the hippocampus and amygdala showed less development in poverty-affected children the researchers found that in cases where the child experienced positive care there was less negative effect on the hippocampus. Difficult and stressful life events only affected the left hippocampus.

Conclusion

Poverty does appear to have a negative effect on brain development in childhood. The quality of caregiving, however, can mediate against some of these harmful effects.

Evaluation of Luby et al. (2013)

Strengths

✓ The measurement of non-clinical variables prior to the MRI scanning provided the researchers with a great deal of background data (triangulation) which contributed to the internal validity of the study: this means that the researchers could check the behavioural, cognitive, and social measures against the MRI results.

✓ The study's findings highlight the importance of good quality care in childhood. These findings could be used to help children of all economic backgrounds by implementing early intervention strategies for children at risk of not receiving proper caregiving.

Limitations

X Attempting to measure complex variables (e.g. nature of caregiving, behavioural responses) is beset with difficulties as these variables are not exact and may be prone to researchers interpreting them in subjective ways.

X The sample is relatively small and difficult to 44eneraliza from; plus it only represents pre-school children who exhibit symptoms of depression, so it cannot explain how poverty may affect non- depressed children.

Reference

Luby, J., Belden, A., Botteron, K., Marrus, N., Harms, M. P., Babb, C., ... & Barch, D. (2013). The effects of poverty on childhood brain development: the mediating effect of caregiving and stressful life events. *JAMA pediatrics, 167*(12), pp.1135-1142.

****

Content 4: Neurotransmitters and their effects on behaviour.

A. Dopamine

KEY STUDY: *Volkow et al. (2004). Dopamine in drug abuse and addiction: results from imaging studies and treatment implications.*

Links to
- **Health.** Biological argument for addiction. This study could be used to critique cognitive and sociocultural research and to help create a biopsychosocial argument of addictive behaviour.

Brief Summary
Drug addiction results in a large and fast increase of dopamine that exceeds the increase produced by other pleasures. This works through the mesolimbic (reward) pathway and results in *incentive salience* (motivation to repeat the act). The researchers in this study chose to focus on cocaine addiction as it is thought to be the most addictive of narcotics.

Aim
To provide an overview of how PET imaging technology has highlighted differences in dopamine (DA) activity in the brains of cocaine addicts compared to controls.

Main findings/Comments
The research takes the form of a review of the existing literature on the topic and summarises some key findings. The key ideas outlined in this article are as follows:

- Cocaine has been associated with an increase in DA and it is thought to be the most addictive of all narcotics. The researchers were interested in understanding why cocaine has such an addictive quality when compared to a less-abused drug: methylphenatidate (MP), a drug prescribed for children with ADHD, which has a similar effect to cocaine.

- The review article looks at studies that used both PET imaging and/or self-reported feelings of euphoria (feeling 'high') and anticipation about taking the drug.

- Both cocaine and MP are taken up swiftly by the brain but cocaine clears from the brain after 20 minutes compared to 90 minutes for MP. This corresponds to the self-reports of cocaine addicts who say that they tend to take cocaine every 20-30 minutes when on a 'binge'.

- PET scans have highlighted activation in areas rich in DA receptors in cocaine addicts compared to controls.

- One study had participants take MP orally or via injection: the results indicated that orally-taken MP was taken up by the brain slowly and gradually (taking 60 minutes), compared to injected MP which hit the brain within 10 minutes.

- Cocaine addicts may take the drug to make up for a decrease in sensitivity in the pathways of the brain associated with reward: in this way it could be said that their increased desire for the drug was not necessarily due to increased liking of the drug but more as a result of being habituated to it and so needing more of it to achieve the same high.

- One PET study cited in the article showed that cocaine addicts had less activity in DA-rich areas of the brain when taking MP compared to non-addicted controls. The controls also reported feeling high more intensely than the addicts. Taking the MP had an additional effect on the addicts: it induced in them a craving for cocaine that was not reported by the controls.

- PET scans show a decrease in DA receptors in addicts which means that they are less likely to be motivated by and open to primary reinforcers such as food, sex, etc. The salience (the level of awareness for) of non-drug related stimuli appears to decrease in cocaine addicts too.

Conclusion

The researchers conclude that for addicts to break the biological addiction to cocaine there should be improved drug therapy which targets the activity of DA more effectively plus a re-training of DA function so that natural and non-drug related activities provide as much stimulation and motivation as cocaine does for them.

Evaluation of Volkow et al. (2004)

Strengths

✓ The article is able to take a broad overview of the topic, drawing from a range of studies, examining results and forming a conclusion that is objective and far-reaching.

✓ Using studies that include self-reports from the participants adds validity to the findings as the participants' responses can then be compared to the PET scans to check for corresponding agreement within the findings.

Limitations

X A review is only as good as the original studies it uses: the researchers will have had no control over the ways in which each piece of research was carried out.

X   PET scans cannot show DA as part of neurotransmission, they can only show which cells are more active in specific regions; therefore a cause-effect explanation cannot be made as to the exact function and activation of DA.

Reference

Volkow, N. D., Fowler, J. S., Wang, G. J., & Swanson, J. M. (2004). Dopamine in drug abuse and addiction: results from imaging studies and treatment implications. *Molecular psychiatry, 9*(6), pp. 557.

****

KEY STUDY: *Guo et al. (2014). Striatal dopamine D2-like receptor correlation patterns with human obesity and opportunistic eating behavior*

Link

- **Excitatory synapse.**
- **Health.** Biological explanation for obesity.

Brief Summary

Dopamine works in many areas of the brain and is related to pleasure, motivation, working memory, intelligence, and reasoning. However, it works in different ways in different parts of the brain.

Opportunistic eating behaviour (eating not only when one is hungry but whenever food is available) and body mass index (BMI) are both positively associated with dopamine in the dorsal striatum, whereas BMI is not associated with dopamine in the ventromedial striatum. The levels of dopamine were measured using binding potential of dopamine to receptors (D2BP).

Aim

To investigate the relationship between levels of dopamine in different parts of the brain and the current obesity epidemic.

Participants

Participants were 22 male and 21 female non-smokers between 18–45 years of age. Those with diabetes, recent weight change, a history of drug abuse, neurological, or psychiatric disorders (including eating disorders) were excluded. Women were excluded if they were pregnant, breastfeeding, or post-menopausal. 23 were non-obese, with an average body weight of 67.5 kg, and an average BMI of 22.4. 20 were obese, with an average body weight of 107.4 and a BMI of 36.1. Both groups were an even mix of male and female, but the obese group was older on average (35 yrs.) than the non-obese group (28 yrs.)

Procedure

All participants gave informed consent. Their body fat was measured, they completed the Three-

Factor Eating Questionnaire (TFEQ) and had fasting blood tests for measurement of insulin resistance. The results of the questionnaire showed levels of opportunistic eating, with the higher score indicating the higher rate of opportunistic eating. They were provided with an energy- balanced diet and consumed all meals as inpatients at a health clinic for at least one day prior to measuring D2BP.

During this day, each participant underwent an MRI scan of the brain. On the following day, two hours after a standard breakfast, each participant had a PET scan of his/her brain. The PET scanning was carried out in 3 sessions over 3.5 hours.

Results

Mean measures	Non-obese (N=23)	Obese (N=20)
BMI	22.4	36.1
Caudate D2BP (dorsal striatum)	24.9	28.2 (sig. correlation)
Putamen D2BP (dorsal striatum	27.0	30.7 (sig. correlation)
Accumbens D2BP (ventromedial)	16.7	18.3 (no sig. correlation)
Opportunistic eating	3.9	6.8

Opportunistic eating has been associated with obesity and these results show that opportunistic eating and obesity are positively associated with dopamine binding to receptors D2BP in the dorsal striatum, a region that supports habit formation. This binding at the receptor site causes a voltage change at the receptor site called a postsynaptic potential (PSP). In the dorsal striatum the PSP produced by dopamine is excitatory, resulting in an excitatory synapse.

Therefore, variations in dopamine neurocircuitry in the lateral striatum may play a role in the development of obesity by increasing a person's inclination to opportunistically overeat when food is freely available.

Another hypothesized role for dopamine in obesity centres on the theory that obese individuals overeat to compensate for reduced reward signalling in the brain. The results also offer some support for this theory, since the ventromedial striatum, and the nucleus accumbens in particular, is thought to support motivation to eat. The lack of positive correlation (and in some parts of the ventromedial striatum, a negative correlation) between BMI and binding of dopamine to the D2BP receptors here may reflect decreased reward signalling, which is a feature in common with addiction

Conclusion

These results suggest that obese people have alterations in dopamine neurocircuitry that may increase their motivation to overeat while at the same time making food intake 'less rewarding', 'more habitual', and less directed towards decreasing hunger.

Evaluation of Guo et al. (2014)
Strengths

- ✓ The research looked separately at both BMI and opportunistic eating, instead of assuming that one includes the other.
- ✓ The results were controlled for the age difference between the two groups.
- ✓ The findings could be used in therapeutic settings for treatment of obesity and overeating.

Limitations

- X This is a small study that only showed a correlation and therefore the results do not demonstrate a direct link between overeating and dopamine.

Reference

Guo, J., Kyle Simmons, W., Herscovitch, P., Martin, A. & Hall, K.D. (2014). Striatal dopamine D2-like receptor correlation patterns with human obesity and opportunistic eating behavior. *Molecular Psychiatry, 19* (10), pp. 1078-1084

****

KEY STUDY: *Romach et al. (1999). Attenuation of the Euphoric Effects of Cocaine by the Dopamine D1/D5 Antagonist Ecopipam (SCH 39166).*

Links to

- **Brain and behaviour.** Neurotransmitters and their effects on behaviour - the effect of an antagonist on behaviour.

Brief Summary

Dopamine works in many areas of the brain and is related to pleasure, motivation, working memory, intelligence, and reasoning. However, it works in different ways in different parts of the brain. This study looks at the link between dopamine and addiction to cocaine, particularly in the ways that dopamine may reinforce (strengthen) the craving for the drug and how the dopamine antagonist ecopipam might be used to treat dependence on cocaine.

An antagonist reduces the action of what would normally happen when something binds with the dopamine receptor by blocking the receptor neurons. Dopamine antagonists block the dopamine receptors which prevents dopamine from binding with receptors in the post-synaptic neuron.

Aim

To investigate the function of the dopamine antagonist ecopipam, in the treatment of cocaine dependence in humans.

Participants

15 participants (3 women, 12 men, aged 26-44 years with a mean age of 34 years) who had been diagnosed as having a cocaine dependence but were otherwise in good health. This was a self-selecting (volunteer) sample, with participants having been obtain through newspaper advertisements and in a treatment clinic.

Procedure

The participants were 50eneralizabi for the two-week duration of the study. The procedure used a 50eneraliza double-blind design with participants being given either a placebo or 10 mg, 25 mg, or 100 mg of ecopipam orally on 4 separate occasions. Two hours after the placebo or ecopipam had been taken a single intravenous injection of 30 mg of cocaine was administered to each participant. The participants were continuously assessed by the researchers who were looking for particular subjective (individual) effects of having taken cocaine per participant e.g. blood pressure readings, heart-rate and cardiovascular measurements. Blood samples were also taken both before and after the cocaine doses.

Data collected included the participants rating their response to having taken the cocaine. They reported feelings and sensations such as experiencing a 'high', feeling 'anxious', 'confused', or 'sedated'; saying they'd had a 'good drug effect', 'bad drug effect', and 'desire to take cocaine'.

Results

The dopamine antagonist, ecopipam, reduced the euphoric, 'high' feelings which normally follow a cocaine hit and also reduced the feelings of anxiety associated with taking cocaine. Participants who took ecopipam expressed less desire to use cocaine than those on the placebo. The most effective dosage of ecopipam was found to be between 25mg and 100mg.

Conclusion

Dopamine antagonists such as ecopipam may be effective in reducing both the effects of taking cocaine and the desire to use it, thus helping to eradicate craving for cocaine.

Evaluation of Romach et al. (1999)

Strengths

✓ The use of a double-blind procedure increases validity as it eliminates demand characteristics and researcher bias.

✓ The well-being of the participants was a strong aspect of this study with continual checks being made on their physical and psychological health and the fact that they were 51eneralizabi for the study means that they were taking cocaine in a safe and secure environment.

Limitations

X A sample of 15 participants is small and means that the data lacks robustness plus the findings are difficult to 51eneraliza to a wider demographic.

X There may have been other reasons as to why the ecopipam group reported fewer feelings of euphoria and craving: the unfamiliar hospital environment may have inhibited their usual response; they may have felt nervous about taking part in a study; they may have not enjoyed staying in a hospital; they may have originally been less addicted to cocaine than the placebo group.

Reference

Romach, M.K., Glue, P., Kampman, K. et al. (1999). Attenuation of the Euphoric Effects of Cocaine by the Dopamine D1/D5 Antagonist Ecopipam (SCH 39166). *Archives of General Psychiatry, 56*(12), pp. 1101–1106. Doi:10.1001/archpsyc.56.12.1101

****

B. Serotonin

KEY STUDY: *Crockett et al. (2010). Serotonin selectively influences moral judgement and behaviour through effects on harm aversion.*

Links to
- **Neurotransmitters and their effect on behaviour.** The function of one agonist and its effect on behaviour.
- **Human Relationships**: Biological explanation for prosocial behaviour.

Brief Summary
High levels of serotonin promote prosocial behaviour. An agonist drug (also known as an 'exogenous' agonist as it is not generated inside the body) will produce a response which is typical for a neurotransmitter if the drug binds to and activates the same receptors in the post-synaptic neuron. Some SSRIs, such as the citalopram used in this study, act as agonists for serotonin, because they inhibit the serotonin transporter and prevent the re-uptake of serotonin into the pre-synaptic neuron and **also** act on the serotonin receptor ($5HT_{2B}$).

Aim
To investigate how serotonin directly affects moral judgement by increasing the motivation of participants to help others and their aversion to personally harming others.

Participants
24 males from the Cambridge area of the UK with a mean age of 25.6 years. The participants were screened for psychiatric and neurological disorders before the study began.

Procedure
The participants were given either an anti-depressant drug that works as a selective serotonin reuptake inhibitor (citalopram), a drug used to treat ADHD and OCD or a placebo. The drugs were administered using a double-blind procedure. The first part of the procedure involved participants being asked to make moral judgements about a series of hypothetical scenarios, for example:

- *Would you push someone in front of a train if it meant saving five other people?* This was the emotionally salient 'personal harm' condition.

- *Would you flick a switch so that a train hit one person instead of five?* This was the less emotionally salient 'impersonal harms' condition. There was no time limit on how long the participants spent thinking about each scenario and making their decisions. The responses were measured according to how many times each participant judged that an action was 'acceptable'.

Results

- The emotionally salient personal harm condition (i.e. which involved participants imagining themselves harming someone else directly) produced the lowest number of 'acceptable' responses from all participants. In other words, participants could not agree to intervene personally to harm another person, even if it meant saving others.

- Participants who had been taking the SSRI citalopram (which acts as an agonist for serotonin) were far more likely to say that harmful actions were unacceptable compared to the other two groups. The moral judgements made by the ADHD medication group and the placebo group were roughly similar, showing no great differences.

Conclusion

Serotonin may induce prosocial behaviour and reduce acts of harm towards others. Serotonin agonists may work to help calm and balance mood, having a positive effect on the well-being of the individual and on their behaviour towards others.

Evaluation of Crockett et al. (2010)

Strengths

- ✓ The procedure involved a double-blind allocation of drugs and placebo which increases the validity of the findings as it means that both researchers and participants did not know what drug was being taken, which should eliminate any bias. That is, neither participants nor researchers could act in accordance with expectations as to the effects of the drug.
- ✓ Using a biological approach to measure prosocial behaviour lends some objectivity and reliability to a topic that is notoriously difficult to test scientifically with a reliable measure.

Limitations

- X The small sample size of 24 males, divided among 3 drug conditions, means that the results are not statistically robust and cannot easily be 53eneralizab; gender bias is also an issue.
- X There may be alternative explanations for the moral judgements made by the participants. They may have held religious principles, had individual differences in morality, personal experience related to specific scenarios or displayed social desirability bias.

Reference

Crockett, M. J., Clark, L., Hauser, M. D., & Robbins, T. W. (2010). Serotonin selectively influences moral judgment and behavior through effects on harm aversion. *Proceedings of the National Academy of Sciences, 107*(40), pp. 17433-17438.

* *

KEY STUDY: *Chan & Harris (2011). Moral enhancement and prosocial behaviour.*

Links to
- **Neurotransmitters and their effects on behaviour.** The role of serotonin in moral and prosocial behaviour.

Brief Summary
Effect of serotonin was to make participants more *emotionally* engaged with a dilemma, short-circuiting what Crockett claims is moral and prosocial behaviour.

Aim
To challenge the findings of Crockett et al. (2010) that serotonin influences prosocial behaviour.

Main findings and comments
The article is written as a response to Crockett et al. (2010), with the main ideas as follows:

- The authors take issue with Crockett et al.'s idea that morality is a function of emotional response to a dilemma: they argue that morality is based on *reasoning*. Reasoning may be based on an individual's assessment of their emotional state but, they argue, its outcome will take the form of a rational decision rather than an emotive, chemically-induced response.

- If someone is a moral person who cares about how they treat others then they will weigh up the pros and cons of specific behaviours and apply their own code of ethics to them. In other words, the serotonin alone will not be enough to prompt prosocial behaviour.

- The authors point out that the scenarios used in Crockett et al.'s (2010) study are unrealistic: how often is someone in the position of having to push a stranger under a train? In this way the original study could lack validity as it may not actually be measuring the effects of serotonin on prosocial behaviour.

- The authors use the example of a passenger, on a flight in 2009, who attacked and disarmed a hijacker, saving the lives of all passengers. They argue that if that person had been in a serotonin-induced state then they would have found such an attack unacceptable, thus bringing about the doom of all the passengers and crew. By using this example, they are questioning the essential dilemma behind Crocket et al.'s scenarios: which of the behaviours (i.e. attacking the hijacker/not attacking the hijacker) actually *is* prosocial? By questioning the nature of prosocial behaviour thus, the authors also raise the issue of prosocial behaviour not being the same thing as moral behaviour.

- They finish by urging caution when it comes to prescribing anti-depressants to treat anti-social behaviour disorders as their effects are unpredictable and may even result in *immoral* or *antisocial* behaviours.

Conclusion
A better definition of morality and how moral decisions are made should be reached before any more research into biological influences on moral reasoning or prosocial behaviour is undertaken.

Evaluation of Chan & Harris (2011)
Strengths
✓ The article takes a critical and detached view of Crockett et al.'s findings, which is useful in research because the original study may have been written in a way that was overly subjective or biased. Offering critiques of other researchers' work provides fresh insight into a topic and opens it up for wider debate and possibly further research in that field.
✓ The article identifies something that the original study did not clarify: that both morality and prosocial behaviour are difficult to 55eneralizabili and measure.

Limitations
X The article does not fully address the idea that biology and decision-making may be linked: they ignore some of the findings of the original study.
X Without actually conducting original research themselves, their critique of Crockett et al. (2010) can only exist at a theoretical level as they have not provided any contradictory empirical evidence.

Reference
Chan, S., & Harris, J. (2011). Moral enhancement and pro-social behaviour. *Journal of Medical Ethics, 37* (3), pp.130-131.

****

KEY STUDY: *Young (2013). The effect of raising and lowering tryptophan levels on human mood and behaviour.*

Links to

- **Abnormal Psychology.** Diathesis-stress model of interaction between biology, cognition and environment in relation to serotonin's effects on mood. Revisits the serotonin hypothesis of the etiology of depression with a nuanced approach.

Brief Summary

Accepts that serotonin results in prosocial behaviour and suggests that positive feedback from this encourages more prosocial behaviour and improves mood and subsequent social interactions.

Proposes more investigation of this link in relation to mental disorders.

Aim

To investigate the role played by tryptophan in the regulation of serotonin and, subsequently, mood and prosocial behaviour.

Main findings and comments

The research takes the form of a review article in which a selection of studies on the topic of interest is examined and evaluated in terms of findings and conclusions made by the researchers.

The main points of the review article are outlined as follows:

- Research on the role of serotonin in the treatment of depression has yielded some contradictory results so that it is still not entirely clear how the brain's chemistry is linked to mood regulation.

- Tryptophan has been shown to promote feelings of calm and is likely to produce agreeable andnon-confrontational behaviour, which in turn leads to fewer situations in which disagreement and conflict abound, thus promoting greater prosocial behaviour.

- A study published in 2002 investigated the effect of lowering tryptophan levels in a sample of males and females from 11 different studies. Most findings showed that, independent of the diagnosis of the patients, mood worsened and people became aggressive and irritable when tryptophan was depleted. In other words, the increased aggression was not part of their mental illness (e.g. depressed patients showed a similar increase in aggression to that of patients with anger-based personality disorders).

- Animal research has shown a link between serotonin and behaviour. For example, low serotonin in lobsters is linked to aggressive behaviour; high serotonin levels has been measured in locusts when they swarm.

- Studies using patients with aggressive forms of schizophrenia who were treated with tryptophan. The control group received a placebo. The results were that the tryptophan group's behaviour improved over the course of the 4-week trial, with fewer aggressive incidents and examples of antisocial behaviour. A similar study with 20 psychiatric patients who had previously shown aggressive behaviour showed that tryptophan was more effective than antipsychotic drugs.

- One study found that tryptophan did *not* have an effect on agreeable mood (although it did seem to produce less quarrelsome behaviour). The authors put this down to the fact that because the participants were not depressed or mentally ill, then their mood-related behaviours already demonstrated a high level of agreeability so there was little room for improvement on this score.

- The authors cite research that has investigated the effect of lowered tryptophan on the ability to recognise facial expressions. Some studies showed that female participants low on tryptophan had an inability to 57recognise fearful facial expressions; another study did not find such a result. One study showed a difference in happiness recognition in healthy women compared to those with depression, which was also found in a later study. However, this happiness-recognition was also accompanied by an inability to 57eneraliz disgust – but only in women.

Conclusion

The recognition of the relationship between serotonin and an increase in prosocial behaviour is very recent and really needs to have more research time devoted to it.

Evaluation of Young (2013)

Strengths

✓ A review article is able to take into account the procedure and results of a wide range of studies, triangulating method and data in order to ascertain the relative validity of a theory, and that is apparent in this research.

✓ The authors of the review article are quick to point out flaws in the methodology and/or findings of the studies they use in their article; they appear to have avoided confirmation bias as they take a properly objective look at research on this tricky topic.

Limitations

X   Some of the research findings cited are so inconclusive as to not really be considered worth reporting on. The authors themselves acknowledge that it is relatively easy to operationalise the variable of expression recognition but that studies in this field have not shown either consistent or interesting results.

X   The samples in some of the studies cited (e.g. 12 in one study) are too small to make 58eneralizability possible and some of the studies use a non-depressed sample, which limits the usefulness of the findings in terms of their application to the treatment of depression.

Reference

Young, S. N. (2013). The effect of raising and lowering tryptophan levels on human mood and social behaviour. *Philosophical Transactions of the Royal Society B: Biological Sciences, 368*(1615), 20110375.

****

C. GABA (Gamma-aminobutyric acid)

KEY STUDY: *Streeter et al. (2010). Effects of yoga versus walking on mood, anxiety, and brain GABA levels: a randomized controlled MRS study.*

Links to

- **Inhibitory neurotransmitters and inhibitory synapses**

Brief Summary

An inhibitory synapse is when the synapse has an inhibitory transmitter released from the pre-synaptic neuron that turns the synapse to inhibitory, which decreases the action potential in the post-synaptic neuron and decreases activity in the synapse. GABA (Gamma-aminobutyric acid) is the main inhibitory neurotransmitter, which means it decreases the receptor neuron's action potential, and therefore makes the synapse inhibitory, and the neurons nearby will not act. It has been associated with relieving anxiety, improving sleep and helping with ADHD. Relaxation exercises, meditation and yoga have also been found to increase levels of GABA.

Aim

To investigate whether changes in mood, anxiety, and GABA levels are specific to yoga or related to physical activity.

Participants

The sample consisted of 34 healthy adults. 19 of the participants were randomly allocated to the yoga group; 15 of the participants were randomly allocated to the walking group.

Procedure

They participants took yoga or walking exercise for 60 mins 3 times a week for 12 weeks. Mood and anxiety scales were taken at weeks 0, 4, 8, 12, and before each magnetic resonance spectroscopy (MRS) scan. Scan 1 was at baseline – before the exercise. Scan 2, obtained after the 12-week intervention, was followed by a 60-minute yoga or walking intervention, which was immediately followed by Scan 3.

Results

The yoga group reported greater improvement in mood and greater decreases in anxiety than the walking group. There were positive correlations between improved mood and decreased anxiety and GABA levels in the thalamus. The yoga group had positive correlations between changes in mood scales and changes in GABA levels. The 12-week yoga intervention was associated with greater improvements in mood and anxiety than a metabolically matched walking exercise.

Conclusion

It may be that yoga could be prescribed as an addition to, or even as a replacement for, medication.

Evaluation of Streeter et al. (2010)

Strengths

- ✓ The procedure took place over 12 weeks, making changes in GABA levels and mood easy to measure and to compare to baseline/prior measurements.
- ✓ Using a biological approach involves objective measures as seen in the MRS scans which increases the reliability of the findings.

Limitations

- X It is unclear as to whether the benefits experienced by the yoga group continued after the duration of the study or whether these benefits were based on other factors e.g. personality, personal circumstances.
- X The participants may have under-reported or over-reported their feelings of anxiety and mood as social desirability bias could have influenced their responses

Reference

Streeter, C. C., Whitfield, T. H., Owen, L., Rein, T., Karri, S. K., Yakhkind, A., ... & Jensen, J. E. (2010). Effects of yoga versus walking on mood, anxiety, and brain GABA levels: a randomized controlled MRS study. *The Journal of Alternative and Complementary Medicine*, *16*(11), 1145-1152.

****

CRITICAL THINKING POINTS: THE RELATIONSHIP BETWEEN THE BRAIN AND BEHAVIOUR

Is it possible to draw cause-effect conclusions based on studies using technology?

The use of brain-imaging technology such as fMRI scanners increases the precision and accuracy involved in measuring specific brain functions and structures, and it is an area of psychological research that has received a lot of interest and investment over the past 20 years or so. However, even sophisticated technology cannot provide a flawless explanation of how brain structure and function affect behaviour as there are still too many unknown variables involved. fMRIs and similar technology can only identify correlations between brain and behaviour, and often these correlations are mediated by the environment and/or cognition. Plus, the research often suffers from ambiguity: for example, Crockett et al. (2010) claim an effect between serotonin and prosocial behaviour, but the 8 participants in the serotonin-induced condition may naturally have been more inclined to prosocial behaviour compared to the other two groups (and with such a small sample it is hard to draw firm conclusions). So what we are learning is just how complex the picture is. Is it ever possible to have certainty about something as individual as human behaviour?

How precise are brain scans?

In order to clarify what is being shown, contrasting colours are added to the brain scan images; but this in itself has the effect of exaggerating differences between areas of the brain, and emphasising activity when there is little. And even if we can see activity, it then has to be interpreted and this is a skilled job. As Bennett & Miller (2010) found in their review article on the reliability of fMRI scanning, some machines appear to be more precise than others: there may be a variety of potential errors in calibration or in response to external factors, such as the light level in the room, which may affect the measurement. They also refer to operator error as a potential source of interference stating that reliability of fMRI scanning may depend on how well researchers handle the equipment and how knowledgeable they are in their understanding of the findings.

Isolating variables in research linking the brain and behaviour is not straightforward.

The biological approach often tries to separate out one variable: the influence on behaviour of one neurotransmitter or hormone, for example, Fisher (2005). Her findings linked the experience of being in love with the activation of dopaminergic pathways in the brain linked to reward and motivation. Is it possible to confidently come to a conclusion such as Fisher's? What about all the other variables of age, gender, ethnicity, socio-economic status, physical health, etc? Being in love may be something that has shared features across age, culture etc., but it is also a unique experience in and of itself that surely cannot be explained simply by looking at the activation of one region of the brain.

TOPIC 2: HORMONES AND PHEROMONES AND THEIR EFFECTS ON BEHAVIOUR

Key Idea: There is a correlation between hormonal and pheromonal activity and human behaviour.

Content 1: Hormones and their effects on behaviour.

A. Cortisol

KEY STUDY: *Fernald & Gunnar (2009). Poverty-alleviation program participation and salivary cortisol in very low-income children.*

Links to
- **Development.** The effect of poverty/socio-economic status (SES) on cognitive development.

Brief Summary
A poverty-alleviation programme lowered levels of the stress hormone cortisol in poor children aged 2-6 years old, especially in those whose mothers also had depression. The poverty alleviation programme was *Oportunidades*, which involved impoverished families being awarded cash (to the value of about 25% of household income) on condition that family members followed specific protocols and routines surrounding care in pregnancy, nutrition, getting immunised, education and health interventions.

Aim
To investigate the extent to which participation in a poverty-alleviation programme affects the levels of cortisol in young, impoverished children.

Participants
A sample of families living in rural Mexico was chosen as the target population: each family had to contain at least one child aged between two to six years old. Of the families in the resulting sample 554 children were taking part in the *Oportunidades* programme and 762 children were there for comparison purposes (control condition). The mean age of the children was 13.9 months.

Procedure
A team of researchers visited the families at home and conducted the following measures:
- A one-hour interview with the mother. The mothers were also assessed using a depression

inventory.
- 25-40 minutes of cognitive tests administered to the child/children.
- Cortisol levels were measured via saliva samples at 3 specific time points within the testing session (i.e. over the course of one testing day).

Results

Children who had been participating in the *Oportunidades* programme showed lower salivary cortisol levels than children in the control group. The programme showed significant effects

Evaluation of Fernald & Gunnar (2009)

Strengths

✓ The researchers were careful to ensure that they themselves did not become a confounding variable by inadvertently increasing a child's stress levels by appearing without warning at the family home. Each researcher spent some time with the child prior to testing, trying to make the child feel relaxed, building a rapport with them. In this way the researchers made efforts to ensure the validity of the findings.

✓ This is a large-scale, real-life measurement of the effects of poverty on stress hormones using a programme that was government-funded; therefore the ecological validity is high and the findings are generalisable to impoverished rural communities throughout Mexico and could be used in similar intervention programmes in other countries.

Limitations

X Using a depression inventory to assess the degree of depression in the mothers does not give a full and detailed insight into the exact nature of the emotional state of each woman and is subject to confirmation bias. Confirmation bias could take the form of the researchers only looking for, or focusing on, information that confirms their hypothesis/objective.

X If the positive effects of a poverty-alleviation programme are only apparent for intensely depressed mothers, then what strategies might work for mothers with mild depression that may become more serious with time? This makes the findings of this research only partially useful.

Reference

Fernald, L. C., & Gunnar, M. R. (2009). Poverty-alleviation program participation and salivary cortisol in very low-income children. *Social Science & Medicine*, *68*(12), pp. 2180-2189.

****

KEY STUDY: *Miller et al. (2007). If it goes up, must it come down? Chronic stress and the hypothalamic-pituitary-adrenocortical axis in humans.*

Brief Summary

Meta-analysis of research into the link between stress and cortisol showed a complex picture of lowered cortisol in relation to chronic stress, as raised cortisol reduces over time. This suggests an interaction between time and environment and cortisol secretion.

Aim

To critically assess the findings of research which links chronic stress and the onset of disease as a result of an excess of cortisol.

Participants

This is a meta-analysis of a range of findings spanning 50 years of research that investigates whether disease can be seen as a result of chronic stress. The researchers used 107 studies involving a total of 8,521 participants. 53% of participants were male, 47% were female, and the mean age was 38.39 years.

Main findings and comments

- Research in this field has shown contradictory findings, with some studies linking high cortisol to stress and other studies claiming opposite results (seen particularly in cases of PTSD and extreme stress). This variation in findings may be linked to extraneous variables, such as type of stressor and individual differences within those who encounter the same type of stressor.

- Time onset is one explanation the authors put forward to explain the often confusing and contradictory findings of different researchers. They state that cortisol is generally raised immediately after a stressor is encountered, but that over time the body is able to re-balance cortisol levels, returning to some semblance of homeostasis. Thus, findings which disagree may simply be as a result of most studies being cross-sectional rather than longitudinal: i.e. one study may measure cortisol at a different time point to another study, so cortisol readings will necessarily be conflicting.

- The authors compared all quantitative data and found that individuals with chronic stress secrete lower levels in the morning, with levels increasing throughout the day, which is the opposite pattern for non-stressed individuals (high in the morning and decreasing as the day progresses). Type of stressor and the nature of the threat also showed different and specific time-related cortisol secretion: e.g. in situations triggering a threat to the person's social identity secretion of cortisol was high during most of the day.

- Not all threats elicit the same biological response: e.g. being involved in war compared to going through divorce. This might affect the validity of the findings if the researchers do not specify the type of threat that the stressor poses, (e.g. being killed in combat as opposed to dealing with the emotional and financial fall-out that divorce brings) and with it identify the specific biological response such a stressor triggers.

- When an individual feels that they can exercise some control over their stress, then morning cortisol was found to be higher, which shows the same pattern as that of non-stressed individuals.

- One finding is that PTSD sufferers were found to secrete lower levels of cortisol in the morning and higher levels in the afternoon and evening when compared with healthy adults who have been exposed to identical chronic stress. Participants with PTSD were found to have high amounts of cortisol circulating around their system.

Conclusion

The relationship between chronic stress and disease may not be as straightforward as previously thought as it appears to be influenced by a range of factors such as type of stressor, nature of threat and the individual's response to the stressor.

Evaluation of Miller et al. (2007)

Strengths

✓ The article takes a critical and detached view of 50 years of research into a biological response to stress giving the authors a clear and objective overview of the available literature, meaning that they were able to look for common flaws in the studies.
✓ The huge sample involved and the use of quantitative analysis means that the authors can claim that their research is robust and reliable.

Limitations

X The authors were unable to determine the exact role played by physical threat, trauma exposure, and stress controllability in the experience of stress and the biological responses triggered by them. They acknowledge that such factors overlap both in research and in life.
X The research lacks a qualitative dimension: it can explain *what* but it cannot explain *why*, which to some extent is a crucial element when looking at how individuals experience stress.

Reference
Miller, G. E., Chen, E., & Zhou, E. S. (2007). If it goes up, must it come down? Chronic stress and the hypothalamic-pituitary-adrenocortical axis in humans. *Psychological Bulletin*, *133*(1), pp. 25-45.

****

KEY STUDY: *Beesley et al. (2018.) Acute Physiologic Stress and Subsequent Anxiety Among Family Members of ICU Patients*

Links to
- **Health.** Elevated cortisol levels are associated with stress and later anxiety.

Brief Summary
An elevated cortisol level upon awakening was a reliable predictor of subsequent anxiety in family members of adult patients in a hospital intensive-care unit.

Aim
To investigate cortisol levels to ascertain whether the degree of stress as a biological response would match the psychological levels of stress in people who had a family member in the ICU (intensive-care unit).

Participants
92 people who had a family member in ICU. The mean age was 54 and the participants were 64% female and 36% male. 71% of the participants had lived with the ICU patient before they were admitted to hospital, and 53% were married to the patient.

Procedure
The participants gave five samples of saliva at different times, spanning 24 hours at the time of their relative/spouse being admitted to the ICU (as soon as they woke up, 30 minutes after waking up and before breakfast, 30 minutes before lunch, 30 minutes before dinner and just before bedtime). There was a 3-month follow-up by telephone to ascertain the degree of psychological stress experienced by the participants using a standardised Hospital Anxiety and Depression Scale (HADS).

Results
Cortisol levels were not found to be positively correlated with anxiety generally. However, those cortisol readings taken when the participants first woke up showed a positive correlation with anxiety.

29 participants (32%) reported symptoms of anxiety at the 3 month follow-up session; 15 participants (16%) reported depression symptoms; and 14 participants (15%) reported PTSD symptoms.

Conclusion

By conducting a biological measure of stress in family members of ICU patients it may be possible to put in place interventions to help alleviate their psychological symptoms, (e.g. anxiety, depression).

Evaluation of Beesley et al. (2018)

Strengths

✓ This is a study carried out in real time, using participants involved in a real situation, and therefore ecological validity of the results is high.

✓ Using both a biological measure (cortisol levels) and a psychological measure (HADS) the researchers were able to triangulate both method and data, which should enhance the validity of their findings.

Limitations

X The findings do not distinguish between acute and chronic stress so they can only represent a biological reading relevant to one day's saliva testing: the type of stress each participant was experiencing at the time is unclear.

X The researchers did not collect data relating to other sources of stress in each participant's life, so their results may have been confounded by this uncontrolled variable.

Reference

Beesley, S. J., Hopkins, R. O., Holt-Lunstad, J., Wilson, E. L., Butler, J., Kuttler, K. G. & Hirshberg, E. L. (2018). Acute Physiologic Stress and Subsequent Anxiety Among Family Members of ICU Patients. *Critical Care Medicine*, *46*(2), pp.229-235.

****

B. Testosterone

KEY STUDY: *Zak et al. (2009) Testosterone administration decreases generosity in the ultimatum game.*

Links to
- **Development.** Role of testosterone in puberty.
- **Human Relationships**. Biological approach to explaining prosocial behaviour.

Brief Summary
In the Ultimatum Game from behavioural economics, men with artificially raised testosterone, compared to themselves on placebo, were 27% less generous towards strangers with money they controlled.

Aim
To investigate the role played by testosterone in prosocial behaviour.

Participants
25 males with a mean age of 20.8 years. The ethnic mix was as follows: 44% Asian; 36% Caucasian; 8% Hispanic; 12% other/not stated.

Procedure
A double-blind procedure was used with half the men receiving testosterone in gel form (Androgel) and half the men being given a placebo. Testosterone levels were measured via blood samples during the experimental phase. The participants took part in the Ultimate Game (UG), a decision- making task borrowed from economic theory that involves making decisions as to whether or not to donate money.

Results
The men who had been given Androgel and thus had heightened testosterone were 27% less likely to donate money than their first, pre-experiment baseline measurement suggested. The testosterone group were also less likely to agree to share money compared to their own baseline measurements.

Conclusion
Men with naturally high testosterone levels may exhibit less prosocial behaviour than those with lower testosterone levels.

Evaluation of Zak et al. (2009)

Strengths

✓ Other research has shown similar findings to Zak et al. (2009): i.e. that prosocial behaviour in the form of generosity can be stimulated by hormonal manipulation, which means that this research has concurrent validity.

✓ This is a well-controlled study using objective measures in which quantitative data was collected, which increases the reliability of the findings.

Limitations

X Using only 25 participants in the sample means that the results are difficult to generalise beyond the immediate demographic.

X The use of the UG as the decision-making measure of the procedure may have given rise to artificial behaviour as it was not the participants' own money that was at stake: it is possible that the participants' decisions did not reflect how they would usually behave regarding donating money, thus affecting the external validity of the study.

Reference

Zak, P. J., Kurzban, R., Ahmadi, S., Swerdloff, R. S., Park, J., Efremidze, L., ... & Matzner, W. (2009). Testosterone administration decreases generosity in the ultimatum game. *PloS One*, *4*(12), e8330.

* *

KEY STUDY: *Inoue et al. (2017). Testosterone promotes either dominance or submissiveness in the Ultimatum Game depending on players' social rank.*

Brief Summary

This adds complexity to the argument that testosterone levels signal dominance in males. Instead, this article argues that testosterone has a variable effect, depending on a man's social status: it may enhance socially dominant behaviour among high-status males, but lead to strategic submission to seniority among lower status males.

Aim

To investigate the extent to which testosterone is associated with high levels of dominant behaviour and low levels of acquiescence.

Participants

70 Japanese students who were all members of the university rugby team with an age range of

18- 23 years. High status among Japanese sports teams at university is linked to length of time served rather than ability and skill, so the fourth-year players would naturally enjoy higher status and first- year players would be expected to acquiesce to (give in to the demands of) the longer-serving players.

Procedure

The participants took part in the Ultimate Game a decision-based task used in economics involving the player being given a sum of money. They must then decide how much of the sum to share with the other player who must then decide to accept or reject the offer. In this game participants played four times, each time with a different player, offering up to 1000 Yen in multiples of 100 Yen during each session. The other player then had a range of 11 possible choices ranging from 100% for their opponent, 0 for themselves to 0 for their opponent and 100% for themselves.

Saliva was taken from each participant just before and just after playing the Ultimate Game. Four hours later the participants answered a questionnaire and received 500 Yen payment for taking part.

Results

The researchers found that the dominant behaviour of the longer-serving players and the raised levels of obedience and acquiescence of the newer players was linked to testosterone levels.

Longer-serving players were less likely to acquiesce if they had high testosterone levels and the newer players were more likely to acquiesce if their testosterone was high as well, which is a surprising finding.

Conclusion

Testosterone may be linked to strategic thinking, as a result of living within hierarchical systems, rather than being solely responsible for aggressive and dominant behaviour.

Evaluation of Inoue et al. (2017)
Strengths

✓ The researchers not only found what they expected: e.g. high testosterone in high status participants linked to dominant play but that first-year rugby team members also had high levels of testosterone and showed acquiescent behaviour. This may mean that they have made a unique finding which warrants further investigation.
✓ This is a well-controlled study using objective measures in which quantitative data was collected, increasing the reliability of the findings.

Limitations

X   The sample is very limited, being restricted to university-age rugby players from Japan so the results are difficult to generalise.

X   The players were not interacting directly and they were making hypothetical decisions which limits the validity of the findings. In a real decision-making situation testosterone levels might be different to those found in this study.

Reference

Inoue, Y., Takahashi, T., Burriss, R. P., Arai, S., Hasegawa, T., Yamagishi, T., & Kiyonari, T. (2017). Testosterone promotes either dominance or submissiveness in the Ultimatum Game depending on players' social rank. *Scientific Reports*, *7* (5335), pp. 1-9.

****

KEY STUDY: *Nave et al (2017) Single-dose testosterone administration impairs cognitive reflection in men.*

Links to

- **Research methods in the biological approach.** This is a double-blind lab experiment with random allocation to groups.

Brief Summary

One-off doses of testosterone lead to an increase in impulsivity and reduction in cognitive reflection. These effects could underlie the already-documented rise in dominance or aggression.

Aim

To investigate the role played by testosterone in cognitive reflection and impulse control.

Participants

243 male university students from the USA.

Procedure

The participants were randomly allocated, via a double-blind procedure, to either the testosterone group or placebo (control) group. On the day of the experiment they gave their first saliva sample at 9.00 am, and then four further samples were taken throughout the session. The participants had to take part in seven different behavioural tasks, one of which was designed specifically to test their cognitive reflection skills, asking three questions designed to test their use of System 2 thinking (effortful and slow) over System 1 thinking (intuitive and fast). The cognitive reflection test included questions such as: *A bat and a ball together cost $1.10. The bat costs $1 more than the ball. How much does the ball cost?* The participants were told that they would be paid $1 for every correctly answered question and a bonus $2 if they answered all three correctly.

Results

The testosterone group achieved significantly lower scores on the cognitive reflection test than the placebo group, making more intuition-based responses than the placebo group. This was true overall and for each of the three cognitive reflection questions separately.

Conclusion

Testosterone may be linked to impaired cognitive reflection.

Evaluation of Nave et al. (2017)

Strengths

✓ The researchers controlled for a variety of possibly confounding variables including maths ability, age and mood which gives their findings validity as they were able to highlight the effect of the independent variable (testosterone or placebo) on the cognitive reflection of the participants.

✓ The researchers ensured that no women were part of the research process to add a further level of control over the procedure: this was done to eliminate the possible confounding variable of testosterone-response based on sexual attraction.

Limitations

X Some of the participants may have needed money more than others so this may have compelled them to try harder to solve the cognitive reflection questions.

X Because they were randomly allocated to each condition, it is possible that the placebo group contained more System 2 thinkers than the testosterone group.

X The questions in the cognitive reflection test are unusual and do not represent the type of cognitive reflection that people generally have to use on a daily basis which means that the study lacks external validity.

Reference

Nave, G., Nadler, A., Zava, D., & Camerer, C. (2017). Single-dose testosterone administration impairs cognitive reflection in men. *Psychological Science, 28*(10), pp. 1398-1407.

****

Content 2: Pheromones and their effects on behaviour.

KEY STUDY: *Zhou et al. (2014). Chemosensory communication of gender through two human steroids in a sexually dimorphic manner.*

Links to
- **Human Relationships**: Biological argument regarding choice of mate.

Brief Summary
Investigated the effect of androstadienone (AND, signalling maleness) on women, and estratetraenol (EST, signalling femaleness) on men and found human visual gender perception was affected by these 'putative' (possible) pheromones. It is not possible to sense pheromones in the same way as sweat or perfume is actively smelt and detected: they are chemical signals that are thought to be transmitted to stimulate sexual attraction or disinterest - AND should attract heterosexual women and homosexual men; EST should attract heterosexual men and homosexual women.

Aim
To investigate the idea that specific male and female steroids act as sex pheromones by presenting visually salient sex-related information.

Participants
24 heterosexual males; 24 heterosexual females; 24 homosexual males and 24 bisexual or homosexual females participated in the study, all adults.

Procedure
The participants were asked to take part in a gender identification task after being exposed to either AND, EST or a placebo over the course of three days of testing. The participants watched a series of figures walking, made up of point-light walkers, in a virtual rendering of the action of the human body in motion, using dots of lights at specific points on the figure, e.g. the head, the centre of the pelvis. They were shown each point-light walking figure for 0.5 seconds and then they had to say whether the walking figure was male or female.

Results
Heterosexual males made more judgements that the walker was female when they had been exposed to EST; heterosexual females made more judgements that the walker was male when they had been exposed to AND; homosexual males made more judgements that the walker was male when exposed to AND (so, heterosexual females and homosexual males showed a similar

pattern of results). The findings for bisexual or homosexual females was not so concrete, making judgements that both the heterosexual females and males made.

Conclusion
Pheromones may be linked to how males and females perceive the sexes based on sexual orientation.

Evaluation of Zhou et al. (2014)
Strengths
✓ The researchers ensured that in all three conditions the substance the participants were exposed to smelled of cloves so as to factor out any preferences for one scent over another which adds a reliable measure of control over the procedure.
✓ Using PLWs rather than images of actual human beings helps to eliminate the possible confounding variable of individual differences regarding who/what is attractive.

Limitations
X These results do not conclusively point to pheromones as being an active part of human sexual selection: it is only possible to infer the role that pheromones may play in mate selection.
X The task lacks ecological validity as it was artificial in nature and does not reflect the array of other variables that may result in judgements pertaining to masculinity or femininity.

Reference
Zhou, W., Yang, X., Chen, K., Cai, P., He, S., & Jiang, Y. (2014). Chemosensory communication of gender through two human steroids in a sexually dimorphic manner. *Current Biology*, *24*(10), pp. 1091-1095.

****

KEY STUDY: *Wedekind et al. (1995). MHC-dependent mate preferences in humans.*

Links to
- **Human Relationships**. Biological argument regarding choice of mate.

Brief Summary
MHC (major histocompatability complex) is a group of genes that, while possibly not pheromones, can be smelt in sweat, and if attraction to those with different MHC than our own is followed by mating (a big 'if'), this maximises the immune responses in offspring, making them stronger.

Aim
To investigate whether females prefer male odours from males with a different MHC from their own.

Participants
49 female students and 44 male students; both groups with a mean age of 25 years. All of the students were from the University of Bern, Switzerland.

Procedure
Experiment, where the male participants were given a plain, cotton T-shirt and were told to wear it for 48 hours, aiming to keep 'odour-neutral', i.e. no deodorant, perfume-free soap, to eat specific foods, avoid sex, alcohol and smoking. The females were then asked to give a rating for six T-shirts which had been specifically chosen, as three of them had been worn by males with a similar MHC to them and the other three by males with a very different MHC from them. The females had to smell the T-shirts by via a triangular hole cut into a cardboard box in which the T-shirt had been placed. Each T-shirt was assessed by the females according to how intense and how pleasant they found their smell. The researchers provided a control in the form of an unworn T-shirt and all smelling was done blind.

Results
The researchers found that women whose MHC was different to the male's MHC found his body odour to be more pleasant than did women with a similar MHC to the male's. However, the finding, was the opposite if the woman was taking an oral contraceptive pill: these women were more attracted to males who had an MHC similar to their own.

Conclusion

Women are normally attracted to males with a different MHC from their own, but the contraceptive pill may interfere with natural mate choice based on MHC dissimilarity.

Evaluation of Wedekind et al. (1995)

Strengths

✓ This was a well-controlled study: as well as the males' behaviour being subject to controls, the females also used a nasal spray for two weeks prior to the study to enhance their sensitivity to smell.

✓ Whether or not MHC genes are pheromones, they act in a similar way to how pheromones act in animals: the results seem to support the idea that humans are naturally drawn to members of the opposite sex who have a different immune system from their own, thereby increasing the chances of stronger offspring and limiting the chances of inbreeding.

Limitations

X Forming a conclusion based on body odour preference is tenuous at best: there may be an array of variables that could have influenced the women's preference that have nothing to do with MHC.

X The males in the task may not have all kept to the demands put upon them by researchers. For example, some may have not been able to deny themselves sex or alcohol. As this was an aspect of the procedure that the researchers could not control, it limits the reliability of the findings.

Reference

Wedekind, C., Seebeck, T., Bettens, F., & Paepke, A. J. (June, 1995). MHC-dependent mate preferences in humans. *Proceedings of the Royal Society, London: Biology, 260* (1359), pp. 245-249.

****

KEY STUDY: *Hare et al. (2017.) Putative sex-specific human pheromones do not affect gender perception, attractiveness ratings or unfaithfulness judgements of opposite sex faces.*

Brief Summary

This study found that exposure to androstadienone (AND) or estratetraenol (EST) had no effect on gender perception.

Aim

To investigate whether AND and EST play a role in the perception of gender and attractiveness of the opposite sex.

Participants

94 (51 female; 43 male) white, heterosexual adults (mean age of 24) from the University of Western Australia.

Procedure

The participants took part in two computer-based tasks while taking in the scent of either AND or EST via a cotton ball taped underneath their nose. The scent was disguised with clove oil and the control condition involved only clove oil being applied to the cotton ball. This was a repeated measures, double-blind design using counter-balancing.

Task 1: The participants were shown 5 images of morphed gender-neutral faces (achieved via blending male and female faces together) and were asked to identify the gender of each face.

Task 2: The participants were shown opposite-sex faces (all Caucasian, hairline and face only on display) and, using a rating scale from 1-10, were asked to rate the level of attractiveness of each photo and also the likelihood of each person shown being unfaithful.

Results

The researchers found no evidence that AND or EST affected gender perception or attractiveness and unfaithfulness ratings.

Conclusion

AND and EST do not appear to function as human pheromones.

Evaluation of Hare et al. (2017)

Strengths

✓ This was a well-controlled study with a counter-balanced design which should eliminate order effects (e.g. fatigue, practice, boredom) from interfering with the results.

✓ The researchers conducted a pilot study before they carried out this study which works to check the validity of the design.

Limitations

X Rating faces (particularly those which have been manipulated by the researchers) shown on a computer is not something that people routinely do as part of everyday life, which makes the study low in external validity.

X The sample includes only white heterosexuals so it cannot demonstrate the ways in which non- Caucasian or homosexual adults may be affected by AND and EST.

Reference

Hare, R. M., Schlatter, S., Rhodes, G., & Simmons, L. W. (2017). Putative sex-specific human pheromones do not affect gender perception, attractiveness ratings or unfaithfulness judgements of opposite sex faces. *Royal Society Open Science*, *4*(3), 160831.

****

CRITICAL THINKING POINTS: HORMONES AND PHEROMONES AND THEIR EFFECTS ON BEHAVIOUR

Are hormone-based studies overly reductionist?

Research using the Biological Approach is often criticised for being reductionist: i.e. for reducing complex human behaviour to the simplest explanation. Fernald & Gunnar's (2009) research on the levels of the stress hormone cortisol in children of poor, depressed mothers may go some way towards establishing a link between a biological manifestation of stress, but it cannot account for the array of other variables that may have induced a stress response in the participants. A phenomenon such as poverty brings with it many possible negative effects so it may be too simplistic to attempt to explain it via biological correlates. Similarly, Inoue et al.'s (2017) findings as to testosterone levels in Japanese college rugby players may be the result of behaviours other than aggression, such as social strategies employed by players living in an extremely hierarchical system.

Do pheromones even exist?

The existence of human pheromones is still debatable. There is scant hard evidence of the existence of sex-based 'invisible' chemicals guiding our mate preferences and gender recognition. Wedekind's (1995) study is not really even a study of pheromones but of MHC and its possible role in mate selection linked to an evolutionary preference for MHC-opposite mates. Biopsychologists have not identified MHC as a pheromone. Hare et al.'s (2017) more recent research seems to thoroughly de- bunk the idea of AND and EST as human pheromones (although some research with animals suggests that pheromones are employed for a variety of purposes). Until some very compelling evidence is provided then the existence of pheromones remains somewhat shrouded in mystery.

What about all the social signals that indicate gender and attraction?

Sociocultural factors arguably play as key a role in attraction as do biological forces. We may be 'primed' to respond to specific hormone-related signals such as AND and EST but surely human beings are more complex than that? Human beings tend to be equally influenced by environmental factors determining who they are attracted to: e.g. the proliferation of female pop stars such as Taylor Swift, Britney Spears and Katy Perry present a fairly homogenised version of what heterosexual males (in the West at least) are supposed to find attractive. This Westernised ideal may not appeal to someone who has grown up in a culture in which a curvy figure, dark skin and curly hair are considered attractive – and this is the influence of cultural norms rather than biology.

****

TOPIC 3: RELATIONSHIP BETWEEN GENETICS AND BEHAVIOUR

Key Idea: It is an interaction between genes and environment that affects human behaviour.

Content 1: Genes and their effects on behaviour.

KEY STUDY: *Caspi et al. (2003). Influence of Life Stress on Depression: Moderation by a Polymorphism in the 5-HTT Gene.*

Links to
- **Abnormal Psychology.** Genetic explanation for inherited predisposition to depression as a response to environmental stressors.

Brief Summary
Looked at the relation between inherited short alleles on the 5HTT serotonin transporter gene and incidences of stress and subsequent depression.

Aim
To investigate whether a functional change in the 5HTT gene is linked to a higher or lower risk of depression in an individual.

Participants
847 participants aged 26 years old split into three groups, depending on the length of the alleles on their 5HTT transporter gene.

Group 1 – two short alleles
Group 2 – one short and one long allele
Group 3 – two long alleles

Procedure
A number of methods was used to ascertain the link between length of allele, stressful life events and depression:

1. Stressful life events occurring after the 21st birthday and before the 26th birthday: assessed using a life-history calendar.
2. The Diagnostic Interview Schedule was used to measure the instances and frequency of depression over the past year per participant.

3. Correlational analyses were calculated between stressful life events and depression, length of alleles and depression and perceived stress and the length of alleles.
4. A further test was done to see if life events could predict an increase in depression over time among individuals with one or two short alleles.

Results

The participants with two short alleles in the 5HTT transporter gene reported more depression symptoms in response to stressful life events than either of the other two groups. Participants with two long alleles reported fewer depression symptoms. Participants with one or two short alleles who had been mistreated as children (e.g. abused or neglected) had scores that could be used to predict depression in adulthood.

Conclusion

There appears to be a correlation between having short alleles on the 5HTT gene and instances of depression linked to stressful life events. Having long 5HTT gene alleles seems to offer protection from stress-related depression.

Evaluation of Caspi et al. (2003)

Strengths

✓ This study used a very large cohort of males and females and the age was controlled in order to isolate the variable of number of stressful life events between the ages of 21 and 26.
✓ It was a natural experiment, with the naturally occurring IV being the length of the alleles, so it would be impossible for demand characteristics to bias this aspect of the study.

Limitations

X Attempting to isolate the action of one gene is a highly complex and difficult undertaking: it is unknown how many other genes may be involved in the experience of stress and subsequent depression.
X The symptoms of depression were self-reported which could produce biased, unreliable results due to a deliberate attempt to mislead the researchers, memory impairment, wanting to please the researchers too much.

Reference

Caspi, A., Sugden, K., Moffitt, T. E., Taylor, A., Craig, I. W., Harrington, H., ... & Poulton, R. (2003). Influence of life stress on depression: moderation by a polymorphism in the 5-HTT gene. *Science, 301*(5631), pp. 386-389.

****

KEY STUDY: *Risch et al. (2009). Interaction Between the Serotonin Transporter Gene (5-HTTLPR), Stressful Life Events, and Risk of Depression.*

Links to
- **Abnormal Psychology.** Critique of genetic argument for depression. Correlation between stress and depression suggests a cognitive/sociocultural explanation.

Brief Summary
Looked at the relation between inherited short alleles on the 5HTT serotonin transporter gene and incidences of stress and subsequent depression.

Aim
To investigate whether a functional change in the 5HTT gene is linked to a higher or lower risk of depression in an individual.

Participants
The researchers conducted a meta-analysis of 14 studies that investigated possible links/interaction between stressful life events, depression and the serotonin 5HTT gene. A total of 14,250 participants comprised the overall sample.

Procedure
Statistical tests were applied to the results of the studies in the meta-analysis.

Results
The researchers found that there was a significant association between stressful life events, such as bereavement or job loss, with depression. However, they did not find that this also had a biological root: no association was found between depression and the 5HTT gene and no interaction was found between stressful life events and the 5HTT gene.

Conclusion
The 5HTT gene alone does not appear to trigger depression, nor does the gene appear to be associated with stressful life events.

Evaluation of Risch et al. (2009)
Strengths
- ✓ This research used a very large sample comprising the quantitative data from a range of studies which means that the findings are robust and reliable.
- ✓ Using an objective, statistical measure to analyse the results of the studies should ensure

that the research is free from researcher bias.

Limitations

X   Very little is really known about the role of neurotransmitters on behaviour so these results are only partially useful and no firm conclusions should be drawn from them.

X   A meta-analysis is a rather 'cold', detached way of measuring human behaviour, particularly a variable so complex and unpredictable as depression.

Reference

Risch, N., Herrell, R., Lehner, T., Liang, K. Y., Eaves, L., Hoh, J., ... & Merikangas, K. R. (2009). Interaction between the serotonin transporter gene (5-HTTLPR), stressful life events, and risk of depression: a meta-analysis. *Jama*, *301*(23), pp. 2462-2471.

****

KEY STUDY: *Yehuda et al. (2016). Holocaust Exposure Induced Intergenerational Effects on FKBP5 Methylation*

Links to

▪   **Health**. Trauma suffered by parents' before conception can result in epigenetic changes that predispose children to a physiological stress response in their own lives.

Brief Summary

Demonstrated an epigenetic association between parental trauma of Holocaust survivors' before conception of their children, with epigenetic alterations that are evident in both exposed parent and children, providing insight into how severe psychophysiological trauma can have intergenerational effects. Epigenetics involves a change in phenotype that is not caused by or does not involve a change in genotype. A range of factors can influence epigenetic change, e.g. disease, diet, age, environment.

Aim

To investigate possible transmission of epigenetic changes in both survivors of the Holocaust and their offspring.

Participants

32 Holocaust survivors (parents) and 22 of their offspring. A control group of 8 Jewish parents who had not experienced the Holocaust and 9 of their children was use for comparison purposes.

Procedure

The participants were given a battery of questionnaires pertaining to mental health, childhood trauma, PTSD, depression and anxiety. Biological measures were taken in the form of blood samples and saliva upon waking and at bedtime.

Results

Holocaust survivors and their offspring showed significant epigenetic changes linked to one specific gene site (FKBP5), which was not seen in the control group. The survivors and their offspring also scored highly for PTSD compared to the controls, who reported a 0% score on this measure.

Conclusion

Experience-dependent epigenetic changes can be seen in both parents and offspring and may be heritable.

Evaluation of Yehuda et al. (2016)

Strengths

✓ The findings seem to provide evidence for the idea that extreme stress experienced by the parent may be transmitted to offspring via specific gene regions.
✓ The researchers used triangulation of method, using both self-reports and biological measures, which increases the validity of the findings.

Limitations

X The sample is small and uneven, with only 17 participants in the control group, which makes it difficult to draw reliable conclusions.
X The study has been criticised for going beyond the slight significance of the results to draw unwarranted conclusions (see https://tinyurl.com/ybzkof9w).

Reference

Yehuda, R., Daskalakis, N. P., Bierer, L. M., Bader, H. N., Klengel, T., Holsboer, F., & Binder, E. B. (2016). Holocaust exposure induced intergenerational effects on FKBP5 methylation. *Biological Psychiatry, 80*(5), pp. 372-380.

* *

KEY STUDY: *Tobi et al. (2018). DNA methylation as a mediator of the association between prenatal adversity and risk factors for metabolic disease in adulthood*

Links to
- **Health.** Genetic inheritance explanation for health problems – obesity, diabetes and schizophrenia. (Only obesity is part of the curriculum.)

Brief Summary
Epigenetic mechanism of DNA methylation in babies, born to mothers who were starving during the Dutch Hunger Winter, affected their later health and life expectancy.

Aim
To investigate the idea that famine experienced during pregnancy can result in long-term deficits in the child born to a starving mother.

Participants
422 people who had been born in 3 cities of the Netherlands between February 1945 and March 1946 (which means that their mothers would have experienced famine during their gestation, as this period coincides with the 6-month Hunger Winter in the Netherlands). 463 sibling controls, born at different dates to the participants, were used for comparison.

Procedure
The participants were interviewed and a series of clinical measures was taken from each of them including height, weight and body mass index (BMI).

Results
The researchers found that, 60 years on, the participants whose mothers had experienced famine had a higher BMI than the controls. Famine experienced by the mothers in the early stages of pregnancy was associated with irregular glucose metabolism in the offspring.

Conclusion
Adverse experience such as famine during pregnancy may result in long-term negative outcomes related to glucose metabolism – resulting in possible obesity – for the child, even into adulthood.

Evaluation of Tobi et al. (2018)
Strengths
- ✓ The use of siblings as a control group means that family environment can be ruled out as a confounding variable, which increases the reliability of the findings.

✓ The findings do go some way towards presenting a compelling and convincing argument for a biological basis for behaviour.

Limitations

X Whole blood samples may not be the best way of measuring BMI or glucose metabolism which means that further research is required before a firm conclusion can be drawn.

X The study bases current findings on events from 60 years ago which means that some caution must be exercised: there are six decades of life experience in between the mother's pregnancy and the measures taken by the researchers and it is possible that the intervening years could have taken their toll in many different ways on each participant.

Reference

Tobi, E. W., Slieker, R. C., Luijk, R., Dekkers, K. F., Stein, A. D., Xu, K. M., ... & Biobank-based Integrative Omics Studies Consortium (2018). DNA methylation as a mediator of the association between prenatal adversity and risk factors for metabolic disease in adulthood. *Science Advances*, 4(1), eaao4364.

****

Content 2: Genetic similarity

KEY STUDY: *McGue et al (2000). Genetic and environmental influences on adolescent substance use and abuse.*

▪ **Health:** MZ (monozygotic, identical twins) and DZ (dizygotic, non-identical twins) male and female twin study into adolescents and gene-environment interaction in drug addiction.

Brief Summary

MZ and DZ male and female twin study into adolescents and gene-environment interaction in drug addiction.

Aim

To investigate the extent to which genetic inheritance can explain the use and abuse of licit (e.g. tobacco) and illicit (e.g. marijuana) drugs in teenagers.

Participants

626 pairs of twins (188 MZ male; 101 DZ male; 223 MZ female; 114 DZ female) from the same birth- year cohort. MZ/DZ status was determined via physical measures e.g. height, weight and appearance, questionnaires and a serological test (to check for the level of antibodies in bodily fluids).

Procedure

The participants were interviewed for a total of 8 hours about their history and experience of licit and illicit drug use, details of their home life; and they also completed a questionnaire.

Results

The researchers found some slight (10%-25%) heritability for illicit drug use being inherited. There were no significant gender differences in heritability of illicit drug use. The main finding was that licit substances show a higher degree of heritability at 40-60%. The importance of shared environment was also a prominent finding: the participants with a well-established habit and history of drug-taking (both licit and illicit) reporting that such drugs were a regular part of family life, with reports of parents or family members openly taking drugs, and drugs being a normal part of the home environment.

Conclusion

Early intervention is needed to mitigate the effects of children being exposed to drug use at home as previous research has also demonstrated that early exposure to drugs in the home can lead to adolescent and lifetime drug use. The environment, therefore, seems to be more influential in determining drug use than genetic inheritance.

Evaluation of McGue et al. (2000)

Strengths

✓ The researchers followed up some of their male participants after 3 years and found that heritability for illicit drugs had increased to 52% which was in line with what they expected: this increases the predictive validity of the study.

✓ The large sample size means that the results are robust and it is easier to generalise the findings to a similar demographic within the USA.

Limitations

X The evidence for genetic inheritance is not fully convincing and the use of self-reports only adds to the lack of objective and convincing empirical evidence for a biological explanation of illicit drug use in particular.

X The sample was over 97% white which means that generalising the findings to other ethnicities is not possible. The parents of the participants were also described as having a reasonably high level of education which ignores an important factor in drug-taking: the use of licit and illicit substances by those whose opportunities are limited due to educational deficits.

Reference

McGue, M., Elkins, I., & Iacono, W. G. (2000). Genetic and environmental influences on adolescent substance use and abuse. American Journal of Medical Genetics Part A, 96(5), pp. 671-677.

****

KEY STUDY: *Lynskey et al. (2010). Genetically informative research on adolescent substance use: methods, findings, and challenges.*

Links to

▪ **Twin and kinship (family) studies**

Brief Summary

Review of research using genetic similarities as the basis for investigation into child and adolescent substance abuse. The study focuses on the epidemiology of drug use and abuse: how often it occurs in adolescents and the possible reasons for this. Such information can be used to assist in devising programmes to help those who use drugs.

Aim

To provide a genetic explanation of drug use and abuse in adolescents via a review of the psychological literature.

Procedure

The researchers reviewed research using twin, adoption and family studies of licit and illicit drug use and abuse. The review was looking for evidence of heritability in drug use in children and adolescents.

Results

▪ **Adoption and family studies** – some compelling evidence that the use of alcohol and other drugs may beexplained using the argument of genetic inheritance as there was a high concordance rate between a biological parent using drugs and their child who had been adopted; environment emerged as a stronger influence when the adopted parent used drugs.

▪ **Twin studies** – these provide some evidence for a genetic inheritance of drug use but the fact that the studies reviewed are of twins reared in the same environment the researchers are not wholly confident that biology is key to drug use: they cite research in which one MZ is a drug user but their twin is not. They also state that the home environment can mitigate possible effects of an inherited propensity for drug use. Some twin research has reported findings that there is wide variety of concordance rates for the heritability of smoking (25%-80%), with older adolescents being more likely to show this heritability.

- The link between heritability and psychopathology – the studies reviewed revealed a high correlation between the abuse of several drugs by the same person and that person's likelihood of developing a psychopathology. This was noted as a feature of some of the twin studies. One study showed that there was a 35% genetic concordance in MZ twins between drug use and behavioural disorders. Another study found that children of MZ twins are more likely to develop both dependence on alcohol and ADHD.

- Use of multiple drugs may be heritable – the review uncovered strong evidence that the dependence on alcohol, smoking and drugs is genetically inherited.

Conclusion

There is a moderate to strong chance that children will inherit their parents' propensity to some form of drug addiction with environment also playing a key role in the development of drug use and abuse.

Evaluation of Lynskey et al. (2010)

Strengths

✓ The use of the review method means that the researchers were able to access a wide variety of research on the topic giving them the means with which to look for shared findings, patterns in data and also the limitations of the studies they were reviewing.

✓ The findings are in line with other research on heritability and drug use, which indicates that heritability for licit drugs shows some convincing evidence.

Limitations

X Many of the studies in the review consisted of adult samples which limits their usefulness in terms of child and adolescent drug use.

X The findings indicate that home environment may work as a protective factor in the heritability of drug use but it does not say *how* this occurs or suggest ways in which to implement this finding.

Reference

Lynskey, M. T., Agrawal, A., & Heath, A. C. (2010). Genetically informative research on adolescent substance use: methods, findings, and challenges. Journal of the American Academy of Child & Adolescent Psychiatry, 49(12), pp. 1202-1214.

KEY STUDY: *Christakis & Fowler (2014). Friendship and natural selection*

Brief Summary

Friends' genotypes are positively correlated, and therefore the argument is that friends are genetically similar.

Aim

To investigate if friends share a similar genotype.

Participants

1,932 participants, giving a sample of 1,367 friendship pairs and comprising 466,608 examples of single nucleotide polymorphism (SNP) samples were taken from the genotype of each participant. A control sample of strangers was used for comparison purposes.

Procedure

The researchers analysed the SNPs of the pairs of friends, using correlational measures to produce a 'kinship coefficient' to show whether or not two alleles from a pair of friends are identical.

Results

Friends showed higher genetic relatedness than strangers, being as genetically similar as fourth cousins. There was no evidence to show genetic relatedness between strangers.

Conclusion

Friendship pairs may come about because they perform an important function in terms of our evolution, e.g. by strengthening particular shared traits.

Evaluation of Christakis & Fowler (2014)

Strengths

- ✓ The researchers used a series of checks (e.g. to ensure that none of the friendship pairs were actually related to each other; controls on the ethnicity of the sample to rule out same-ethnicity preferences), making this a highly reliable study.
- ✓ The results of this study showed a similar pattern to studies investigating the heritability of schizophrenia and bipolar disorder. This finding breaks new ground in the field of genetics as it is based on a variable that is not connected to inherited traits from parents, rather on a shared genotype between non-related individuals.

Limitations

X While the researchers took pains to exert a good level of control over the study it is overly reductionist to explain friendships using SNP samples as the quality of friendships is hugely varied and subject to change.

X The researchers claim that shared genetic traits between friends may have been an evolutionarily useful mechanism, but this claim is difficult to support with empirical evidence and can only be inferred from the results.

Reference

Christakis, N. A., & Fowler, J. H. (2014). Friendship and natural selection. Proceedings of the National Academy of Sciences, 111(Supplement 3), pp. 10796-10801.

****

Content 3: Evolutionary explanation for behaviour.

KEY STUDY: *Singh (1993). Adaptive significance of female physical attractiveness: role of waist-to-hip ratio.*

Links to

▪ **Human Relationships**. Evolution and long-term mate choice. Males prefer young, healthy and fertile females; females prefer older and financially stable men.

Brief Summary

Males choose female partners whose small (0.7) waist-to-hip ratio suggests fertility.

Aim

To investigate the role played by the waist-hip-ratio (WHR) in determining how attractive a woman is rated by a man.

Participants

106 male university students aged 18-22 years old. 74 of the sample were white; 34 were Hispanic.

Procedure

The participants were shown 12 line drawings of an identical female who differed only in regard to her WHR and her weight (underweight, normal or overweight). The participants then had to rank all 12 figures in order of most to least attractive. They were then asked to choose their top and bottom 3 figures using categories such as sexiness, healthiness and childbearing potential.

Results

Figures with the lowest WHR and of a 'normal' body weight were found to be the most attractive and the healthiest. The highest WHR across the categories was found to be least attractive, with the overweight women being ranked as the least attractive of all categories. The 'normal' body weight was preferred to the 'underweight' category by 30% difference in ranking scores.

Conclusion

Men appear to prefer a woman's body shape to show a low WHR as long as she is generally deemed to be 'normal'. This may be linked to an evolutionary preference for healthy mates who also exude powerful attraction signals.

Evaluation of Singh (1993)

Strengths

- ✓ The use of a replicable procedure in controlled conditions and quantitative data make this a reliable study.
- ✓ The findings of this study have some practical application as they indicate that men do not prefer thinner women: this information could be used to inform a range of services from the fashion industry to advertising, as well as contributing to health service providers, e.g. eating disorder clinics.

Limitations

- X The findings do not explain why some men prefer large women, older women, thin women, disabled women. Nor do they explain homosexuality or lesbianism.
- X There is the possibility that the participants were affected by demand characteristics which could be manifest in some of them responding in the way they felt they 'should' respond (i.e. succumbing to society's ideal) rather than how they really felt about preferred female shape.

Reference

Singh, D. (1993). Adaptive significance of female physical attractiveness: role of waist-to-hip ratio. Journal of Personality and Social Psychology, 65(2), pp. 293-307.

****

KEY STUDY: Dixson (2016). Waist-to-hip ratio.

Links to

- **Human Relationships**. Evolution and long-term mate choice. Males prefer young, healthy and fertile females; females prefer older and financially stable men.

Brief Summary

Review of research suggests preferred waist-to-hip ratio (WHR) varies cross-culturally.

Aim

To critically assess Singh's (1993) claim that men find a low (0.7) WHR universally attractive in females.

Procedure

Dixson (2016) is a review article written as a critique of Singh (1993) whose research concluded that males tend to find the 0.7 WHR the most attractive measurement for women and that this response is formed from an evolutionary preference for young, healthy, fertile females.

Main Comments and Findings

- Dixson (2016) argues with the idea that the preference for the 0.7 WHR is assumed to be universal, regardless of culture. His review article finds examples of male preferences which do not accord with Singh's claims. Although Singh's (1993) has been replicated with similar results in several different countries (e.g. Germany, New Zealand), these are predominantly industrialised, individualistic cultures where similar ideals of attractiveness prevail.

- Some examples of contradictory research findings include the Matsigenka people in Peru who showed preference for a larger (0.9) WHR; the Bakossi (Cameroon), a rural community in which the males preferred women with a more masculine, 'tubular' shape (i.e. a WHR of 0.8, lacking the 'hourglass' shape), and a hunter-gatherer tribe in Tanzania, the Hadza, who also reported a
0.9 WHR as their preference.

- Other research findings involve the idea that height related to weight is more significant for some cultures and that judging a woman's attractiveness via her body fat or BMI is more relevant than a WHR ideal. Men from Zulu tribes, for example, stated a strong preference for females with a high BMI. Interestingly, males of Zulu origin who subsequently moved to the UK did not share this high BMI ideal, preferring instead what most British males state is their ideal - lower BMI and a slimmer shape. In this way, Dixson argues, the low WHR preference as stated by Singh (1993) is only a product of cultural identity and is not shared cross-culturally.

Conclusion

WHR is too simplistic and reductionist a way to measure male preference for female body shapes: understanding ecological context and the ways in which various aspects of body shape, type, BMI and image work in unison is a much better way of understanding how different cultures evolve different ideals in terms of physical attractiveness.

Evaluation of Dixson (2016)

Strengths

✓ The use of a review article means the author was able to consider a range of studies from different cultures, giving him scope to look for patterns and for examples that contradict prevailing ideas on the topic.

✓ Dixson's article opens up the debate regarding culture and evolution by highlighting the importance of understanding that there is not necessarily one universal explanation for a behaviour that may at first sight appear to be a shared evolutionary mechanism.

Limitations

X   It is not clear how the examples from tribal or remote cultures were originally obtained: in emic research it is possible for the researcher to become overly close to the people they are studying, which could result in a biased account of behaviours.

X   This is a very tricky topic to investigate even when primary data is being used: using secondary data means that the researcher is even more distanced from what is already a very difficult variable to measure as it involves making claims about present behaviour using ultimate causes to explain this behaviour.

Reference

Dixson, B.J.W. (2016). Waist-to-hip ratio, in T.K. Shackelford, V.A. Weekes-Shackelford (eds.), Encyclopedia of Evolutionary Psychological Science. Springer: Switzerland

****

KEY STUDY: Conroy-Beam & Buss (2016). Do mate preferences influence actual mating decisions?

Links to

- **Human Relationships**. Evolution and long-term mate choice. Males prefer young, healthy andfertile females; females prefer older and financially stable men.

Brief Summary

Stated mate preferences have a causal role in real-life mate choices.

Aim

To investigate whether what people say they want in a partner is reflected in their real-life choice of long-term partner.

Participants

214 newly married heterosexual men and women (i.e. 107 couples in total) who had been married for less than a year and were living in the Midwest of the USA. The mean age for males was 27 years old and for females it was 26.

Procedure

The participants were initially asked, individually, to provide ratings, using a 7-point scale, describing their ideal partner. Each couple was interviewed by a researcher asking them about their relationship history and their life together. An independent rater then gave each participant an individual rating on a range of measures: their attractiveness, height, age, salary and their overall value as a mate. The researchers then used a complex statistically correlational analysis of their data to ascertain the extent to which stated partner preferences were seen in their choice of actual real-life partner.

Results

The preferences stated by the participants were reflected in their choice of real-life mate.

Conclusion

What people say they want in a mate appears to be a valid predictor of the person they end up with on a long-term basis.

Evaluation of Conroy-Beam & Buss (2016)

Strengths

✓ The researchers used a sophisticated, computerised method of analysing their data, which means that the results are objective and free from bias.

✓ Using an interview as part of the research process means that the quantitative results could be viewed in conjunction with the qualitative data, providing more in-depth and insightful explanation.

Limitations

X The sample all came from the same area of the USA and may therefore have shown similar preferences for mates. If a wider demographic had been used, then more variance might have been evident and the results would have been more generalisable.

X The study lacks ecological validity for several reasons: the couples may have felt as if they had to be on the 'best behaviour' during the interviews and therefore showed a social desirability effect; an independent rater cannot fully understand the mate value of an individual in one brief meeting; using computational models to form conclusions about mate preferences is highly artificial and ignores the complexity, depth and unpredictability of actual relationships.

Reference

Conroy-Beam, D., & Buss, D. M. (2016). Do mate preferences influence actual mating decisions? Evidence from computer simulations and three studies of mated couples. Journal of Personality and Social Psychology, 111(1), pp. 53-66.

****

CRITICAL THINKING POINTS: THE RELATIONSHIP BETWEEN GENETICS AND BEHAVIOUR

Isn't trying to explain the etiology of depression too difficult for any one explanation?
Depression is a complex and unpredictable mood disorder that affects approximately 25% of the population at any given time. Because depression is so prevalent in 21st century life, it should be easy to quantify and measure; but the reality of attempting to explain how and why depression develops is beset with difficulties. One person's experience of depression may have similar features to another's but it is also likely to be experienced in a way that is unique to that individual.

Using a genetic approach to explain depression is appealing, as it provides a concrete and objective account based on ideas such as an inherited predisposition to the condition in a large number of the depressed population. Caspi et al.'s (2003) findings that participants with two *short alleles on the 5HTT transporter gene reported more depression symptoms in response to stressful life events provides a clear, biological link between the disorder and genetics, pointing to a possible biological basis for depression. The evidence is only partially objective, however, as the self-report aspect of the study means that the participants may not have given unbiased responses that would reduce the validity of this aspect of the measure. Research in this field can attempt to explain **what** may be happening in the brains of depressed people but it falls short of explaining **why** some people develop depression and others do not (even if they share the same genetic predisposition to it).*

Research in this field may be overly deterministic.

Biological determinism involves the prediction of an outcome based on biological evidence. An example is the use of twin studies such as McGue et al. (2000) in which MZ and DZ twins were interviewed as to their licit and illicit drug use. The finding that licit drug use appeared to have a higher concordance rate in MZ twins than illicit drug use could provide some evidence for the idea that drug use has a biological basis: that the behaviour of one MZ twin is correlated to the behaviour of the other MZ twin due to their identical DNA. What this study does not do is to provide clear biological evidence alone in support of nature over nurture. The fact that a higher concordance rate for licit drug-taking in MZ twins was found may instead be based on the fact that MZ twins are more likely to spend greater amounts of time together than DZ twins (who may be of the opposite sex) and thus are more likely to share activities. The higher rate for licit drug use agreement may also have something to do with the fact that people are more likely to admit to smoking tobacco than to smoking marijuana which could be a confounding variable in the research process.

Can a genetic explanation be used to explain something as personal as mate preference?

*Research by Singh (1993) reinforces the idea that heterosexual men see a low waist-hip-ratio of 0.7 as the ideal body shape for women. This may be partly based on an evolutionary preference for females who appear young and fertile, but it may be in large part to the influence of the media and social conditioning. The ideal female body shape has fluctuated over the centuries, from the fleshy 'Rubenesque' form to the boyish shapes of the 1920s and 1960s. Men may **say** that they prefer the conventional WHR shape but this could be due to social pressure. For example, even in an objective research setting some men may feel that they cannot express their preference for overweight women or muscular women. As ideas about gender and appearance are increasingly being challenged by younger people it may be that the 0.7 WHR 'perfect' shape becomes as outdated as the idea that men enjoy the 'chase' and women enjoy being 'pursued' in courtship rituals.*

****

TOPIC 4 (EXTENSION): THE ROLE OF ANIMAL RESEARCH IN UNDERSTANDING HUMAN BEHAVIOUR.

Key Idea: To what extent the results of animal research can be generalised to give insight into human behaviour.

Content 1: The value of animal models in research to provide insight into human behaviour.

A. The relationship between the brain and behaviour (Example: neuroplasticity)

KEY STUDY: *Rosenzweig et al. (1972). Effects of environmental enrichment and impoverishment on rat cerebral cortex.*

Links to
- **Development.** The influence of poverty/socio-economic status on cognitive development. See Luby et al. (2013).

Brief Summary
Study into neuroplasticity of rats' brains in response to environmental stimuli.

Aim
To investigate the effects of a highly stimulating environment compared with the effects of an impoverished environment on rats' brain growth and chemistry.

Procedure
Three male rats were randomly assigned to one of three conditions. One rat remained in the laboratory cage with the rest of the colony; another was assigned to the 'enriched' environment cage; and the third was assigned to the 'impoverished' cage. There were 12 rats in each of these conditions for each of the 16 experiments.

The three different environments were:
1. The standard laboratory colony cage - several rats in an adequate space with food and water always available.
2. The impoverished environment - a slightly smaller cage isolated in a separate room in which the rat was placed alone with adequate food and water.
3. The enriched environment - 6-8 rats in a large cage furnished with a variety of objects with

which they could play.

The rats lived in these different environments for various periods of time, ranging from four to 10 weeks. They were then humanely killed so that autopsies could be carried out on their brains to determine if any differences had developed.

Results
The cerebral cortex (responsible for the five senses plus memory, learning, movement) of the enriched rats was significantly heavier and thicker than the impoverished rats. The enriched environment rats produced larger neurons than the impoverished rats and the synapses of the enriched rats' brains were 50% larger than those of the impoverished rats.

Conclusion
An enriched environment may contribute to neural branching and to enhanced brain function.

Evaluation of Rosenzweig et al. (1972)
Strengths
✓ It has been found (Bennett, 1976) that learning itself is enhanced by enriched environmental experiences and that even the brains of adult animals raised in impoverished conditions can improve when placed in an enriched environment.
✓ The findings of this study – that stimulation appears to encourage cortical health and function – could be applied to therapeutic settings for conditions such as dementia.

Limitations
X Rats' brains are not as complex as human brains, which means that the results are not fully generalisable to humans.
X Although the rats were 'killed humanely' there are still some ethical concerns surrounding the use of animals in research such as this. Rats are intelligent creatures who appear to be sensitive
to their environment so a study such as this one does pose some ethical dilemmas as to the use of animals in psychological research.

Reference
Rosenzweig, M. R., Diamond, M. C., Bennett, E. L., Lindner, B., & Lyon, L. (1972). Effects of environmental enrichment and impoverishment on rat cerebral cortex. *Developmental Neurobiology*, *3*(1), pp. 47-64.

****

KEY STUDY: *Wexler (2010). Neuroplasticity, cultural evolution and cultural difference.*

Brief Summary

The main difference between animals and humans is the *extent* to which neuroplasticity occurs in humans. It is far greater than in animals.

Aim

To provide a review of research that considers how the environment shapes the brain and the ways in which changes to the environment may impact on the individual.

Procedure

A review article that considers a range of research findings.

Main Comments and Findings

- Human brains are much more alert and receptive to sensory input than those of other mammals: humans have more neurons; neurons take longer after birth to form connections, meaning that the environment plays much more of a key role in shaping human brains than brains of non-human mammals.

- Only humans are fully capable of shaping and modifying their environment to the extent that they do: this results in more variety within the human species, comprising a range of complex internal mental processes and cross-cultural differences in brain structure and function.

- Neurons prefer tasks that they are used to: some examples from animal research shows that kittens raised in darkness with daily exposure to black and white vertical lines developed brain cells that only recognised similar vertical line arrangements. Such findings demonstrate that mammals develop concrete perceptual structures that are linked to the environment in which they are reared.

- Research using monkeys showed that infant monkeys deprived of maternal contact preferred a fake 'cloth' mother to a wire mother with milk: the conclusion being that the monkeys were in need of the comfort that the cloth mother offered which would in turn increase external stimulation and, subsequently their brain development. Adult rats who were licked more by their mother showed a lowered stress response and increased spatial awareness than less- licked rats. Examination of the rats' brains indicated neuroplasticity in the hippocampus, with longer neurons being evident in this group.

- Human neuroplasticity research shows that practice at particular tasks showsfar-reaching changes in brain structure and function: research on mirror neurons demonstrates that even subtle stimuli can result in a mirroring. For example, seeing someone cry stimulates mirroring in the regions of the brain associated with emotion. Intense practice on the violin produces increases in the development of the somatosensory and motor areas of the brain associated with the intricate finger movements of players – but only in the right hemisphere of the brain. Piano players who use both hands showed symmetrical development over both hemispheres. People blind from birth show a compensation for this deficit by having their brains direct sound and touch information to the visual areas of the brain.

- The review also considers the role of culture in shaping human brains: immigrants to a new culture may suffer mental disorders such as depression because the cultural environment in which they grew up, the one that shaped their brain, differs from their new cultural environment. This may cause a clash of internal processes and external forces which may lead to a psychopathological response.

Conclusion
Both animals and humans show neuroplasticity, but in human brains it is more complex.

Evaluation of Wexler (2010)

Strengths
✓ The findings cited by the author raise some interesting ideas about the interaction of sociocultural, biological and cognitive factors, arguing for a holistic understanding of neuroplasticity.
✓ The recommendations made by the author could serve to inform governments and other institutions that immigrants face a range of challenges adapting to their new culture and thereby avoid the onset of depression or other mental disorders.

Limitations
X The evidence for culture as a key influence on brain development is not completely convincing: culture is a multi-faceted variable which affects each individual in a variety of ways. It is possible that immigrants feel depressed purely because they miss their home country and face a series of difficult challenges in settling into a new one.
X The author has not really broken new ground by highlighting that human brains are more complex than non-human mammals.

Reference
Wexler, B. E. (2010). Neuroplasticity, cultural evolution and cultural difference. World Cultural Psychiatry Research Review, 5, pp. 11-22.

KEY STUDY: *Murphy et al. (2014). Effects of diet on brain plasticity in animal and human studies: mind the gap.*

Links to
- **Development.** The influence of poverty/socio-economic status on cognitive development. See *Luby et al. (2013).*
- **Health.** Determinants of health and protective factors.

Brief Summary

Diet changes the brain in animals and humans, showing an interaction between environment and neuroplasticity.

Aim

To provide a review of research that considers the ways in which diet may affect neuroplasticity and subsequently cognition in both animal and human research.

Procedure

A review article that considers a range of research findings on the effects of a calorie restricted diet.

Main Comments and Findings
- A range of animal and human studies involving a calorie restricted (CR) diet is considered by the authors. Overall, the benefits of a CR diet seem to be positive, both for animals and humans: an extended lifespan has been seen in rats plus a reduction in disease and delays in age-related conditions probably as a result of an increase in and a strengthening of synapses.

- Research using mice showed that there was an increase of neurotransmission related to the hippocampus (associated with learning and memory performance). One study showed that mice on a CR diet for one week displayed an improvement in mood (manifest in a decreased fear response) and a study using rats on a CR found similar improvement in anxiety when exposed to an anxiety-linked stimulus. Rats on a CR diet also became more resilient to age-related impairments, with improvements to their working memory, learning and spatial awareness.

- Human studies have demonstrated that a CR diet brings enhanced executive functioning with a study of aged participants performing better at memory tasks. CR may also be implicated in the prevention or delay of Alzheimer's disease.

- Intermittent fasting (IF) is another approach to investigating the link between diet and neuroplasticity. Rats on IF showed an improvement in hippocampal function and resilience. Mice who had been put on a 9-hour fast showed mood improvement and a reversal in lost synaptic density.

- Some foods may enhance neuroplasticity and blood flow to key brain regions associated with cognitive function: turmeric (which has anti-bacterial and anti-inflammatory qualities), red grapes, nuts, yeast, fish (particularly oily fish rich in omega-3 fatty acids to strengthen neural membranes) and blueberries are some of the foods implicated. Studies using humans suggest that higher fish intake reduces depression and the onset of dementia.

Conclusion
Both animal and human research suggests a link between diet and neuroplasticity.

Evaluation of Murphy et al. (2014)
Strengths
✓ The use of both animal and human research findings in this review show that there may be shared effects between diet and neuroplasticity amongst species.
✓ The findings could be used in therapeutic settings such as for treatment of obesity as well as dementia and for people with learning difficulties.

Limitations
X The over-reliance on animal studies means that the results are not wholly generalisable. Carrying out some of the procedures used in animal studies would not be ethical with human participants so some of the effects of diet can only be generalised to same-species animals.
X The findings that a CR diet and IF are beneficial for a range of functions could be abused by people with eating disorders as a justification for an extreme diet regime.

Reference
Murphy, T., Dias, G. P., & Thuret, S. (2014). Effects of diet on brain plasticity in animal and human studies: mind the gap. *Neural Plasticity*, Article ID 563160.

****

B. Hormones and pheromones and their effects on behaviour (Examples: ACTH and cortisol)

KEY STUDY: *Barr et al. (2004). Rearing condition and rh5-HTTLPR interact to influence limbic-hypothalamic-pituitary-adrenal axis response to stress in infant macaques.*

Links to
- **Health.** Health problems: this is a biological correlation with a stressor (separation) leading to stress, which in turn led to raised and then lowered cortisol levels and compromised health, as chronic/repeated stress is associated with a number of disorders.

Brief Summary
Adrenocorticotropic hormone (ACTH) and cortisol levels of infant macaque monkeys rose when initially separated from their mother soon after birth and fell after chronic separation. This effect was intensified by a short allele on the serotonin-transporter gene, showing an interaction between genetic inheritance, stress and hormone effect.

Aim
To investigate whether the conditions in which infant macaque monkeys are raised affects levels of ACTH and cortisol.

Animal subjects
The researchers used 208 infant macaque monkeys who had either been reared by their mother (MR) or their peers (PR). PR involves a lack of parental care and no opportunity to learn how to behave socially, which may in turn give rise to increased anxiety.

Procedure
At 6 months old the monkeys were put in isolated conditions for a period of 4 full days (96 hrs), which involved no physical or visual contact with other monkeys. The researchers took blood samples from the monkeys at baseline (before separation), and at 1hr, 2hrs and 96 hrs, which they used to measure ACTH and cortisol levels. Researchers measured the length of the alleles on the 5HTT serotonin transporter, with the monkeys possessing either one long and one short allele (l/s) or two long alleles (l/l). Because animals with the xl/l and s/s genotype were rare, they were excluded from all analyses.

Genotype by rearing

Rearing condition	l/l allele	l/s allele	Total
MR	96	45	141
PR	57	10	67

Results

Type of rearing (genotype)	ACTH levels at baseline	Cortisol levels at baseline
MR (l/l)	Lower	Next highest
MR (l/s)	Highest	Highest
PR (l/l)	Equal lowest	Lower
PR (l/s)	Equal lowest	Lowest
Type of rearing (genotype)	**ACTH levels at end of separation** *(all lower than at baseline)*	**Cortisol levels at end of separation** *(all higher than at baseline)*
MR (l/l)	Lower	Highest
MR (l/s)	Next highest	Next highest
PR (l/l)	Lowest	Lower
PR (l/s)	Highest	Lowest

At 1 hr and 2hrs, the levels of ACTH and cortisol had risen significantly over the baseline, but by 96 hrs they dropped, ACTH to below the baseline and cortisol to just above. There was an interaction between type of rearing and genotype, with peer-reared (l/s) monkeys having the very lowest cortisol levels both at baseline and at the end of the separation period, but their ACTH spiking to become the highest of the group after an hour, and remaining the highest, though it dropped in real terms after 96 hrs.

The MR (l/s) monkeys' results were quite similar to the MR (l/l) monkeys' results, with basic parenting seeming to mediate the effects of the l/s allele genotype on both cortisol and ACTH

Conclusion

Being reared in an environment where parental care is absent may result in a blunting of the stress response in terms of cortisol levels. This may be due to a dysfunctional biological response to stress brought on by impoverished rearing conditions. This has been found in human studies. Moreover, recent human studies demonstrate gene x environment interactions, whereby the risk for developing psychopathology or neuropsychiatric disease in the face of stressful life events is more marked among carriers of certain gene variants, including a short allele on the 5-HTT serotonin transporter gene. Barr et al.'s study also demonstrates this.

Evaluation of Barr et al. (2004)

Strengths

✓ Although this research uses animals, similar results have been seen in humans. For example, traumatised and depressed children have lower waking levels of cortisol compared to control samples.

✓ The findings of this study provide some key pointers in terms of the impact of deprivation: this could be used to inform government and other relevant institutions that provide interventions for children in the care system or those who have suffered abuse or neglect.

Limitations

X The researchers could only use data from 10 PR monkeys, which they themselves point out is too small a sample to provide robust statistical results.

X Because the cortisol levels were low for both baseline and separation conditions in the PR monkeys it is unclear as to what the specific role of the stress hormone is related to in isolation/separation. It may be that other biological factors are more significant in the experience of isolation, but this study cannot suggest what these might be.

Reference

Barr, C. S., Newman, T. K., Shannon, C., Parker, C., Dvoskin, R. L., Becker, M. L., ... & Suomi, S. J. (2004). Rearing condition and rh5-HTTLPR interact to influence limbic-hypothalamic-pituitary-adrenal axis response to stress in infant macaques. *Biological Psychiatry, 55*(7), pp. 733-738.

****

KEY STUDY: *Shively et al. (2007). Social stress, visceral obesity, and coronary artery atherosclerosis: product of a primate adaptation.*

Brief Summary

A review of research into elevated cortisol in monkeys that concluded that elevated cortisol, due to stress, resulted in weight gain.

Aim

To investigate the extent to which social stress may be linked to obesity and related disease.

Procedure

A review article that considers a range of research findings.

Main Comments and Findings

▪ The authors' focus is on the damage that visceral fat can do to both humans and animals:

this type of fat lies deep within the body, in tissues and organs and is therefore potentially highly dangerous and may be linked to a range of diseases such as coronary heart disease and diabetes. This review article looks over research in the field and considers the extent to which social stress may contribute to – among other things - the over-production of glucose stored as energy in fat cells. This stored energy which is not burnt off by the body is concentrated as fat cells and, ultimately, as visceral fat. Visceral fat may lead to obesity in particular body regions such as the abdomen.

- Research in this field has tended to use macaque monkeys as they provide the most suitable human-substitute model with which to investigate this topic. Female monkeys have been the focus of the bulk of research in this field as they have shown themselves to be particularly vulnerable to social stress and the attendant health issues that accompany it. The female macaque monkey is highly sensitive to social hierarchies: e.g. who is the most dominant monkey, who is the next dominant, and so on down the hierarchy with decreasing dominance and increasing subordination.

- Subordinate monkeys in typical packs tend to have higher levels of cortisol, the stress hormone, in their system; they tend to be the victims of higher-status monkey's aggressive acts; they are groomed less by other monkeys; they spend more time in isolation than other monkeys. Thus lower-status subordinate female monkeys experience long-term and intense levels of social stress on a daily basis.

- Research has usually focused on packs of 3-5 monkeys living off the equivalent of a typical American diet: i.e. one that has moderate amounts of fat and cholesterol, meaning that the monkeys are not in starvation or famine mode. From a range of studies reviewed, the authors were able to gather findings that point to a link between social stress and visceral obesity: the subordinate female monkeys had higher levels of cortisol which can itself lead to an 'emergency' storing of energy in fat cells; they had a higher number of fat cells than other monkeys; higher cholesterol; higher risk of heart disease and ovarian dysfunction. These females also showed a higher sympathetic nervous system functioning, e.g. raised heart rate, which could in turn damage their artery walls. The authors point to social stress being the root of this negative state.

Conclusion
There may be a link between social stress and visceral obesity.

Evaluation of Shiveley et al. (2009)
Strengths
✓ Research using primates other than macaques has shown similar findings, which may point to

stress as a cause of obesity in more than one species.

✓ Given the proliferation of obesity and its related diseases in the Western world, the findings outlined by the authors should be taken seriously: any research which raises questions about the dangers of stress and a high fat/sugar diet may help to convince people to take up a healthier lifestyle.

Limitations

X The authors themselves point out that the causal pathways between the variables of stress, visceral fat, cortisol etc. are not fully clear so that current research can only point to possible correlation, not causation.

X The use of animal studies cannot be generalised fully to human beings, so the findings remain theoretical in terms of how useful they are when applied to people.

Reference

Shively, C. A., Register, T. C., & Clarkson, T. B. (2009). Social stress, visceral obesity, and coronary artery atherosclerosis: product of a primate adaptation. *American Journal of Primatology, 71*(9), pp. 742-751.

****

KEY STUDY: *Jackson et al. (2017). Hair Cortisol and Adiposity in a Population-Based Sample of 2,527 Men and Women Aged 54 to 87 Years*.

Links to

▪ **Health.** Determinants of health, risk factors, health problems, explanations of health problems.

Brief Summary

Long-term stress in humans is related to weight gain around the stomach area. (Confirming results of animal studies.)

Aim

To investigate the relationship between stress, cortisol levels and obesity.

Participants

2,527 participants were obtained from an English study of ageing. They were aged 54-87 years old and 98% of them were white.

Procedure

The researchers took measurements from the participants' hair to determine their levels of cortisol, the hormone associated with stress. The height, weight, BMI and waist measurements were taken from each participant. The researchers also took into account the following variables per participant: sex, level of affluence and job status, whether they smoked or not, if they had diabetes or arthritis.

Results

Cortisol levels were positively correlated with weight, BMI and waist circumferences. The obese participants (measured by their BMI of 30) had significantly higher levels of cortisol and significantly larger waist circumferences than non-obese participants. High levels of cortisol were associated with ongoing and persistent obesity.

Conclusions

Chronic exposure to elevated cortisol concentrations, assessed in hair, is associated with markers of adiposity and with the persistence of obesity over time. Consistently high levels of cortisol appear to be associated with the type of obesity that is long-lasting and persistent. These results confirm the findings of animal studies and therefore confirm the use of animal studies in generating hypotheses to be tested on humans. E.g. *Shively et al. (2007).*

Evaluation of Jackson et al. (2017)

Strengths

✓ This study used a longitudinal design, which increases its validity, as the researchers were able to track changes over time, enabling them to observe and measure the relationship between stress and obesity at different time intervals.

✓ The researchers used a large sample, which means that the quantitative data obtained is reliable and robust.

Limitations

X   The methodology is reductionist as it measures the complex variable of stress using cortisol found in hair as a marker of stress levels. This is an overly simplistic method to use to ultimately explain something as varied and differentiated as the experience of stress.

X   The sample is almost exclusively white and is limited to the upper age ranges of the population which means that the results are not generalisable beyond this demographic and cannot explain how stress may affect younger people and those from different ethnic groups.

Reference

Jackson, S. E., Kirschbaum, C., & Steptoe, A. (2017). Hair cortisol and adiposity in a population-based sample of 2,527 men and women aged 54 to 87 years. *Obesity, 25*(3), pp. 539-544.

C. The relationship between genetics and behaviour (Examples: stress and genetic disease)

KEY STUDY: *Weaver et al. (2004). Epigenetic programming by maternal behaviour.*

Links to
- **Development.** Influences on cognitive and social development, the role of nurturing in resilience.

Brief Summary

Behavioural epigenetics: rat pups raised by nurturing mothers were less sensitive to stress as adults. Those deprived of nurturing showed epigenetic changes and later went on to become worse mothers. Acquired epigenetic modifications can be inherited and passed on to offspring; this is not just learned behaviour.

Aim

To investigate how maternal behaviour in rats, seen through licking and grooming of their offspring, may be linked to epigenetic changes within the offspring measured in DNA methylation (a process which is necessary for normal development in an organism).

Animal subjects

Lab-born and raised rats from the Charles River laboratories in Canada.

Procedure

The researchers were interested in seeing the differences in DNA methylation of rat pups depending on whether the pups had been raised by a mother that scored high on licking and grooming (LG) and arched-back nursing (ABN) or by one that scored low. DNA methylation was measured by the researchers from the rats being one week old and continued during the course of the rats' lives. To test the reversibility of the LG-ABN nurturing the researchers implemented a cross-fostering strategy whereby rats who had been raised either by a high or a low LG-ABN mother were fostered by mothers with the opposite nurturing style of high or low LG-ABN.

Results

Rat pups that had experienced high levels of LG-ABN mothering showed more differences in their DNA methylation than the pups who had experienced low LB-ABN mothering. This effect was reversed when the pups were cross-fostered with a rat mother who presented the opposite nurturing style to that of their biological mother. The DNA methylation changes were observed to be long-lasting, going from the first week of the pups' lives well into adulthood. The high LG-ABN pups exhibited a reduced stress response compared to the low LG-ABN pups.

Conclusion

Epigenetics can change the state of specific genes and this can occur through learnt experiences either early or later in life. These changes are also reversible.

Evaluation of Weaver et al. (2004)

Strengths

- ✓ This study is ground-breaking in that it demonstrates a clear link between epigenetics and nurture, providing insight into gene-environment interactions across a lifespan.
- ✓ These findings reflect similar results from studies of other animals and plant life, i.e. that maternal responses to stress and attack become 'programmed' within the offspring: such observations have contributed to the field of evolutionary psychology and provide valuable insight into adaptation across species.

Limitations

- X The results, though interesting, cannot be generalised to humans who have more complex DNA than rats.
- X The sample of rats used was taken from a laboratory facility so the experience of nurture and stress is likely to be different to animals in the wild.

Reference

Weaver, I. C., Cervoni, N., Champagne, F. A., et al. (2004). Epigenetic programming by maternal behavior. *Nature Neuroscience*, 7(8), pp. 847-854.

****

KEY STUDY: *Nithiantharajah & Hannan (2006). Enriched environments, experience- dependent plasticity and disorders of the nervous system.*

Brief Summary

Interaction of genes and environment – environmental enrichment improves outcome in genetic diseases, such as Huntington's in mice.

Aim

To provide an overview of research into the link between enriched environments (EE) and observed improvements in a range of genetic diseases.

Procedure
A review article discussing findings from a range of studies in the field.

Main findings and comments

- An enriched environment (EE) for lab animals such as rats and mice would typically involve a highly stimulating cage environment including a variety of different objects, running wheels, tunnels, mazes, exploratory devices, etc. The presence of other animals might also provide social enrichment. Such stimuli are thought to contribute to improved cognition, brain plasticity, and lead to a heightened stimulation of the senses among other effects.

- It is thought that EE may be responsible for neurogenesis (the development of new neurons), neurotransmission, the strengthening of neuronal circuits and pathways and the brain being able to use existing pathways more efficiently.

- Findings related to the effects of an EE on specific diseases in lab animals include the following:
  - **Huntingdon's disease** - improvements in spatial memory and movement; decrease in the loss of grey matter volume in the cortex.
  - **Parkinson's disease** - improved movement.
  - **Alzheimer's disease** - better memory and learning capacity; increased synaptic activity.
  - **Epilepsy** - fewer seizures; an increase in spatial learning skills; neurogenesis.

Conclusion
Living in an enriched environment may contribute to the delay or improvement of some genetic disease symptoms.

Evaluation of Nithiantharajah & Hannan (2006)

Strengths
- ✓ A review article is useful as a method as it enables the researchers to use a wide variety and number of published studies in order to produce an informed overview of the main findings of the topic in a manner that is time-efficient and involves some degree of objectivity.
- ✓ Although the research cited in the article is animal-based it could still be used to inform therapeutic settings in the treatment of diseases such as Huntingdon's in humans. It is a non- invasive and relatively inexpensive measure to take in the treatment of genetic diseases, by introducing puzzles, games and movement-based tasks for sufferers of the particular disease tackled.

Limitations
X   The research leaves some important questions unanswered, such as whether or not there is

a 'critical period' within which EE has the most impact on the brain.

X   The experience of rats or mice living in EEs cannot begin to represent the multiple, often complex environments that human beings may find themselves in, and therefore the findings are limited in generalisability.

Reference

Nithiantharajah, J. & Hannan, A. J. (2006). Enriched environments, experience-dependent plasticity and disorders of the nervous system. *Nature Reviews Neuroscience, 7*(9), pp. 697-709.

****

KEY STUDY: *Lassi & Tucci (2017). Gene-environment interaction influences attachment-like style in mice.*

Links to

- **Development.** Developing an identity - attachment style affected by genes.

Brief Summary

Gene-environment interaction influences attachment in mice.

Aim

To investigate whether maternal behaviour in mice produces a complementary attachment style in the offspring.

Animal subjects

A total of 8 litters of mouse pups born to either a 'good' mother (exhibiting positive maternal behaviours) or 'bad' mother (exhibiting negative maternal behaviours). Each litter contained between 6-10 pups: 4 litters were raised by 'good' and 'bad' biological mothers; 4 litters were raised by 'bad' foster mothers. The total sample size was 140: 64 pups had been fostered and 76 were raised by their biological mothers.

Procedure

The researchers used a modified version of a study (Ainsworth, 1969) known as the Strange Situation (SS) in which a young infant undergoes testing for separation anxiety, stranger anxiety, exploratory behaviour and reunion behaviour under such conditions as the mother leaving them alone or with a stranger. Because the SS is a research method designed for human behaviour it was adapted accordingly to observe mouse-equivalent behaviours, such as how much the pup explored the stranger and how much the mother groomed the pup.

Results

The mice that had been raised by their biological mothers exhibited behaviours that are synonymous with a secure, positive attachment to the parent, e.g. preferring the mother to a stranger.

The offspring of foster mothers did not show a full set of secure attachment behaviours, exhibiting some signs of insecure attachment, e.g. showing little exploration of the mother when reunited with her. Most of the pups who had been raised by their biological mothers displayed a higher number of secure attachment behaviours compared to those raise by foster mothers, in line with their genotype. Pups raised by foster mothers showed attachment styles that were linked to the genetic paternal line, so fostered pups who had 'good' biological fathers were more likely to show secure attachment.

Conclusion

Epigenetics may contribute to attachment style in infancy that can determine the degree of an individual's mental health in adult life.

Evaluation of Lassi & Tucci (2017)

Strengths

- ✓ The results of this study agree with previous research (e.g. guinea pigs seek proximity to their mother; maternal presence lowers stress in offspring), so it could be said to have concurrent validity.
- ✓ This was a well-designed study with a good level of control involved: e.g. 4 groups per condition with an equal number of litters per condition meaning that it is replicable and should give reliable results.

Reference

Lassi, G., & Tucci, V. (2017). Gene-environment interaction influences attachment-like style in mice. *Genes, Brain and Behavior*, *16*(6), pp. 612-618.

****

Content 3: Ethical considerations in animal research

A. The relationship between the brain and behaviour (Example: neuroplasticity)

Rosenzweig's study (already used in the previous section) may be used to answer questions from this topic also.

See above for:
Rosenzweig et al. (1972). Effects of environmental enrichment and impoverishment on rat cerebral cortex. The rats were killed in order to weigh the cerebral cortex of each, and this raises ethical questions, as does their raising in captivity for the purpose of experimentation.

****

KEY STUDY: *British Psychological Society (2012). Guidelines for Psychologists Working with Animals.*

Brief Summary
Guidelines for working with animals: Replace animals with other alternatives. Reduce the number of animals used. Refine procedures to minimise suffering.

Aim
To provide ethical guidelines to be followed by psychologists working with animals.

Main points
- **Replace** the use of live animals wherever possible. This might be achieved via the use of pre-existing video or film footage of past experiments using animals or via the use of computer- generated images (CGI) of animals in simulated forms.

- **Reduce** the number of animals used in research. This might be achieved by using the smallest possible number of animals per study. The BPS advises that researchers should ensure that their experiments are well designed, with a good level of control, using standardised procedures and appropriate statistical tests (in which a good level of statistical power is possible so that the stats are robust to analysis). They also suggest the use of pilot studies to ensure that any flaws with study design can be addressed and acted on before the study itself is conducted.

- **Refine** procedures to minimise the suffering of the animals. This might be achieved in a number of ways: by not overcrowding caged animals and also ensuring that individual animals are not kept in isolation; the normal eating and digestion processes of animals must be considered if this is part of the procedure, particularly so if the procedure involves deprivation of food. Researchers should aim to limit the levels of deprivation or aversive stimuli; field studies should be utilised wherever possible; when in the wild conducting a field study, researchers should aim for minimal disruption and interference with the animal's natural habitat. If the animal undergoes any surgical procedures as part of the research process then proper pre and post- surgical care and monitoring must be used to ensure humane treatment is adhered to.

Reference

British Psychological Society (2012). *Guidelines for Psychologists Working with Animals.* BPS: Leicester, UK

****

KEY STUDY: *Xu et al. (2015). Macaques Exhibit a Naturally-Occurring Depression Similar to Humans.*

Brief Summary

Refine procedures: Not only is breeding and keeping animals in cages for research purposes unethical, it means that the results lack ecological validity. Xu et al. used macaque monkeys to investigate the natural occurrence of depression in socially stable groups under natural conditions.

Aim

To investigate depression as a naturally occurring condition in monkeys.

Animal subjects

Macaque monkeys living at a research base in China in environmental conditions that closely resembled what they would experience in the wild. As per conditions in the wild the monkeys were housed in colonies consisting of around two males and 16-22 females, with offspring of under six months. Having observed the monkeys over a period of seven months, the researchers identified a total of 20 female monkeys that consistently displayed signs of depression, e.g. slumped posture, little interest in food or sex. A control group of 20 female, non-depressed monkeys was used for comparison purposes.

Procedure

The monkeys were observed over a period of 31 months, which consisted of eight days of observation, using three observers, for a total of 5000 hours. The monkeys were filmed and then the three observers rated their behaviours. Behavioural categories included feeding behaviours, sex-related behaviours, conflict behaviours and several others. Biological measures were taken in the form of metabolic analyses of the monkeys.

Results

Non-depressed monkeys spent more time drinking, resting, perching on branches and moving along perches and the floor than the depressed monkeys. Depressed monkeys did not receive as much friendly grooming as the non-depressed group nor did they groom other monkeys as much. The non-depressed monkeys took more care of their young, nursing them for longer than the depressed monkeys. The non-depressed monkeys were also seen to be more independent and 'self-directed' as shown in behaviours such as scratching their limbs. The depressed monkeys' metabolic data demonstrated disturbances in their metabolism of amino acids.

Conclusion

It is possible to study monkeys in near-natural conditions in order to establish a phenotypical presentation of depression.

Evaluation of Xu et al. (2015)

Strengths

✓ This study has high inter-rater reliability with a score of 85% agreement for each behaviour, plus monkeys were scored by blind observers (i.e. the observers did not know if they were observing depressed or non-depressed monkeys), which means that the issue of researcher bias was controlled for.

✓ This study uses a more relevant model of depression than other animal studies as it is the closest representation so far of how depression may develop in human beings.

Limitations

X The biological data (metabolic) was only taken once which means that the balance of objective, clinical data and the more qualitative, behavioural data was uneven, which makes the correlation between biology and depressed behaviour deficient in robustness.

X The results do not explain why some monkeys exhibit depressed behaviour, so they form only a partial understanding of depression in primates.

Reference

Xu, F., Wu, Q., Xie, L., Gong, W., Zhang, J., Zheng, P., ... & Fang, L. (2015). Macaques exhibit a naturally-occurring depression similar to humans. *Scientific Reports, 5, Article 9220*, pp. 1-10.

B. Hormones and pheromones and their effects on behaviour (Examples: ACTH and cortisol)

Two of the studies already used in the earlier sections can be used here.

See above for:

Barr et al. (2004). *Rearing condition and rh5-HTTLPR interact to influence limbic-hypothalamic- pituitary-adrenal axis response to stress in infant macaques.* Monkeys were forcibly held down to have blood taken to measure ACTH and cortisol levels. Baby monkeys were separated from their mothers after birth.

British Psychological Society (2012). *Guidelines for Psychologists Working with Animals.* Gives guidelines regarding refining procedures to minimise suffering. Use saliva swabs for short-term measurement of cortisol levels, and hair concentration measurement for longer-term measures.

****

KEY STUDY: *Stanton et al. (2015). Maternal behaviour and physiological stress levels in wild chimpanzees.*

Links to
- **Health.** Determinants of health, risk factors; health problems, explanations of health problems.

Brief Summary
Investigated the effect of maternal stress on the glucocorticoid levels of infant chimpanzees by examining and measuring faecal glucocorticoid metabolite (FGM) concentrations of mothers and babies in the wild.

Aim
To investigate the relationship between maternal chimpanzee behaviour towards their young and physiological stress levels.

Animal subjects
12 female chimpanzees (who were lactating) with infants between the ages of 6 months and 4 years. The sample was obtained from a larger community of chimps living in a national park in Tanzania, Africa that has been under constant observation since 1960.

Procedure

The chimpanzees were observed over the course of 55 months by more than one researcher. Each sampling session was conducted over two days with one mother and her young being the focus of that observation for a total of five hours per day. The chimpanzee mothers were observed on the first day of the sampling session recording their behaviour with family members and mate; their proximity to family members; the types of sounds they made; their sexual behaviours. On the second day of the sampling session the researchers took FGM samples from the mothers.

Results

High FGM concentrations (denoting periods of high stress) were associated with periods of greater interaction between mothers and their young. The mothers also spent more time nursing their young when their FGM levels were high. The female offspring of the chimp mothers also received more attention from their mothers when the FGM was high, with the male offspring, who were socially more advanced, interacting more with others.

Conclusion

Elevated stress levels in chimpanzees may be linked to an increase in positive maternal behaviours, though such behaviours themselves, if the offspring are demanding, may be stressful.

Evaluation of Stanton et al. (2015)

Strengths

- ✓ The study used a tightly controlled time sampling method with behaviours being sampled at one, five and 15-minute intervals.
- ✓ The study is high in ecological validity as the chimps were in their natural habitat, performing unforced behaviours.

Limitations

- X The use of time sampling could mean that some useful data is lost if it is performed outside of the specific time sampling sessions.
- X It is not clear as to why stress should result in more chimpanzee maternal care behaviour as this study uses correlational data, which cannot point to cause and effect.

Reference

Stanton, M. A., Heintz, M. R., Lonsdorf, E. V., Santymire, R. M., Lipende, I., & Murray, C. M. (2015). Maternal behavior and physiological stress levels in wild chimpanzees (Pan troglodytes schweinfurthii). *International Journal of Primatology, 36*(3), pp. 473-488.

C. The relationship between genetics and behaviour. (Examples: stress and genetic disease)

Some studies already used to explore the role of animal research in understanding human behaviour may be used to answer questions from the ethics topic also.

See above for:

Weaver et al. (2004). *Epigenetic programming by maternal behaviour.*
Some new-born rat pups were removed from their birth mothers and 'adopted' by other mothers. Rats were anaesthetised for removal of hippocampal material and for infusions into the brain, and had blood taken regularly and were restrained to induce stress.

British Psychological Society (2012). *Guidelines for Psychologists Working with Animals.*
Replace animals by studies of humans. Instead of stressing animals, choose humans already being treated for stress or depression and investigate heritability in children at time of birth.

****

KEY STUDY: Scheinost et al. (2016). Does prenatal stress alter the developing connectome?

Brief Summary
Summary of human studies into correlation between pre-natal maternal stress and epigenetic changes in the infant. **Can be used to demonstrate that mouse studies into maternal stress are no longer necessary.**

Aim
To consider research into possible links between stress experienced by pregnant women and the developing brain of the foetus.

Procedure
This is a review article that uses a range of studies on this topic.

Main findings and comments
- MRI studies of new-born and young infants have highlighted a range of possible associations between prenatal stress exposure (PNSE) and brain region dysfunction. A Singapore study using babies aged 6-14 days old found that the infants whose mothers had experienced high levels of stress had less robust right amgydalas, a brain region associated with vulnerability to stress and depression.

- Women with high anxiety levels were also found to have babies that showed a slower hippocampal development in their first six months compared to non-anxious mothers. Other research findings using fMRI methodology have demonstrated that high PNSE has an association with irregularities in brain regions associated with the regulation of emotion and with disorders such as depression: e.g. the anterior cingulate cortex, the medial orbitofrontal cortex and the amygdala.

- Research which has focused on older children reports similar findings to those using infants. In California, an MRI study of 35 mother-and-child pairs found that mothers who had experienced high PNSE had children with a lower volume of grey matter in various brain regions including the prefrontal cortex, a region associated with executive functioning and impulse control.
  Similar research using MRI has found that the children of depressed mothers have thinner cortical volume and thickness, conditions that have been associated with adult depression.

Conclusion
Exposure to stress in the womb is a risk factor for the developing foetus and may have long-term epigenetic effects on the brain, resulting in disorders such as depression and anxiety.

Evaluation of Schienost et al. (2016)
Strengths
✓ The study uses research that is MRI or fMRI-based which means that the findings are objective and reliable.
✓ The findings of this review article could be applied to a variety of health and therapeutic settings so that women who may be vulnerable to PNSE might be targeted with some form of intervention to help protect the unborn child.

Limitations
X The studies used in the article tend to be based on small samples, which makes the results lacking in robustness and statistical power.
X Some of the studies use retrospective self-reports from the mothers which may be subject to unreliable memory, social desirability bias or misinterpretation, making the findings less valid.

Reference
Scheinost, D., Sinha, R., Cross, S. N., Kwon, S. H., Sze, G., Constable, R. T., & Ment, L. R. (2016). Does prenatal stress alter the developing connectome? *Pediatric Research*, *81*(1-2), pp. 214-226.

CRITICAL THINKING POINTS: THE ROLE OF ANIMAL RESEARCH IN UNDERSTANDING HUMAN BEHAVIOUR.

Is there any point in using animals to investigate human behaviour?

Animals have been used in psychological research in huge numbers over the years, with the first use probably being Pavlov and his famous salivating dogs. Biopsychology is the obvious branch of psychology to use animals in research as: a) they have a brain similar in some ways to the human brain; and b) it is possible to go beyond ethical constraints that would apply if human subjects were used. A great deal of research has been done in the field of motivation and addiction using animal subjects, providing some fascinating insights into ideas linked to brain regions associated with learning, addiction and reward. Ethical considerations aside, the question remains, how like these lab animals are we, and if results cannot be generalised to humans then why continue using animals? For example, the brains of human embryos show a larger thalamus and cerebral cortex than rat embryos at the same stage of development. A fully mature human brain has many more neurons than a mature rat brain and is thus capable of more sophisticated and complex tasks.Research by Scheinost et al. (2016) uses the findings of brain imaging studies on babies and children, which are far more compelling and meaningful than similar findings on animals would be as the former have a direct application to human behaviour and experience.

Animal studies can provide a useful precursor to studies on human behaviour.

Shively et al. (2009) reviewed research into elevated cortisol in monkeys and concluded that elevated cortisol, due to stress, resulted in weight gain. This finding was supported by Jackson et al. (2017), who found that long-term stress in humans is related to weight gain around the middle. By initially using an animal sample, in conditions manipulated by the researcher (which would be unethical if using humans) it is possible to see that some aspects of animal behaviour can inform and provide insight into human-equivalent behaviour. This is particularly true when the animals used are closer to us in terms of shared DNA, as mice are, for example.

The use of animals in some studies may be inhumane.

Whilst the majority of studies conducted since ethical guidelines were introduced adhere to the humane treatment of animals, there are still some procedural aspects of particular studies which may be unpalatable when the treatment of the animal is considered. Barr et al.'s (2004) procedure involved monkeys being forcibly held down to have blood taken to measure ACTH and cortisol levels. In this same study, baby monkeys were separated from their mothers after birth, which has been shown to be a highly stressful and traumatic experience for them. The BPS guidelines (2012) stipulate that animals must only be used when no other alternative is possible and where any suffering the animals may experience can be set against the value of the insight and knowledge the research brings. It could be argued that sufficient research had already been carried out in the field of stress and cortisol levels, rendering Barr et al.'s (2004) study unnecessary.

* *

Should we use animals to learn about human behaviour?

Cc. images from pixabay.com

Cognitive Approach

Ethics

Methods

Cognitive processing

Reliability of cognitive processes

Emotion and cognition

Cognitive processing in a technological (digital/modern) world

Models of memory

Reconstructive memory

The influence of emotion on cognitive processes

Influence (positive and negative) of technologies on cognitive processes

Schema theory

Biases in thinking and decision-making

Methods used to study the interaction between technologies and cognitive processes

Thinking and decision-making

Discuss

Outline

Describe

To what extent?

Explain

Evaluate

COGNITIVE APPROACH
TOPIC 1: Cognitive processing
Key idea: There is a correlation between cognitive processes and human behaviour.

Content	Research	Use in Cognitive Approach	Links to
Models of memory	Classic **Atkinson and Shriffrin (1968)**	Multi-store memory theory, visually represented in a model, of how information flows through three static memory stores, each having different capacities and durations.	**Biological Approach:** HM's case study (Milner et al., 1968; Corkin, 1997) is evidence for the existence of separate memory stores.
	Glanzer & Cunitz (1966)	Demonstrated that the U-shape of the serial position curve (described as a 'bimodal serial position curve') is caused by two separate stores for short-term and long-term memories. This supported the MSM.	**Biological Approach:** HM's case study (Milner et al., 1968; Corkin, 1997) is evidence for the existence of separate memory stores.
	Critique/Extension **Baddeley & Hitch (1974)**	The theory that, rather than being a static store, short-term memory is a complex information processor. This is the working memory model (WMM).	
	Robbins et al. (1996)	Found that chess used the visuo-spatial sketchpad and this suffered no interference from rapid repetition of the word see-saw (using the phonological loop), but random number generation or tapping numbers on a keypad reduced the ability to make chess moves. This supported the WMM.	
	Recent **Schneider & Niklas (2017)**	Looked at the impact of working memory and IQ on academic achievement.	

Further resources
TED talk by Peter Doolittle (2013). How your working memory makes sense of the world.
https://tinyurl.com/njcvn58

COGNITIVE APPROACH

Topic 1: Cognitive processing

Key idea: There is a correlation between cognitive processes and human behaviour.

Content	Research	Use in Cognitive Approach	Links to
Schema theory	Classic **Bartlett (1932)**	Schemas constructed from culture and past experience shape our perceptions of current experiences, resulting in memories that are culturally and experientially relevant.	**Abnormal Psychology:** Etiology of abnormal psychology – negative cognitive schemas shape perceptions of people suffering from depression. **Development:** Cognitive schemas shape learning and cognitive development.
	Critique/Extension **Alba & Hasher (1983)**	Meta-analysis that evaluated schema theory as an explanation for memory and concluded that a detailed representation of a complex event or complex material is stored in memory, and what is retrieved depends on a variety of circumstances, with distortion less common than suggested in some studies.	
	Recent **Thimm (2017)**	Study that investigated the relationship between early maladaptive schemas, mindfulness, self-compassion and psychological distress in adolescents.	**Etiology of abnormal psychology** – cognitive explanation for disorders.

Further resources

Useful *Youtube* video on Piaget's schema assimilation and accommodation

https://www.youtube.com/watch?v=3-A9SgbAK5I

COGNITIVE APPROACH
TOPIC 1: Cognitive processing
Key idea: There is a correlation between cognitive processes and human behaviour.

Content	Research	Use in Cognitive Approach	Links to
Thinking and decision-making **A. Dual process and dual system theories.**	Classic **Tversky & Kahneman (1974)**	Heuristics and biases – review and overview of the main heuristics that affect thinking and decision-making under System 1.	**Rational and intuitive thinking**
	Critique/Extension **Pavkov & Lewis (1989)**	Study showing how cognitive biases in mental health diagnoses lead to racist diagnoses. Especially relevant are confirmation bias and availability heuristic.	**Abnormal Psychology:** Factors influencing diagnosis - the role of cognitive biases in diagnosis.
	Recent **Evans (2003)**	Review of dual process theories.	**Rational and intuitive thinking**
B. Theory of planned behaviour and theory of reasoned action.	Classic **Ajzen (1971)**	Theory of reasoned action (TRA). Study into using the Prisoner's Dilemma game to investigate the effectiveness of persuasive communication designed to change behaviour.	**Rational thinking**
	Critique/Extension **Conner & Heywood-Everett (1998)**	Theory of planned behaviour (TPB) applied to mental health interventions.	**Abnormal Psychology:** Factors influencing treatment – how TPB can be applied to treatment.
	Recent **Conner et al. (2013)**	Socio-economic status (SES) moderates the effectiveness of TPB as an explanation for health behaviour because the intention-health behaviour relationship is weaker in people from lower SES groups.	**Health:** Health promotion -How sociocultural factors mitigate the cognitive theory of planned behaviour when applied to health.

Further resources

Review of TRA and TPB. Ajzen, I. & Fishbein, M. (2005). The Influence of Attitudes on Behavior, in D. Albarracín, B. T. Johnson, M. P. Zanna (eds.), *The handbook of attitudes.* Mahwah, NJ: Lawrence Erlbaum. https://tinyurl.com/ybn32lvx

TEDX talk by Colleen McCulla. The power of intention.
https://www.youtube.com/watch?v=FgzROef3Z6s

*TEDX talk by
Colleen McCulla*

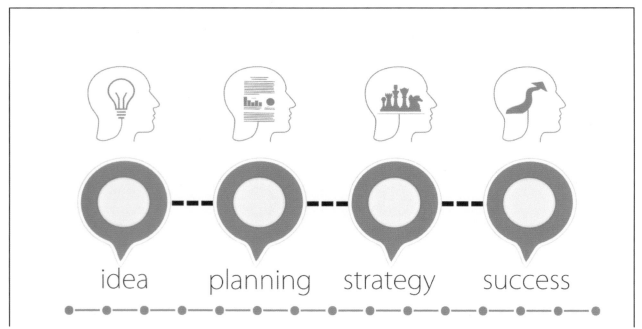

Planning and rational thinking
CC image from pixabay.com

COGNITIVE APPROACH

Topic 2: Reliability of cognitive processes

Key idea: The extent to which the cognitive processes of memory, thinking and decision-making are reliable.

Content	Research	Use in Cognitive Approach	Links to
Reconstructive memory **A. Eyewitness testimony**	Classic **Loftus & Palmer (1974)**	Post-event leading questions can lead to mis-remembering of an event by eyewitnesses.	
	Critique/Extension **Yuille & Cutshall (1986)**	In real situations, rather than lab experiments, memory for events is more resistant to post-event leading questions than previously suggested.	
	Recent **Vredeveldt (2017)**	Eyewitnesses who were interviewed in pairs made significantly fewer errors and remembered more information than those interviewed separately.	
B. Schema theory *These studies are from the schema theory topic, above.*	Classic **Bartlett (1932)**	Schemas constructed from culture and past experience shape our perceptions of current experiences, resulting in memories that are culturally and experientially relevant.	**Abnormal Psychology:** Etiology of abnormal psychology – negative cognitive schemas shape perceptions of people suffering from depression. **Development:** Cognitive schemas shape learning and cognitive development. (See also Piaget, 1932)

Content	Research	Use in Cognitive Approach	Links to
	Critique/Extension **Alba & Hasher (1983)**	Meta-analysis that evaluated schema theory as an explanation for memory and concluded that a detailed representation of a complex event or complex material is stored in memory, and that what is retrieved depends on a variety of circumstances, with distortion less common than suggested in some studies.	
B. Schema theory (cont'd)	Recent **Thimm (2017)**	Study that investigated the relationship between early maladaptive schemas, mindfulness, self-compassion and psychological distress in adolescents.	**Abnormal Psychology:** Etiology of abnormal psychology - cognitive explanation for disorders.

Further resources
California Innocence Project on eyewitness misidentification.
https://tinyurl.com/glwt7c8

TED talk by Elizabeth Loftus (2013). How reliable is your memory?
https://www.ted.com/talks/elizabeth_loftus_the_fiction_of_memory

Innocence Project

Loftus. The fiction of memory

COGNITIVE APPROACH

Topic 2: Reliability of cognitive processes

Key Idea: The extent to which the cognitive processes of memory, thinking and decision-making are reliable.

Content	Research	Use in Cognitive Approach	Links to
Biases in thinking and decision-making	Classic **Tversky & Kahneman (1973)**	Availability heuristic (an example of a cognitive bias): people judge the frequency of something by the ease with which the examples come to mind (availability). In the study, participants judged frequency by the ease with which the famous names were recalled. *(Their 1974 article also covers other heuristics.)*	
	Critique/Extension **Pavkov & Lewis (1989)**	Study showing how cognitive biases in mental health diagnoses lead to racist diagnoses. Especially relevant to confirmation bias and availability heuristic.	**Abnormal Psychology:** Factors influencing diagnosis - the role of cognitive biases in diagnosis.
	Recent **Sundali & Croson (2006)**	Representativeness heuristic and its relationship to gambling: examples of 'hot hand' and 'gambler's fallacy' biases.	

Further resources

BBC Health Check radio interview with Daniel Kahneman (2012). Thinking, fast and slow.

http://www.bbc.co.uk/programmes/p00mmnj2

TED talk by Dan Ariely (2008). Are we in control of our own decisions?
https://tinyurl.com/mqe5xyo

(Note: the speaker is a behavioural economist – not a psychologist. The theories of dual systems and of cognitive biases in thinking and decision- making owe a lot to behavioural economics.)

BBC interview with Daniel Kahneman

COGNITIVE APPROACH

Topic 3: Emotion and cognition

Key Idea: How emotion influences memory, thinking and decision-making.

Content	Research	Use in Cognitive Approach	Links to
The influence of emotion on cognitive processes. **A. Memory**	Classic **Brown & Kulik (1977)**	Flashbulb memories (FBM) are memories for the circumstances in which one first learned of a surprising and emotionally arousing event. This study suggests that they are more vivid and accurate than other memories.	
	Critique/Extension **Neisser & Harsch (1992)**	Noted that research into FBM relies on self-report, with no external check on validity of responses. They interviewed participants about the 1986 Challenger space shuttle disaster one day after it happened and again two-and-a-half years later, and found significant differences between the two accounts. Suggests FBM is vivid, but not accurate.	
	Recent **Stone et al. (2015)**	Compared FBM for two public political events across two cultures, Japanese and Australian, and concluded that different factors may determine event memory accuracy and FBM confidence across cultures.	**Sociocultural approach:** Cultural origins of behaviour and cognition – culture and its influence on behaviour and cognition.

Content	Research	Use in Cognitive Approach	Links to
B. Thinking and decision-making	Classic **Tiedens & Linton (2001)**	Investigated how emotion affects decision-making, with emotional certainty leading to heuristic processing, and emotional uncertainty resulting in systematic processing.	
	Critique/Extension **Slovic et al. (2007)**	Affect heuristic – a clear outline of the theory and examples of how the heuristic affects thinking and decision-making.	
	Recent **Lerner at al. (2015)**	A review of research into how emotion affects decision-making.	

Further resources

TEDx talk by Julia Galef (2016). Why you think you're right, even if you're wrong. https://tinyurl.com/jndfol8

Highfield, R. (15 Dec 2006). 9/11 Study reveals how flashbulb memories form. *The Telegraph* https://tinyurl.com/y7wez3hw

Telegraph article on flashbulb memories

Flashbulb memories

(Image cc licensed from pixabay.com)

COGNITIVE APPROACH
TOPIC 4 (HL extension): Cognitive processing in a technological world
Key idea: Digital/modern technologies have an influence on cognitive processes.

Content	Research		Use in Cognitive Approach	Links to
The influence of technologies on cognitive processes – cognitive processing. *Example:* **memory.**	Classic **Rosen et al. (2011)**		Examined the direct impact of text message interruptions on memory in a classroom environment and found the effects to be a slight, but significant, reduction in memory.	
	Critique/Extension **Sparrow et al. (2011)**		Negative effect on memory of digital technology and using search engines.	
	Recent **Blacker et al. (2014)**		Found that action video games cause improvements to information stored in visual working memory.	
The influence of technologies on cognitive processes – reliability of cognitive processes. *Example:* **memory.**	Classic **Rosen et al. (2011)**		Examined the direct impact of text message interruptions on memory in a classroom environment and found the effects to be a slight, but significant, reduction in memory.	
	Classic **Hembrooke & Gay (2003)**		Investigated the effects of multitasking on learning. Found that students who had their laptops open during a lecture remembered less of the content than a control group who kept them closed.	
	Critique/Extension **Sparrow et al. (2011)**		Negative effect on memory of digital technology and using search engines.	
	Recent **Blacker et al. (2014)**		Found that action video games cause improvements to the quantity and quality of information stored in visual working memory.	**Development:** Developing as a learner – cognitive development.

Content	Research	Use in Cognitive Approach	Links to
The influence of technologies on cognitive processes – emotion and cognition. (cont'd) *Example:* **memory.**	Classic **Gerardi et al. (2008)**	Evaluated the effectiveness of virtual reality exposure therapy (VRET) for treatment of PTSD in an Iraq war veteran and found it to be effective.	**Abnormal Psychology:** treatment of disorders – individual (cognitive) therapy for PTSD.
	Critique/Extension **Morina et al. (2015)**	Meta-analysis of VRET research with phobias and later follow-up, to check efficacy in real-life situations. Found VRET to have real-life application in changing emotion and memories associated with phobia.	**Abnormal Psychology:** treatment of disorders – individual (cognitive) therapy for phobias.
	Recent **Freeman et al. (2017)**	Review of research into VRET as a replacement for more traditional therapy for all classes of mental disorders. Also exploration of its use for better assessment and understanding of disorders.	**Abnormal Psychology:** treatment of disorders - individual (cognitive) therapy.

Further resources

Gillihan, S.J. (13 August 2018). Does Technology in the Classroom Help or Harm Students? *Psychology Today* article on divided attention in the classroom. Follow the links at the end to a recent study.
https://tinyurl.com/ycdnpb9u

Hattenstone, S. (7 Oct 2017). 'After, I feel ecstatic and emotional': could virtual reality replace therapy? *The Guardian.*
https://tinyurl.com/y9vnp2je

Psychology Today.

TEDx talk by Marilyn Flynn and Skip Rizzo (2010). Treating Post Traumatic Stress with Virtual Reality.
https://www.youtube.com/watch?v=V9EF8v-w5Xc

TEDx talk on PTSD and VRET

TED talk by Tom Gruber (2017). How AI *(artificial intelligence)* can enhance our memory, work and social lives. *(Note the bias introduced by his business background as co-founder of 'Siri'.)* https://tinyurl.com/y6wa36ca

TED talk by Tom Gruber

VRET for PTSD

Cc. image from pixabay.com

COGNITIVE APPROACH
TOPIC 4 (HL extension): Cognitive processing in a technological world
Key idea: Digital/modern technologies have an influence on cognitive processes

Content	Research	Use in Cognitive Approach	Links to
Methods used to study the interaction between technologies and cognitive processes – cognitive processing.	Example 1 **Rosen et al. (2011)**	Lab experiment conducted in a classroom during a lecture: IV = number of texts received and sent (3 groups, low, medium and high); DV = score on test based on lesson content.	
	Example 2 **Blacker et al. (2014)**	Lab experiment: IV = whether participant trained on and played an action video game or a non-action video game; DV = performance on visual working memory tasks.	
Methods used to study the interaction between technologies and cognitive processes - reliability of cognitive processes.	Example 1 **Hembrooke & Gay (2003)**	Field experiment conducted at a university during a lecture: IV = whether or not a laptop was used during the lecture; DV = performance on a test.	

Content	Research	Use in Cognitive Approach	Links to
Methods used to study the interaction between technologies and cognitive processes - reliability of cognitive processes. (cont'd)	Example 2 **Sparrow et al. (2011)**	A series of four lab experiments on digital technology and memory. **Expt 1**. IV = level of difficulty of trivia questions; DV = reaction times on the Stroop-like task, to either computer or non-computer terms. **Expt 2 & 3.** IV = whether or not participants believed the computer would save the search statement typed in (and, for Expt. 3, in which folder it would be saved); DV = memory for the exact wording of the search statement (and in Expt. 3 for where it had been saved). **Expt 4.** Non - traditional design.All participants were given statements to save to folders and then tested on which they remembered best: the statement or where it had been saved.	
	Example 1 **Gerardi et al. (2008)**	Case study of VRET therapy used to treat a 29 year-old Iraq war veteran PTSD sufferer	**Abnormal Psychology:** Psychological treatment
	Example 2 **Morina et al. (2015)**	Meta-analysis of VRET research with phobias and later follow-up, to check efficacy in real-life situations. 132 studies reduced to 14 key studies focusing on either fear of heights or fear of spiders	**Abnormal Psychology:** Psychological treatment

Further resources
Youtube film (2015). Systematic review and meta-analysis.
https://www.youtube.com/watch?v=04E8JiXY2s4

Youtube film on systematic review

Technologies and memory
(Image a composite of two cc licensed images from
Pixabay.com)

Key Studies

The studies in the rest of this chapter are all summaries, in order, of the cognitive studies named in the overview above. It is not suggested that you use all of these, but it is a comprehensive and inclusive list that would allow you to teach and study cognitive psychology at pre-university and year 1 university level. The full reference is given underneath each summary, and virtually all of these are available freely online. Happy reading!

****

COGNITIVE APPROACH KEY STUDIES

TOPIC 1: COGNITIVE PROCESSING

Key Idea: There is a correlation between cognitive processes and human behaviour.

Content 1: Models of memory.

KEY STUDY: *Atkinson & Shiffrin (1968). Human memory: A proposed system and its*
control processes.

Links to
- **Biological Approach.** HM's case study (Milner, 1966; Corkin, 1997) provides evidence for the existence of separate memory stores.

Brief Summary
Multi-store memory theory, visually represented in a model, of how information flows through three static memory stores, each having different capacities and durations.

Aim
To provide an explanation in model form of how information flows through three stores, each having a different capacity and duration.

The Multi-Store Model of memory comprises the following three stores, each of which have specific functions in terms of how much information they can hold, how long they can each hold that information for and how information may be lost or retained in the memory:

- **The Sensory Register.** This is the initial point at which a memory may be formed: the five senses (sight, sound, touch, smell, taste) pick up information from the environment for just a fraction of a second's duration although the capacity for holding sensory information is huge, possibly infinite. If this information is paid attention to, then it is transferred to short-term memory.

- **Short-term memory (STM).** The duration of STM is between about 18- 30 seconds with information in this store being encoded acoustically (sounds) and structurally (by sound, by the look of the words or items). STM is thought to be able to hold 7 items at a time, plus or minus two (known as 'Miller's magic number 7). If information is rehearsed in STM, e.g. by repeating it several times, then it will pass into Long-Term Memory. There are two types of rehearsal: maintenance rehearsal is simplistic and may involve simply repeating or 'drilling' pieces of information, (e.g. learning a formula needed only for an exam and then discarding it once the exam is over), or by elaborative rehearsal which involves deeper processing of the information, (e.g. learning lines for a play may require the information to be encoded using a variety of techniques and may well embed recall of the lines for many years to come). If information is not rehearsed in STM it may be 'pushed out' or displaced by incoming information.

- **Long-term memory (LTM).** This is thought to have a huge capacity and duration, both of which are difficult to measure. LTM encodes information semantically (via its meaning). Items in long-term memory can be hard to retrieve as they may become inaccessible which could lead to the decay of those memories.

Explanation of the model

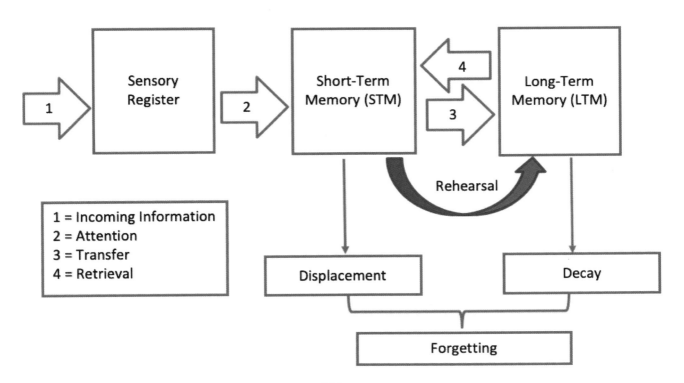

140

Conclusion

Human memory is composed of distinct and separate memory stores, which are independent of each other but are capable of working together in the process of encoding, storing and retrieving memories.

Evaluation of Atkinson & Shiffrin (1968)

Strengths

✓ There is research support for the idea of memory having separate stores: e.g. Glanzer & Cunitz (1966) lab experiment and case studies of brain damage leading to memory deficits, e.g. the case of H.M.

✓ The model is clear and straightforward, helping to explain the process of memory via distinct stages.

Limitations

X The model may be over-simplistic: human memory is surely more complex and dynamic than is suggested by the Multi-Store Model.

X The model cannot account for how a memory may not necessarily need to be rehearsed in order for it to transfer into LTM.

Reference

Atkinson, R. C., & Shiffrin, R. M. (1968). Human memory: a proposed system and its control processes in K. W. Spence, & J. T. Spence (Eds.), *The Psychology of Learning and Motivation: advances in research and theory*, Vol. 2, pp. 89-195. New York: Academic Press.

****

KEY STUDY: *Glanzer & Cunitz (1966). Two storage mechanisms in free recall.*

Links to

▪ **Biological Approach.** HM's case study provides evidence for the existence of separate memory stores. (Milner, 1966; Corkin, 1997)

Brief Summary

Demonstrated that the U-shape of the serial position curve (described as a 'bimodal serial position curve') is caused by two separate stores for short-term and long-term memories. This supported the MSM.

Aim

To investigate the serial position effect as evidence for there being two separate stores of memory: short-term memory and long-term memory.

Participants
46 males who were all enlisted in the US army.

Procedure
Each participant was individually shown 15 lists each containing 15 words. There were three conditions of the independent variable:

- Immediate recall after being shown the list.
- Recall after a 10-second interference task (the Brown-Peterson technique of counting in threes backwards from a given number).
- Recall after a 30-second interference task as outlined above.

The words were never shown in the same order per condition so that each participant received a different set of lists and a different sequence of delay conditions.

Results
Participants in the immediate recall condition showed the expected 'U' curve of the serial position effect: i.e. more items recalled from the beginning and the end of the list. Participants in the 10- second delay condition showed a similar primacy effect to the immediate recall group but much less of a recency effect. The biggest difference between the immediate recall and the 30-second delay condition was that the primacy effect was high for both groups but the 30-second delay condition, out of all the conditions, showed that the recency effect had disappeared with fewest items recalled from the end of the list.

Conclusion
By preventing rehearsal with a 30-second interference task items from the end of the list have not been rehearsed in the STM (which does happen with items earlier on the list) so cannot pass into the LTM and so the recency effect is prevented. In other words, there appear to be two separate memory stores at work.

Evaluation of Glanzer & Cunitz (1966)
Strengths
- ✓ This is a well-controlled lab experiment with a standardised procedure, which makes it high in reliability.
- ✓ The results of the study support Atkinson & Shiffrin's (1968) multi-store model of memory.

Limitations

X   The sample cannot be generalised to females or males who do not fit the demographic: i.e. male and within the age range of army recruits.

X   The procedure lacks ecological validity due to the artificial conditions in which it was conducted.

Reference

Glanzer, M., & Cunitz, A. R. (1966). Two storage mechanisms in free recall. *Journal of Verbal Learning and Verbal Behavior, 5*(4), pp. 351-360.

****

KEY STUDY: *Baddeley & Hitch (1974). Working memory.*

Brief Summary

Theory that, rather than being a static store, short-term memory is a complex information processor. This is the working memory model (WMM).

Aim

To improve upon the Multi-Store Model of memory by focusing on the dynamic nature of working memory.

Explanation of the model

- The **central executive** is the most important component of the model as it directs the phonological loop and visuo-spatial sketchpad (known as 'slave systems') to carry out tasks and to operate according to their function, relaying their information to LTM. The central executive decides which information is attended to and to which parts of the working memory that information should be sent. Rather than as a

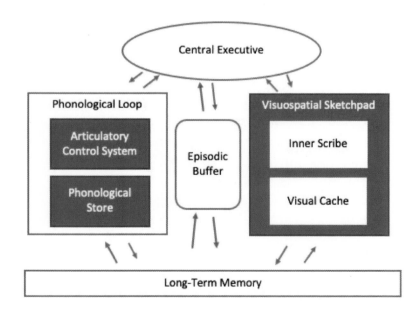

memory store, the central executive acts like a command system that controls attention processes. The central executive enables the working memory system to selectively attend to some stimuli and ignore others.

- The **phonological loop** is the part of working memory that deals with spoken and written material. It consists of two parts: the **phonological store**, the 'inner ear', which holds information in speech-based form (i.e. spoken words) for 1-2 seconds - these enter the store directly. The other is the **articulatory control system**, the 'inner voice', which converts written words into spoken code so they can enter the phonological store, rehearsing information as part of the process. Information is circulated around the 'loop' of this system so that it is possible to remember a phone number by repeating it to ourselves over and over.

- The **visuo-spatial sketchpad** deals with the visual appearance of items, e.g. faces, a landscape and our location in relation to other objects as we move around. The visuo-spatial sketchpad allows people to picture things in their mind so that recall is aided visually via the **inner scribe**, and then stores this information in the **visual cache** which may be linked to LTM.

- The **episodic buffer** was added to the model in 2000: it acts as a way of arranging information in easily-understood sequences, communicating with the components of the WMM and LTM.

Conclusion
STM can be understood and explained via its own model rather than simply seeing it as a unitary store.

Evaluation of Baddeley & Hitch (1974)
Strengths
✓ The WMM explains STM in a way which highlights the dynamic nature of this type of memory with its focus on a range of ever-changing tasks and demands.
✓ The model has found some support in research such as in dual-task studies.

Limitations
X The role of the central executive is vague and has been criticised by psychologists as being inaccurate in terms of where in the brain it is located (Baddeley & Hitch suggested it resides in the frontal lobes; this has been challenged empirically).
X The process by which memories are transferred to LTM is not fully explained.

Reference
Baddeley, A. D., & Hitch, G. (1974). Working memory. In *Psychology of Learning and Motivation, Vol. 8,* pp. 47-48. New York: Academic Press.

****

KEY STUDY: *Robbins et al. (1996). Working memory in chess.*

Brief Summary
Found that chess used the visuo-spatial sketchpad and this suffered no interference from rapid repetition of the word see-saw (using the phonological loop), but random number generation or tapping numbers on a keypad reduced the ability to make chess moves. This supported the WMM.

Aim
To investigate the role of working memory in chess moves.

Participants
Twenty male chess players were recruited from the Cambridge City and Cambridge University Chess Clubs. They were all male and ranged in ranking from weak club player to grand master. The 20 subjects were divided into two groups—weaker players (n= 12) and stronger players (n= 8). Eighteen of the subjects were 30 years of age or less.

Procedure
The participants were shown a chessboard containing 16 black and white chess pieces, arranged as if mid-game. They were given 10 seconds to memorise the placing of the pieces and then they had to recreate the exact placing of each piece on an empty chess board, being given as much time as they needed to do this.

There were four conditions of the independent variable:

- **Articulatory-loop suppression:** the participants had to repeat the word 'the' in time to a metronome whilst in the 10-second memorisation phase of the procedure.
- **Visuo-spatial sketchpad suppression:** the participants had to press keys on a calculator in time to a metronome whilst in the 10-second memorisation phase of the procedure.
- **Central executive suppression:** the participants had to call out a sequence of letters at random in time to a metronome whilst in the 10-second memorisation phase of the procedure.

- **Control:** no suppression task.

Results
Participants in the central executive and visuo-spatial suppression conditions performed more poorly, with worse recall of chess positions, than those in the Control or Articulatory Loop suppression conditions. Participants who had been categorised as stronger chess players prior to the procedure performed significantly better than those categorised as weaker players.

Conclusion
Working memory for chess positions does not appear to be affected by verbal processing suppression, but visual suppression does appear to create an 'overload' effect, preventing visual material from being recalled as easily.

Evaluation of Robbins et al. (1996)
Strengths
✓ This is a well-controlled lab experiment with standardised procedure, which makes it high in reliability.
✓ The blocking of the operation of the visuo-spatial sketchpad did produce a difference in conditions, supporting the idea of the different slave systems within the WMM.

Limitations
X This is a biased sample from which generalisations are difficult: the sample size is small; the sample were all male; the sample's IQ and intellectual ability is likely to have been much higher than a sample taken from the general population.
X The procedure may have exerted some pressure on the participants which possibly affected their ability to use their WM in the same way they might have done under less pressing circumstances.

Reference
Robbins, T. W., Anderson, E. J., Barker, D. R., Bradley, A. C., Fearnyhough, C., Henson, R., ... & Baddeley, A. D. (1996). Working memory in chess. *Memory & Cognition, 24*(1), pp. 83-93.

****

KEY STUDY: *Schneider & Niklas (2017). Intelligence and verbal short-term memory/working memory: Their interrelationships from childhood to young adulthood and their impact on academic achievement.*

Brief Summary
Looked at the impact of working memory (WM) and IQ on academic achievement.

Aim
To investigate whether WM is a stronger predictor of achievement than IQ.

Participants
193 children from Southern Bavaria in Germany who had been recruited in 1984 at the age of four.

Procedure
Originally, 205 4-year-old children from Southern Bavaria were recruited for the study in 1984, and another 25 children joined a year later. Children were assessed annually until they were 12 years old. Two follow-up assessments were carried out at about 18 years old, and again in 2003 when they were 23 years of age. The researchers used the assessments at age 6, 8, 10, 18, and 23 (t1 to t5). A total of 193 children were still available at t3, and 151 participants at t5, indicating that the drop-out rate was rather low for this long period of time. The tests comprised psychometric intelligence tests: e.g. a standard IQ test; WM tests, e.g. word-span recall and academic achievement tests of the type that schools might administer, e.g. comprehension, maths. Statistical analyses were then applied to the data to look for correlations between the variables tested.

Results
There was a strong positive correlation – seen consistently over time – between verbal and non- verbal and IQ and WM.
Conclusion
If working memory is strong in children from a young age it can act as a predictor for their future academic achievement, seen via high IQ scores.

Evaluation of Schneider & Niklas (2017)
Strengths
✓ The use of a longitudinal design means that the research could generate a huge amount of quantitative data which can then be compared with itself across time, giving the results high reliability and internal validity.

✓ The findings that link IQ to WM reinforce the idea that working memory is a dynamic and flexible tool that works hard to solve 'here and now' cognitive problems.

Limitations
X IQ tests may not sufficiently measure intelligence in its various forms: some people may be highly intelligent but may not perform well on IQ tests (e.g. due to issues such as the nature of the questions or the cultural bias that most IQ tests involve).
X WM tests such as word-span recall are very simplistic and do not measure the full extent of working memory.

Reference
Schneider, W., & Niklas, F. (2017). Intelligence and verbal short-term memory/working memory: Their interrelationships from childhood to young adulthood and their impact on academic achievement. *Journal of Intelligence*, 5(2), pp. 26-45.

****

Content 2: Schema theory

KEY STUDY: *Bartlett (1933). Remembering: A study in experimental and social psychology.*

Links to
- **Abnormal Psychology.** Etiology of abnormal psychology – negative cognitive schemas shape perceptions of people suffering from depression.
- **Development.** Cognitive schemas shape learning and cognitive development.

Brief Summary
Schemas constructed from culture and past experience shape our perceptions of current experiences, resulting in memories that are culturally and experientially relevant.

Aim
To investigate the effect of a culturally-specific schema on participants with a different cultural background to that of the stimulus provided.

Participants
Male undergraduate students from the University of Cambridge in the UK.

Procedure
In one version the participants read a native American folk tale called 'War of the Ghosts' twice over to themselves and then reproduced the story after a time lapse of 15 minutes. A different process was then implemented, known as **serial reproduction**, in which one participant read the story then reproduced it in writing; this was then read to a second person who then wrote his own memory of the story which was then read to a third person and so on.

Results
The story was reconstructed in order to fit the participants' own cultural schemas (this was true if the participant had reproduced the story alone or via serial reproduction). The story was reconstructed in the following ways:

- **Omission of the irrelevant, unfamiliar and unpleasant:** ghosts were soon dropped from the re-telling of the story as they do not fit with the way that adult males see the world, particularly in relation to war. Details such as a contorted face were omitted as they may have caused unpleasant memories.
- **Transformation of the material:** 'canoes' became 'boats' and 'paddling' became 'rowing' as it was surmised that these references were more familiar to the participants; puzzling details such as the spirit wound were re-interpreted as a flesh wound with words such as 'therefore' and 'because' inserted to explain the events.
- **Transposition of details from one part of the story to another:** which involved swapping roles played by characters in the story: e.g. one of the warriors was presented by the participants as begging to be taken home, rather than deciding to go home himself as in the original story.

Conclusion
Cultural schemas play an active role in the way that information is reconstructed in the memory.

Evaluation of Bartlett (1933)
Strengths
- ✓ Bartlett's study explains the phenomenon of schematic reconstruction of memory: e.g. two people who witness the same event may give very different accounts of what they have seen.
- ✓ Schemas are relevant in several branches of psychology and can explain the ways in which people may process information: e.g. depressed people are described as having a negative self- schema; children use schemas to build their knowledge of the world.

Limitations

X   This is very old research: university students in the UK are much more aware of wider multi-cultural issues and the availability of information means that these results would probably not be seen if the study was replicated today: e.g. it is unlikely that 21st century participants would not understand 'canoes' or would be put off by the more gruesome aspects of the story.

X   Exact details of the sample and the procedure are vague which means that reliability is low as the study would be difficult to replicate precisely.

Reference

Bartlett, F. C., & Burt, C. (1933). Remembering: A study in experimental and social psychology. *British Journal of Educational Psychology*, *3*(2), pp. 187-192.

****

KEY STUDY: *Alba & Hasher (1983). Is memory schematic?*

Brief Summary

Meta-analysis that evaluated schema theory as an explanation for memory and concluded that a detailed representation of a complex event or complex material is stored in memory, and what is retrieved depends on a variety of circumstances, with distortion less common than suggested in some studies.

Aim

To evaluate the idea that schemas influence memory.

Procedure

A meta-analysis of research in the field.

Main Comments and Findings

After critically evaluating the studies chosen for the meta-analysis, the researchers identified four encoding processes and one retrieval process, which are common to all schema theories. These processes are:

- **Selection** - the process of selecting some information for representation.
- **Abstraction** – a process that stores the meaning of a message, though not its surface (grammatical) structure.
- **Interpretation** – a process through which relevant knowledge is used to aid understanding.

- **Integration** – a process by which a unitary memory representation is formed from the products of the previous operations.
- **Reconstruction (a retrieval process)** – using whatever details are accessible, together with general knowledge, to reconstruct the episode.

The review then focused on the adequacy of schema theory in accounting for three fundamental characteristics of memory: accuracy, incompleteness and distortion. The main findings from this analysis were that people's memories are much more vibrant, rich and detailed than selection and abstraction allow for.

The researchers also found that material does not have to be integrated in order to be recalled and that people tend to be aware of information that has been distorted by their schema, much more so than acknowledged by research in this field.

Conclusion
Schemas do not, on their own, account for what is remembered: the type of encoding at the time of the event; the way that the information is recalled. Context at the time and when recalling all contribute to the production of a memory.

Evaluation of Alba & Hasher (1983)
Strengths
- ✓ The use of a meta-analysis gives the researchers access to a large number of studies, increasing reliability.
- ✓ The findings challenge the idea that the human memory is so easily influenced by schema, highlighting the idea that it is much more nuanced and complex than previous research such as Bartlett's (1933) suggests.

Limitations
- X Using a meta-analysis means only having access to secondary data which reduces the level of control.
- X The researchers might have succumbed to confirmation bias, only selecting findings from the studies they reviewed that agreed with their own ideas.

Reference
Alba, J. W., & Hasher, L. (1983). Is memory schematic? Psychological Bulletin, 93(2), pp. 203-231.

****

KEY STUDY: *Thimm (2017). Relationships between early maladaptive schemas, mindfulness, self-compassion, and psychological distress.*

Links to

- **Abnormal Psychology:** Etiology of abnormal psychology – cognitive explanation for disorders.

Brief Summary

Study that investigated the relationship between early maladaptive schemas, mindfulness, self-compassion and psychological distress in adolescents.

Aim

To investigate the relationship between early maladaptive schemas (EMS), mindfulness, psychological distress and self-compassion.

Participants

212 university students from Norway, with a mean age of 22 years: 74% female; 26% male. The students were awarded course credit for participating in the research.

Procedure

The participants completed four separate questionnaires which measured their responses via forced-choice answers (e.g. 'Yes/No'; 'Sometimes/Never') and rating scales. The questionnaires were on the following topics:

- **The Young schema questionnaire** – this asks a range of questions which are designed to measure the degree of EMS in the respondent: e.g. feelings of self-worth, the extent to which the person feels that they have suffered emotional deprivation, feelings of social isolation.

- **The five-facet mindfulness questionnaire** – this measures the extent to which the respondent expresses feelings of living in the present and of taking a non-judgemental attitude towards themselves and what is going on in their lives.

- **The self-compassion scale** – this offers the respondent a 1-5 rating scale by which to express how forgiving they are of themselves.

- **The brief symptom inventor** – this is a range of 53 psychological symptoms that could be linked to maladaptive behaviour.

Results

The researchers found a negative correlation between EMS and mindfulness, i.e. the participants who expressed a more negative, pessimistic outlook about themselves were less likely to use mindfulness. Low EMS scores also showed a correlation with psychological distress but the researchers found that this could be mediated by mindfulness or self-compassion.

Conclusion

Forming a negative self-schema early on in life (an EMS, in other words) may be linked to negative attitudes such as low self-worth and a pessimistic outlook.

Evaluation of Thimm (2017)

Strengths

✓ The use of a range of questionnaires incorporates triangulation of data, which increases the internal validity of the findings.
✓ Questionnaires are easy to replicate in large numbers, providing robust data that is high in reliability.

Limitations

X Using only questionnaires means that the validity of the findings is compromised: participants may succumb to social desirability bias and the findings lack explanatory power as there is no qualitative data.
X The questionnaires covered some socially sensitive topics which could possibly distress some participants as they could exacerbate feelings of low self-worth and cause them to dwell on negative aspects of their lives.

Reference

Thimm, J. C. (2017). Relationships between early maladaptive schemas, mindfulness, self-compassion, and psychological distress. International Journal of Psychology and Psychological Therapy, 17, pp. 1-15.

****

Content 3: Thinking and decision-making

A. Dual-process and dual systems theories

KEY STUDY: *Tversky & Kahneman (1974). Judgement under uncertainty: Heuristics and biases.*

Links to
- **Rational and intuitive thinking**

Brief Summary
Heuristics and biases – review and overview of the main heuristics that affect thinking and decision- making under System 1 thinking. Related to **rational** and **intuitive thinking**, especially intuitive, which is the result of heuristics.

Aim
To provide an overview of the ways in which a range of heuristics may affect the processes of thinking and decision-making. (Note: this study can also be used for biases in thinking and decision- making).

Main comments and findings
The authors of this paper review a range of research in which they themselves have tested a range of heuristics, looking for evidence of ways in which System 1 thinking (effortless, fast, a short-cut to the answer) may operate when tested under specific conditions. What follows is a sample of their observations:

- The **representative heuristic** is based on the idea that one event is representative of other events very similar to it, using the idea of how *probable* something is according to the individual's prior knowledge of it. Tversky and Kahneman set up a study in which pps were asked to guess the occupations of people from a set of particular details. They were also given base-rate information: e.g. that 70% of the descriptions had referred to engineers, while 30% had referred to lawyers. The actual description given could apply equally well to either engineers or lawyers. For example, one typical description might be something like: *John is a 30 year-old married man with two children. He has high ability and motivation and promises to be quite successful in his field. He is well-liked by his colleagues.* Logic would assume that base-rate information would be used and that the participant would say that John is an engineer as 70% of the descriptions were of engineers. The participants, however, did not do this: they judged that there was an equal chance of John being either an engineer or a lawyer.

- Another **representativeness study** presented participants with this scenario: *Steve is very shy and withdrawn, invariably helpful, but with little interest in people, or in the world of reality. A meek and tidy soul, he has a need for order and structure, and a passion for detail. Does Steve work as a musician, a pilot, a doctor, a salesman or a librarian?* The researchers found that most of the participants chose librarian, presumably because his personality characteristics matched some of the stereotypical features of this job. In this way, the representative heuristic could explain stereotypes: a quick and easy way of categorising someone without having to expend too much effort.

- The **availability heuristic** works by people tending to judge an event using the probability of its occurring: e.g. a middle-aged man with chest pains might be assumed to be a heart attack but a four-year-old child with similar pains would not elicit the same response as four-year-old children do not tend to have heart attacks. Tverksy and Kahneman investigated the availability heuristic by presenting participants with lists of 19 famous people and 20 less famous people to memorise. In theory, the participants should have been able to recall more of the less-famous names simply because they occurred more frequently than the non-famous names. What actually occurred was that the participants recalled more of the famous names, with the inference being that because they were well-known they were more available to access in their memory.

- **Adjustment and anchoring** involves an initial value or starting-point in an information-processing task determining how the final value is arrived at. The researchers tested high school students asking them to estimate, in their heads one of the following: 8x7x6x5x4x3x2x1 or 1x2x3x4x5x6x7x8. Of course, each answer is the same as the numbers are identical per list.

- What Tversky and Kahneman found was that the descending list (8x7x6 etc.) produced a much higher estimate than the ascending scale (1x2x3 etc.) with the researchers concluding that the first value anchored the value as either high or low and that this is what caused the adjustment to the estimations.

Conclusion
Heuristics provide a short-cut method of thinking and decision-making, but this can sometimes be at the cost of accuracy and result instead in intuitive thinking.

Evaluation of Tversky & Kahneman (1974)

Strengths

✓ The authors present a very appealing and accessible version of how people think, which makes for entertaining reading: the examples of research they include in their article are fascinating whilst also being very easy to relate to and to replicate, if desired.

✓ The article includes several examples of research which helps to validate their theory as one set of findings agrees with other sets of findings.

Limitations

X The methods employed by Tversky and Kahneman are not scientific as they lack precision and some objectivity (e.g. the 'librarian' question depends on the degree to which participants are aware of the expected traits of a librarian in the first place).

X The research lacks ecological validity as they were conducted in lab conditions so they cannot explain how people operate heuristics in real-life situations.

Reference

Tversky, A., & Kahneman, D. (1974). Judgement under Uncertainty: heuristics and biases. *Science, 185*(4157), pp. 1124-1131.

****

KEY STUDY: *Pavkov & Lewis (1989). Psychiatric diagnoses and racial bias: An empirical investigation.*

Links to

- **Abnormal Psychology.** Factors influencing diagnosis - the role of cognitive biases in diagnosis.
- **Intuitive thinking**

Brief Summary

Study showing how cognitive biases in mental health diagnoses lead to racist diagnoses. Especially relevant are confirmation bias and availability heuristic, which can result in **intuitive thinking.**

Aim

To investigate whether a patient's skin colour determines the diagnosis they are given by mental health professionals.

Participants

The researchers selected their participants from the patient database covering four mental health hospitals in Chicago, USA. The demographic was two thirds male, two thirds in the 18-34 years age range, with neighbourhoods that represented both black-dominant and white-dominant populations in the sample.

Procedure
The researchers interviewed the participants while they were still in hospital. One of the interviews was diagnostic in nature and was conducted by an expert who had not been told what it was that the researchers were investigating. The researchers conducted the other interview, which it focused on social-psychological measures, such as how socially integrated the patient was and how aware they were of their condition.

Results
The researchers found that their hypothesis was confirmed: black patients were more likely to be given a diagnosis of schizophrenia than white patients, particularly in hospitals located in black- dominant neighbourhoods.

Conclusion
Patients may be being wrongly diagnosed simply due to the colour of their skin.

Evaluation of Pavkov & Lewis (1989)
Strengths
✓ The use of a range of hospitals in the research means that comparisons could be made based on the demographic of the sample.
✓ Interviews provide rich, thick data which has strong explanatory power, and which provides the insight and detail that experimental methods cannot.

Limitations
X There are a range of extraneous variables involved in this research: using four separate hospitals containing a wide variety of staff, patients, equipment, location issues, etc., means that it is difficult to draw meaningful conclusions from the findings.
X The participants may have exaggerated their response in the interviews, or they may have underplayed specific aspects of their response which would impair the validity of the findings.

Reference
Pavkov, T. W., Lewis, D. A., & Lyons, J. S. (1989). Psychiatric diagnoses and racial bias: an empirical investigation. *Professional Psychology: Research and Practice, 20*(6), pp. 364-368.

KEY STUDY: *Evans (2003). In two minds: dual-process accounts of reasoning.*

Links to
- **Rational and intuitive thinking**

Brief Summary
Review of dual process theories.

Aim
To investigate evidence for dual-process as an explanation of reasoning.

Method and Findings
A review of research into dual processing, using three examples to demonstrate the theory. One of the examples used in this study is the Wason card selection task, which provides evidence for dual- process accounts of reasoning because the task is so sensitive to its content and the context in which it is presented.

A. Abstract task (Wason, 1966)
This task demonstrates what can happen when heuristics interfere with abstract reasoning. Participants were presented with four cards, showing one side only, as below. They were instructed that every card had a letter on one side and a number on the other side.

| A | D | 3 | 7 |

Condition 1 (Positive)
Participants were given the rule 'If there is an A on one side of the card, then there is a 3 on the other side of the card.' They were then asked which of the cards they needed to turn over in order to find out whether the rule was true or false. The correct answer is 'A and 7'.

Condition 2 (Negative)
The rule was changed to 'If there is an A on one side of the card, then there is not a 3 on the other side of the card.' They were then asked which of the cards they needed to turn over in order to find out whether the rule was true or false. The correct answer is now 'A and 3'.

Task Results

Condition 1: Most participants replied 'A and 3' or 'only A'. They seemed to ignore the importance of not finding an A on the back of the 7 and they showed what is known as a 'matching bias' - only choosing cards mentioned in the statement. Participants sometimes chose an irrelevant card, such as a 3. In the majority of studies, only between 10-20% of participants got the right answer.

Condition 2: Participants appeared to find this easier than the former task, with the majority of them supplying the right answer.

B. Thematic Task (Griggs and Cox, 1982)

This task was designed to see if context and content, which reduced the abstract element of the first task, would reduce the number of errors made. The task was as follows:

Drinking beer	Drinking coke	22 years of age	16 years of age

Participants were told to imagine that they were police officers observing people drinking in a bar and given this instruction: 'If a person is drinking beer, then that person must be over 18 years of age.' They were then asked which of the cards they needed to turn over to ensure that all beer drinkers were 18 or older. (The correct answer is 'Drinking beer' and '16 years of age'.)

Thematic Task Results: Most participants got the correct answer.

Conclusion

This review concluded that performance on the abstract task is strongly affected by a System 1 heuristic, the 'matching bias': abstract thinking is more difficult and time-consuming than System 2 thinking, so the participants reverted to System 1, which is less effortful, and more intuitive. With the thematic task, the correct answer is strongly cued by relevant prior knowledge of the world, reflecting System 1 processes. This example of two different tasks provides important evidence for dual-process accounts of reasoning because performance on the task depends on the context in which it is presented.

Evaluation of Evans (2003)

Strengths

✓ The authors have put together a careful analysis of research in the field, allowing them to make good comparisons of studies and to draw meaningful conclusions as to dual-process systems.

✓ The research cited does seem to point to System 1 and System 2 thinking as being different, giving the theory validity.

Limitations

X There are details missing in the review: e.g. no information as to sample demographic or size and some procedural details are missed out which means that it is not easy to state that the findings are generalisable or reliable.

X The research lacks explanatory power as it describes what each system does but not how or where in the brain these systems might reside.

References

Cox, J. R., & Griggs, R. A. (1982). The effects of experience on performance in Wason's selection task. *Memory & Cognition, 10*(5), pp. 496-502.

Evans, J. S. B. (2003). In two minds: dual-process accounts of reasoning. *Trends in Cognitive Sciences, 7* (10), pp. 454-459.

Wason, P. (1966). Reasoning, in B.M. Foss (ed.), *New Horizons in Psychology.* Harmondsworth: Penguin.

****

B. Theory of planned behaviour and theory of reasoned action

KEY STUDY: *Ajzen (1971). Attitudinal vs. normative messages: An investigation of the differential effects of persuasive communications on behavior.*

Brief Summary

Theory of reasoned action (TRA). Study into using the Prisoner's Dilemma game to investigate the effectiveness of persuasive communication designed to change behaviour. Related strongly to **rational thinking**.

Aim

To use the Prisoner's Dilemma game to investigate the effectiveness of persuasion in the attempt to change someone's behaviour.

Participants

216 male and female participants were divided equally and at random into the six groups employed in the experiment. The players in the same group were always of the same sex.

Method

A two-person Prisoner's Dilemma game was implemented. The Prisoner's Dilemma is a game in which a cooperative outcome is unanimously preferred to the competitive outcome obtained when each player focuses on self-interest. The two players make repeated choices between the alternatives cooperation (X) and competition (Y). The combined choices of the two players determine the payoff to each. It is called the Prisoner's Dilemma as it stems from the idea that if two criminal co-conspirators are arrested for a crime they committed together, they can be 'played off' against each other by a detective: the detective will try to persuade them, separately, to 'grass' on their partner; but if they both keep quiet then they will receive a much-reduced sentence, (i.e. the best outcome is for each prisoner to cooperate, at a distance, with each other).

In this experiment, the two players were seated at opposite sides of a table, separated by a partition. In the cooperative condition the group members were instructed to consider themselves to be partners, i.e. to cooperate with each other. In the competitive condition they were told to do better than the other person, i.e. to compete with them.

After receiving the instructions, the groups played the game for 4 moves after which they were asked to complete a questionnaire. On the front page of the questionnaire was a persuasive message which promoted either cooperation or competition. The complete text on the front page was recorded and played back while the participants read it. When all participants had filled out the questionnaires, the game was resumed and played for an additional 20 moves.

The experimental design was as follows:
Competitive Groups
- Standardised introductory statement plus **attitudinal** message advocating competition.
- Standardised introductory statement plus **normative** message advocating competition.
- Standardised introductory statement only (control group).

Cooperative groups
- Standardised introductory statement plus **attitudinal** message advocating cooperation.
- Standardised introductory statement plus **normative** message condoning cooperation.
- Standardised introductory statement only (control group).

The questionnaires provided measures of:
- Attitude towards cooperation
- Attitude towards competition
- Social normative beliefs

- Motivation
- Behavioural intention

Results

Before the participants had been exposed to the persuasive messages, there were no significant differences between the gaming behaviours. When the players in the control groups were oriented towards cooperation, normative behaviour (i.e. wanting to fit in with the group) and the motivation to cooperate carried the most weight in the game. When they were persuaded to be competitive, attitude carried the most weight in the game. There was also some influence across components: the normative message had an effect on attitude towards the behaviour in the cooperative condition; the attitudinal message had an effect on normative beliefs in the competitive condition.

Conclusion

The way in which a persuasive message (attitudinal or normative) is presented has an effect on the motivational orientation of the players (cooperation or competition). Therefore, it is important to gear the message not only to the behaviour but also to the orientation of the person undertaking the behaviour. Showed that presentation of a message can affect rational thinking.

Evaluation of Azjen (1971)

Strengths

✓ The findings of this study have good applicability for advertising, schools and government-funded health promotions (knowing how to persuade people to change their behaviour is crucial for all of these institutions).

✓ The standardised procedure means that this experiment is replicable and can be tested for reliability.

Limitations

X The study does not shed light on how normative beliefs develop or what motivates people to comply with perceived norms.

X The Prisoner's Dilemma game is an abstract, theoretical concept, making it hard to use in research, thus lowering the external validity of the findings.

Reference

Ajzen, I. (1971). Attitudinal vs. Normative messages: an investigation of the differential effects of persuasive communications on behavior. *Sociometry*, pp. 263-280.

****

KEY STUDY: *Conner & Heywood-Everett (1998). Addressing mental health problems with the theory of planned behaviour.*

Links to
- **Abnormal Psychology.** Factors influencing treatment – how the theory of planned behaviour can be applied to treatment.

Brief Summary
Theory of planned behaviour (TPB) applied to mental health interventions.

Aim
To investigate the extent to which TPB might influence the treatment of Asian and non-Asian patients.

Participants
65 GPs (general practitioners, i.e. doctors) from 39 different practices in Bradford, West Yorkshire (U.K.); 18 female, 47 male; 10 Asian, 55 non-Asian. This was a purposive sample chosen because
Bradford has an Asian population of 18%, and the doctors working there had experience of treating Asian patients for mental health conditions.

Method
The GPs were sent a questionnaire which measured their responses via a -2 to +2 rating scale. The questionnaire (which asked the GPs about both Asian and non-Asian patients) was structured so that the GPs were responding to questions per section on the following issues:

- Whether they intended to refer a patient to mental health services.
- How well they understood the different cultural aspects of patients reporting of mental health conditions: e.g. Asian patients are more likely to report mental health symptoms in ways which are somatic, (i.e. as a physical rather than a psychological condition).
- How influenced they were by colleagues' attitudes towards the topic of race and mental health.
- Whether practical obstacles, such as long waiting lists or costly treatment, might stop them referring a patient for mental health treatment.
- One final question asked the GPs to state how many (Asian and non-Asian each) patients they had referred to mental health services over the past year.

Results

The GPs were significantly more likely to refer non-Asian patients to mental health services, regardless of whether the GP was Asian or not. The GPs also seemed unaware that non-Asian patients might present somatic symptoms rather than psychological ones. They felt that non-Asian patients would be more likely to benefit from mental health services. They also thought that Asian patients over-used their doctor's practice, that they were more likely to present somatic symptoms, have communication difficulties and less positive outcomes if referred to mental health services.

Conclusion

The Theory of Planned Behaviour can go some way towards explaining behaviour in medical settings.

Evaluation of Conner & Heywood-Everett (1998)

Strengths

✓ The use of rating scale questionnaires generates quantitative data which is straightforward to compare and analyse.
✓ Using a purposive sampling method means that the researchers did not waste time collecting data which was not useful: their specific sample meant that they were able to focus on the research aim in a time-efficient way.

Limitations

X Asking doctors about their intentions to refer patients or not to mental health services is not the same as measuring their actual referral behaviour.
X The use of a purposive sample means that the findings are only generalisable to the immediate demographic: they do not represent the attitudes of GPs in other regions of the U.K.

Reference

Conner, M., & Heywood-Everett, S. (1998). Addressing mental health problems with the theory of planned behaviour. *Psychology, Health & Medicine*, 3(1), pp. 87-95.

****

KEY STUDY: *Conner et al. (2013). Moderating effect of socioeconomic status on the relationship between health cognitions and behaviors.*

Links to
- **Health.** Explanations of health problems, and effectiveness of health promotion programmes. How sociocultural factors mitigate the cognitive theory of planned behaviour when applied to health.

Brief Summary
Socio-economic status (SES) moderates the effectiveness of TPB as an explanation for health behaviour, as the intention-health behaviour relationship is weaker in people from lower SES groups

Aim
To investigate correlations between SES and intention, self-efficacy and behaviour.

Participants
826 school-children aged 11-12 years, at the start of the study, from 20 schools in the North of England. Each school's SES was measured to give a guideline as to the background of each participant.

Method
This was a prospective study, conducted over the course of two years. The participants filled in questionnaires at specific intervals over the course of the two years. The questions, using rating scales, covered the following points:

- The intention to not smoke.
- Self-efficacy surrounding not smoking.
- Smoking behaviour itself in the specific time period.

Results
SES was a reliable predictor of whether the participants were more or less likely to smoke: as SES increased so the intention to smoke and actual smoking behaviour decreased. Lower SES participants did not show the same pattern, with their earlier intentions not to smoke unrelated to subsequent smoking behaviour.

Conclusion
Shows how SES can affect rational thinking and behaviour: low SES may interfere with good health intentions and prevent individuals from making healthy choices.

Evaluation of Conner et al. (2013)

Strengths

✓ This study was one of three prospective studies carried out as part of this research, with the following two studies agreeing with this study's findings, showing good concurrent validity.

✓ Data from a sample of 826 participants at regular intervals over two years makes the findings robust and reliable.

Limitations

X The sample may be biased as a good portion of the initial sample of 1209 participants dropped out and it is likely that these participants were more likely to be smokers from the start, to have weaker intention to not smoke, weaker self-efficacy over not smoking and lower SES.

X The participants may have under or over-reported their intention to not smoke as well as their actual smoking behaviour due to social desirability bias.

Reference

Conner, M., McEachan, R., Jackson, C., McMillan, B., Woolridge, M., & Lawton, R. (2013). Moderating effect of socioeconomic status on the relationship between health cognitions and behaviors. *Annals of Behavioral Medicine*, *46*(1), pp. 19-30.

****

CRITICAL THINKING POINTS: COGNITIVE PROCESSING

Are models of memory overly reliant on machine reductionism to explain behaviour?
The Multi-Store model of memory and the Working Memory model are useful ways of conceptualising a complex cognitive process. However, they are, perhaps, too simplistic in their depiction of what is still, to some extent, a mysterious and unpredictable process. Models of memory attempt to use machine reductionism – the idea that the mind can be compared to a machine such as, say, a computer – in ways which are illustrative and descriptive. This does have its uses as technology has not developed to the extent that mental processes can be observed in the same way that fMRI scanning can highlight the structure and function of the brain. The problem with taking a machine reductionist approach, however, is that complex processes such as memory can only be inferred from the observed outcomes of experiments (which are themselves artificial and contrived). What models of memory cannot explain is why some memories are lost while others seem to persist over time regardless of how interesting or emotional those memories might be. The role of rehearsal goes some way towards suggesting how long-term memories are formed, but it cannot shed light on why and how unrehearsed memories may endure over the years. It could be argued that models of memory represent a

good starting point from which to conceptualise memory, but they lack dynamism and flexibility so they can only ever be a partial explanation of this particular cognitive process.

Could schema theory be used as part of a self-help programme?

In recent years the idea of everyone developing a 'life story schema' has been suggested. A 'life story schema' refers to the mental organisation used to produce a life story narrative that includes only those memories that are relevant for encoding and/or retrieval, providing a bridge between selected life events and the self. This concept could be very useful for people who have mild depression or low affect as it could help them focus on the positive aspects of their life so that they are able to filter events through life-affirming representations rather than dwelling on unhappy events from the past which may in turn produce a negative self-schema. The therapist or life coach could encourage an attitude of looking to the future rather than living in the past, and they could encourage the client to frame negative events from the past into opportunities to learn from mistakes or to simply draw a line under what cannot be undone in a process of starting afresh. This application of schema theory might help to counteract the idea that it is too vague to be practically useful.

Is technology making us all System 1 thinkers?

There are times when only System 1 (S1) will do: when making snap decisions while driving; choosing which flavour ice-cream to get; responding to a friend asking, 'How do I look?' (Although one's response to this last question sometimes does require careful consideration!) S2 is useful when writing long essays, when deciding whether or not to buy a particular house, when pondering questions such as 'What is the nature of existence?' and the like. But are we becoming overly reliant on S1? The last 20 years has seen a massive boom in technology to the extent that a generation of people cannot remember life pre-internet or mobile phones. Social media and a plethora of channels through which to consume media dominate our lives. It could be argued that this tidal wave of information and choice is robbing us of S2 thinking and replacing it with an abundance of S1: bitesize tweets that by their very nature can only relay one message; switching between social media sites, TV channels, music streaming. It is possible to order almost anything online today and have it delivered within hours in some cases. We can find a date with the swipe of a screen and make judgements simply based on the appearance of one person over another. (No need to read someone's online profile – takes too long). There is no empirical evidence to prove whether or not the 'swipe' generation will turn out to be poorer thinkers than 'analogue' types: perhaps this quick- fix thinking is simply making us all more efficient, streamlined thinkers?

****

TOPIC 2: RELIABILITY OF COGNITIVE PROCESSES

Key Idea: The extent to which the cognitive processes of memory, thinking and decision making are reliable.

Content 1: Reconstructive memory.

A. Eyewitness testimony.

KEY STUDY: *Loftus & Palmer (1974). Reconstruction of automobile destruction: An example of the interaction between language and memory.*

Brief Summary
The theoretical background is the theory of the reconstructive nature of memory. Post-event leading questions can lead to mis-remembering of an event by eyewitnesses.

Aim
To investigate how information provided after an event can influence eyewitness testimony.

Participants
45 college students from the University of Washington, USA, for Experiment 1; 150 participants from the same university for Experiment 2.

Procedure
Two laboratory experiments were used for Experiment 1 and Experiment 2; both of them used an independent measures design.

The following table presents the results of Experiment 1 (mean of highest and lowest speed estimates) and Experiment 2:

Condition	Speed mph	Broken glass?	
		Yes	No
Smashed	40.8	16	34
Contacted	31.8	7	43

Conclusion
Leading questions can alter the memory of events and lead to unreliable eyewitness testimony.

Evaluation of Loftus & Palmer (1974)

Strengths

✓ This study represents part of Elizabeth Loftus's pioneering work in calling to attention the unreliability of eyewitness testimony under certain conditions: this and other research of hers has had a huge influence on the questioning of eyewitnesses by police.

✓ The standardised procedure and control of variables make this study easy to replicate which increases its reliability.

Limitations

X Watching a traffic accident for a few seconds on a film screen is nothing like experiencing the event in real life, so the study lacks ecological validity.

X Loftus and Palmer have themselves pointed out that the participants might have been prone to response bias: i.e. the nature of the words may have prompted the participants to think that a high or low speed estimate was expected of them depending on the verb they were presented with.

Reference

Loftus, E. F., & Palmer, J. C. (1974). Reconstruction of Automobile Destruction: an example of the interaction between language and memory. *Journal of Verbal Learning and Verbal Behavior*, *13*(5), pp. 585-589

****

KEY STUDY: *Yuille & Cutshall (1986). A case study of eyewitness memory of a crime.*

Brief summary

In real situations, rather than lab experiments, memory for events is more resistant to post-event leading questions than previously suggested.

Aim

To investigate how information provided after an event can influence eyewitness testimony.

Participants

13 eyewitnesses who had been present at various vantage points during a shooting outside a gun shop in Vancouver, Canada. The sample was composed of 3 females and 10 males with an age range of 15-32 years.

Procedure

The police had interviewed the eyewitnesses at the time of the crime: they asked them to give a verbatim account of what they had seen and then asked them a series of questions after this account had been given. Four to five months after the incident the researchers interviewed the witnesses in the same way that the police had: i.e. first a verbatim account and then questions. Unlike the police, however, the researchers asked each participant two misleading questions: 'Did you see a/the broken headlight on the thief's car?' and 'Did you see a/the yellow panel of the car?' The researchers alternated between 'a' and 'the' to attempt to mislead the witnesses into giving false information ('the' suggests that the headlight was broken or the panel was yellow; there was in fact no broken headlight and the panel of the car was blue).

Results

The following table shows the number of details recalled by eyewitnesses taken from police interviews and researcher interviews:

Type of detail	Police interview	Researcher interview
Action details	392	551
Person descriptions	180	267
Object descriptions	77	238
Total	649	1056

The researchers found 60% more detail from their own interviews compared to the police interviews and a high degree of accuracy (82%) when the interviews were compared to those given four or five months previously to the police. The misleading information in the form of leading
questions had no effect on the accuracy of the eyewitness testimony: the eyewitnesses were not misled by the false information.

Conclusion

Leading questions do not always lead to unreliable eyewitness testimony: in real conditions it seems that accuracy of recall is preserved.

Evaluation of Yuille & Cutshall (1986)

Strengths

✓ This study used a real-life incident with actual eyewitnesses to a shocking crime, making it high in ecological validity.

✓ The researchers successfully challenged previous lab-based research which claimed that eyewitnesses can be misled by leading questions and information given after the event.

Limitations

X   Using a sample of only 13 participants limits the generalisability of the findings.

X   This was a time-consuming study involving a great deal of data being amassed and analysed, making it difficult to replicate, particularly as the event was a unique, one-off incident.

Reference

Yuille, J. C., & Cutshall, J. L. (1986). A case study of eyewitness memory of a crime. *Journal of Applied Psychology, 71*(2), pp. 291-301

****

KEY STUDY: *Vredeveldt (2017). When discussion between eyewitnesses helps memory.*

Brief Summary

Eyewitnesses who were interviewed in pairs made significantly fewer errors and remembered more information than those interviewed separately.

Aim

To investigate whether discussion between eyewitnesses improves or impedes recall of the event.

Participants

80 students from a college in the Netherlands who formed a total of 40 pairs of witnesses. The sample consisted of 20 males and 60 females. Participants were then randomly allocated: 20 pairs in the nominal condition (which meant that they were interviewed without their assigned partner
present) and 20 pairs in the collaborative condition (interviewed together for one of the interviews). Some of the pairs had known each other for some time (the average was 15 months acquaintance). Only four of the pairs said that they did not know each other at all.

Procedure

The participants watched a video lasting eight minutes which depicted a violent scene from a TV drama. Participants in the nominal condition were then interviewed separately about what they had just seen on the video. Participants in the collaborative condition were interviewed separately
for the first and the third interview and interviewed together for the second interview. In the collaborative interview the participants were encouraged to work together to remember as

many details as they could. The procedure allowed participants free recall together with asking them open-ended questions to provide qualitative data and structured, closed questions to generate quantitative data.

Results
The following graph shows the number of correct details recalled by participants in each condition.

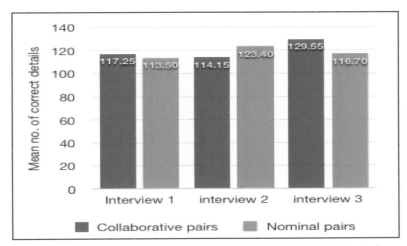

Mean number of correct details remembered in each condition

The participants in the collaborative condition recalled more correct details on average than the nominal pairs – but this was not statistically significant. The collaborative pairs did not tend to repeat information but instead produced new and fresh details after the second interview. In the second interview there were 114.15 correct details on average in the collaborative condition, of which 26.95 (23.6%) were new. They also made fewer errors than the nominal pairs.

Conclusion
Collaboration between eyewitnesses does not, as police tend to assume, lead to inaccuracy of detail or the invention of facts; rather, it appears to minimise errors and to add extra insight to each person's memory of the event.

Evaluation of Vredevelt (2017)
Strengths
✓ The use of both qualitative and quantitative measures involves triangulation which

increases the validity of the findings.

✓ The findings have direct applicability to police procedural settings and could therefore be used to enhance the quality and accuracy of eyewitness testimony.

Limitations

X A lot of the collaborative pairs already knew each other so it is likely that they felt relaxed in each other's company: this would not necessarily be true of real-life eyewitness experience (sharing with a stranger may inhibit recall).

X There was no real jeopardy in this artificial situation: in a real-life eyewitness situation it is likely that people would feel some degree of stress, anxiety and emotion which could interfere with their recall of the event.

Reference

Vredeveldt, A., Groen, R. N., Ampt, J. E., & Koppen, P. J. (2017). When discussion between eyewitnesses helps memory. *Legal and Criminological Psychology*, *22*(2), pp. 242-259.

****

B. Schema theory.

The studies already used to explore cognitive processing and schema may be used to answer questions from this topic also.

See above for:

Bartlett (1932). *Schemas constructed from culture and past experience shape our perceptions of current experiences, resulting in memories that are culturally and experientially relevant.*

Alba & Hasher (1983). *Evaluated schema theory as an explanation for memory and concluded that a detailed representation of a complex event or complex material is stored in memory, and what is retrieved depends on a variety of circumstances, with distortion less common than suggested in some studies.*

Thimm (2017). *Study that investigated the relationship between early maladaptive schemas, mindfulness, self-compassion and psychological distress in adolescents.*

Content 2: Biases in thinking and decision-making.

The studies already used to explore cognitive processing and thinking and decision-making may be used to answer questions from this topic also.

See above for:

Tversky & Kahneman (1973). *Availability heuristic (an example of a cognitive bias): people judge the frequency of something by the ease with which the examples come to mind (availability). In the study, participants judged frequency by the ease with which the famous names were recalled. (Their 1974 article also covers other heuristics.)*

Pavkov & Lewis (1989). *Study showing how cognitive biases in mental health diagnoses lead to racist diagnoses. Especially relevant to confirmation bias and availability heuristic.*

****

KEY STUDY: *Sundali & Croson (2006). Biases in casino betting: The hot hand and the gambler's fallacy.*

Background
Representativeness heuristic and its relationship to gambling: examples of 'hot hand' and 'gambler's fallacy' biases.

Aim
To investigate the relationship between the 'hot hand' and the gambler's fallacy biases.

Participants
The researchers used security videotapes from a large casino in Nevada, USA: no gamblers were identifiable on the tapes as the cameras shot from overhead, with actual players not visible: the camera instead filmed the bets being made (which was possible as the chips were colour-coded).

Procedure
This was a non-participant naturalistic observation of gamblers betting at roulette. Roulette involves a dealer, a wheel and a layout. The wheel is divided into 38 even sectors, numbered 1-36, plus 0 and 00. Each space is red or black, with the 0 and 00 coloured green. The researchers watched the security video footage which lasted a total of 18 hours (3 x 6 hour sessions) of play

at a single roulette table. Since the house advantage on (almost) all bets at the wheel is the same, there is no economic reason to bet one way or another (or, for that matter, at all).

The researchers were interested in the following behavioural measures:

- Placing bets randomly: this makes sense as any number is equally as likely to come up as any other number. (Each turn of the wheel is a new event and does not depend on what has come before or is to come after it.)

- Using the gambler's fallacy: this is evidence of a cognitive bias as it assumes that there is a pattern or structure to which numbers come up, e.g. 'I won't bet on 15 as it has come up the last 5 times in a row so it's unlikely to come up next'. The true nature of randomness means that 15 could come up every time the wheel is turned, as each turn of the wheel is a new and independent event.

- Using the 'hot hand' fallacy: this is evidence of a cognitive bias that assumes that a previous win/loss on number 15 will predict future wins/losses on 15. It operates along the lines of a gambler thinking, 'That number isn't working for me today/I am so lucky today'.

Results
- **Gambler's fallacy:** approximately half of the gamblers showed the gambler's fallacy by decreasing their betting on a number that had come up frequently. The other half showed the opposite behaviour and increased their betting on a number that had come up frequently.
- **Hot hand:** of 139 gamblers, 62 bet consistently with the hot hand bias and bet on more of the numbers that had won after winning with those numbers.
- **Correlation between the two biases**: 42 gamblers who acted consistently with the gambler's fallacy also acted consistently with the hot hand bias.

Conclusion
Gamblers may rely on the representative heuristic, highlighting the idea that their gambling behaviour is not based on logic but is instead dependent on biased thinking.

Evaluation of Sundali & Croson (2006)
Strengths
- ✓ The use of naïve participants means that demand characteristics and participant expectations were not in danger of confounding the results.
- ✓ The use of two independent analysts to view the video footage and check the findings

means that the study has inter-rater reliability.

Limitations

X   The study demonstrates clearly that gamblers tend to use cognitive biases when gambling, but it does not provide solutions as to how to treat this dysfunctional type of thinking which is what would be of real use to gambling addicts.

X   Gamblers who used the 'hot hand' bias may simply have been feeling lazy or unimaginative in their choice of bet rather than succumbing to the representative heuristic.

Reference

Sundali, J., & Croson, R. (2006). Biases in casino betting: The hot hand and the gambler's fallacy. *Judgment and Decision Making, 1*(1), pp. 1-12.

****

CRITICAL THINKING POINTS: RELIABILITY OF COGNITIVE PROCESSES

Could research on the reliability of eyewitness testimony be a victim of its own success?

Elizabeth Loftus is a renowned world expert on the misleading of eyewitnesses by police, usually because the police are unaware that their questioning of witnesses can be a confounding variable in the pursuit of a conviction, not because they wish to subvert justice. Loftus's research (alone or in partnership with others) has broken boundaries and raised concern about the accuracy and reliability of eyewitness testimony: rightly so, too, given the various miscarriages of justice that have resulted from witnesses being questioned badly. It could be argued, though, that because the work of Loftus and others is now regarded with such reverence (see her TED talks for evidence of how compelling she is and how much she is respected), researchers and those directly involved in eyewitness testimony have become rather complacent about how eyewitnesses should be questioned. Perhaps it is time to review the theories, particularly now that we live in a very different world to that of 1974 when her famous 'car crash' research was conducted. Recent studies such as Vredeveldt (2017) demonstrate that well-established ideas (e.g. witnesses should not be allowed to confer) have been found to be fallible: the time may well be ripe for fresh research into eyewitness testimony.

What is a schema, anyway?

The term schema is used throughout cognitive psychology to express the idea that we all carry in our heads 'mental representations' of 'things', 'people' and 'actions'. If that last sentence sounded clumsy and rather immature, well, that's because schema theory is a little clumsy and immature itself. At a basic level the idea of schemas make sense: everyone has a specific set of

references that
they call on to make sense of stimuli presented on a daily basis. An example often given is, 'It has four legs, a tail and it barks – it's a dog'.

But there is a lot of overlapping of schemas, sometimes to the extent that it is difficult to know where one schema begins and the other ends: e.g. My schema for 'Italian food' contains pasta, pizza, parmesan but it is also part of my 'holiday in Rome' schema and my 'favourite restaurant' schema plus my 'cooking' schema and my 'cheese' schema'. The problem with having such fluid and all- encompassing schemas is that, as a psychologist, one may end up asking, 'Is there much point in persisting with schema theory? What can it actually tell us about how the mind works?' Bartlett's (1932) work on the influence of cultural schemas on memory is hopelessly outdated and uninformative on several key procedural details, and yet it is still used widely (by IB Psychology teachers for a start!) as evidence of schema theory in action. What is a schema then? A collection of ideas? A method for sorting information? Or just an over-worked concept that doesn't really stand up to close analysis? You can decide that for yourself (using a suitable schema of course).

Cognitive biases have real and serious consequences.

Any quick internet search will reveal that racial bias continues to make its presence felt. For example, research considered in this section – Pavkov & Lewis – highlighted this by focusing on the medical profession in 1989, with black patients being more likely to receive a diagnosis of schizophrenia than white patients. This is a worrying trend and it reveals the extent to which racism and prejudice may be at the heart of the very institutions that should be protecting and caring for people. This type of bias may operate at a conscious or an unconscious level, but the fact that it operates at all is something that governments and health authorities should be concerned about and should prompt real steps in order to address and improve this imbalance in diagnosis.

A diagnosis of schizophrenia can label someone as it carries with it a certain stigma which could affect job and other prospects: it may also involve a course of medication, which – if the diagnosis is incorrect – can have terrible consequences for the misdiagnosed person. Doctors and other health professionals must be mindful of the dangers of diagnosing and treating patients according to ethnicity or other broad markers like gender, age or socio-economic status, as they hold in their power the potential to affect their patients' lives forever.

****

TOPIC 3: EMOTION AND COGNITION

Key Idea: How emotion influences memory, thinking and decision-making.

Content: The influence of emotion on cognitive processes.

A. Memory.

KEY STUDY: *Brown & Kulik (1977). Flashbulb memories.*

Background
Flashbulb memories (FBM) are memories of the circumstances in which one first learned of a surprising and emotionally arousing event. This study suggests that they are more vivid and accurate than other memories.

Participants
The researchers recruited a volunteer sample from Harvard University consisting of 40 Caucasian Americans and 40 African Americans; the age range was 20-60 years old.

Procedure
The participants were given questionnaires asking them about their memories surrounding the details of when they first found out about the death of eight famous people including John F. Kennedy and Martin Luther King. They were also asked to recall an incident from their own lives in which they had experienced a sudden, unexpected shock, e.g. the death of someone close to them, a serious medical diagnosis, etc. They were then asked to write a free recall of the circumstances in any form or order and at any length. They were also asked to rate how important the event was to them.

Results
The Caucasian Americans (39/40) reported the strongest FBMs about the assassination of John F. Kennedy; for the African Americans (40/40) this was also a very strong FBM. 69 out of the 80 participants reported FBMs linked to personal shock. Race was a factor, with more African Americans having FBMs connected the deaths of important black figures, e.g. Malcolm X and more Caucasian Americans having FBMs for white leaders, e.g. Gerald Ford.

Conclusion
FBMs are vivid memories which can be recalled instantly. They will vary in strength according to

the significance of the event to the person recalling it, and they depend on the person experiencing surprise and strong emotion at the time of forming the memory.

Evaluation of Brown & Kulik (1977)

Strengths

✓ The use of leaders with high significance for either the black or white communities enabled the researchers to identify the relationship between personal significance and flashbulb memory.

✓ The researchers used a standardised procedure, with all participants experiencing the same stimuli which means that the study is replicable which increases its reliability.

Limitations

X There are issues with the sample: it is small; it is drawn from a very elite establishment and it used volunteers (this tends to attract similar personality types), making it difficult to generalise the results.

X The participants may have exaggerated their FBMs of same-race leaders as a way of identifying with others in their ethnic group.

Reference

Brown, R., & Kulik, J. (1977). Flashbulb memories. *Cognition, 5(*1), pp. 73-99.

****

KEY STUDY: *Neisser & Harsch (1992). Phantom flashbulbs: False recollections of hearing the news about Challenger.*

Background

Noted that research into FBM relies on self-report, with no external check on validity of responses. They interviewed participants about the 1986 Challenger space shuttle disaster one day after it happened and again two-and-a-half years later and found significant differences between the two accounts. Suggests FBM is vivid, but not accurate.

Aim

To challenge the idea that flashbulb memories are accurate.

Participants

44 first-year student participants (30 female; 14 male) who had witnessed the explosion of the Challenger space shuttle on television on January 28 1986.

Procedure
The participants were given questionnaires on the morning after the disaster had taken place. The questionnaire asked them to give a free-recall description of how they came to hear of the disaster followed by several pre-determined questions pertaining where they were, who they were with, etc. when they first heard or saw the news of the disaster. They were also asked to estimate how much time they had spent discussing the disaster or following media coverage of it. 32-34 months later the participants filled in the same questionnaire, but this time they were also asked to rate their level of confidence in the accuracy of their memory on a 1-5 scale. They were also asked if they had ever filled in the questionnaire in the past.

Results
When participants were questioned one day after the disaster, 21% reported hearing about it on TV. However, two-and-a-half years later (32-34 months), 45% of them reported hearing about it on TV. Their memories of how they knew about the Challenger explosion had changed over time.
Moreover, in this second interview, some of them reported being at certain events when they heard, although such events were not taking place at the time. It is also interesting to note that 25% of the sample claimed that they had never filled in a questionnaire on the topic before. The level of confidence in the memories was also high – for both accurate and inaccurate memories.

Conclusion
FBMs may be vivid, long-lasting and meaningful to the person recalling them but they are not necessarily accurate or reliable, although people persist in sticking to their version of what happened.

Evaluation of Neisser & Harsch (1992)
Strengths
- ✓ The use of a longitudinal design means that the researchers were able to compare participants' original responses with later responses, which is the test-retest method for external reliability of a measure.
- ✓ The findings demonstrate that previous research into FBMs neglected to scrutinise their accuracy, which is an important finding, particularly in an eyewitness context, (e.g. if a witness were reporting on a crime committed some time ago).

Limitations
- X The usefulness of this research may be limited: if people are highly confident of the accuracy of their FBMs (even when their errors are pointed out to them), then there may be

little that can be done to remedy this.

X   The study focuses on how people form memories of an event which did not directly involve them, so the findings cannot be generalised to all emotional or shocking (particularly personal) events.

Reference

Neisser, U., & Harsch, N. (1992). Phantom flashbulbs: False recollections of hearing the news about Challenger. In E. Winograd & U. Neisser (Eds.), *Emory symposia in cognition, 4. Affect and accuracy in recall: studies of "flashbulb" memories* (pp. 9-31). New York: Cambridge University Press.

****

KEY STUDY: *Stone et al. (2015). Remembering Public, Political Events: A Cross-Cultural and Sectional Examination of Australian and Japanese Public Memories.*

Links to

▪   Sociocultural approach: Cultural origins of behaviour and cognition – culture and its influence on behaviour and cognition.

Background

Compared FBM for two public political events across two cultures: Japanese and Australian and concluded that different factors may determine event memory accuracy and FBM confidence across cultures.

Aim

To assess to what extent emotion plays a role in recalling significant past events, using a cross-cultural perspective.

Participants

245 university students from Sydney (40) and Tokyo (205).

Procedure

The researchers used the real-life resignations of both the Japanese and the Australian Prime Minister in 2010: both events occurred within a short time of each other and both were strikingly similar (each Prime Minister resigned as a result of not following party political ideology). Each participant filled in a questionnaire 3-5 weeks after the respective Prime Minister's resignation. The questionnaire included measures of how accurate the participant's memory was; how confident they were in their memory of the event; emotions connected to the event; how much rehearsal they had done of the event.

Results

There were differences in the way that the participants recalled the events: the Japanese recalled the event more negatively than the Australians, who tended to take a more positive outlook. It was found that positive emotions were associated with better accuracy for the Australian participants but that negative emotions improved the accuracy of the Japanese participants' recall. High confidence in memory of the event was found only in Australian participants.

Conclusion

FBMs may be influenced by culture: collectivist cultures appear to utilise a more negative view of past events than individualistic cultures and this seems to improve accuracy of recall.

Evaluation of Stone et al. (2015)

Strengths

✓ Using two very similar public events means that the researchers controlled for some possible extraneous variables.

✓ The questionnaires included a measure of how independent/interdependent each participant felt which was then correlated with the other measures, increasing the internal validity of the study (independence is associated with individualistic cultures; interdependence is associated with collectivist cultures).

Limitations

X Using questionnaires is one way of demonstrating what participants think/feel but as a method they lack depth and insight.

X The results state that Japanese people tend to view the past negatively which may perpetuate cultural stereotypes and may in fact be based on misinterpretation of the Japanese participants' responses.

Reference

Stone, C. B., Luminet, O., & Takahashi, M. (2015). Remembering Public, Political Events: A Cross-Cultural and-Sectional Examination of Australian and Japanese Public Memories. *Applied Cognitive Psychology*, *29*(2), pp. 280-290.

****

B. Thinking and decision-making

KEY STUDY: *Tiedens & Linton (2001). Judgment under emotional certainty and uncertainty: the effects of specific emotions on information processing.*

Background
Investigated how emotion affects decision-making, with emotional certainty leading to heuristic processing, and emotional uncertainty resulting in systematic processing.

Aim
To investigate how emotion may trigger heuristics or deeper processing.

Participants
118 university students from Stanford University, USA (61 male; 57 female).

Procedure
The participants were asked to write about something that had happened in their own lives. There were 4 possible conditions within the study's design:

- Whether the event prompted **positive** or **negative** emotions.
- Whether the event was based on **certainty** or **uncertainty**.

In the negative certain condition participants were asked to remember, relive, and vividly recall a negative event that had made them feel disgusted; in the negative uncertain condition participants were asked to recall an event that made them feel scared. The positive certain condition asked for recall of a happy event whereas the positive uncertain condition asked for recall of a hopeful event. Participants were also asked to predict what may occur in the year 2000, under each of the four conditions listed.

Results
In the certainty condition participants tended to use heuristics more readily than in the uncertainty condition. Participants who were induced to feel a certainty-associated emotion were more certain about their Year 2000 predictions than were participants who were induced to feel uncertainty- associated emotions. Certainty in one domain, (e.g. emotion experienced), was found to be replicated in further experiments conducted by the researchers while uncertainty was shown to prompt deeper processing of the information, (also supported by further experiments in this study).

183

Conclusion
Uncertainty may trigger deeper processing, possibly because it causes people to question what they know and to analyse available information.

Evaluation of Tiedens & Linton (2001)
Strengths
✓ There is much triangulation of data in this study as the researchers conducted four separate experiments, increasing the validity of the findings.

✓ By focusing on the influence of emotion on thinking and decision-making the researchers have included an important element that is often lacking in this field of research, with much literature on this topic regarding humans as little more than information-processors.

Limitations
X The four conditions of the IV are rather vague and difficult to operationalise.

X People's response to the emotional manipulation by the researchers is something that is difficult to control for as everybody will have a different idea of what 'disgust' or 'hopeful' means, therefore the findings may be affected by participant variables.

Reference
Tiedens, L. Z., & Linton, S. (2001). Judgment under emotional certainty and uncertainty: the effects of specific emotions on information processing. *Journal of Personality and Social Psychology*, *81*(6), pp. 973-988.

****

KEY STUDY: *Slovic et al. (2007). The affect heuristic.*

Background
The affect heuristic – a clear outline of the theory and examples of how the heuristic affects thinking and decision-making.

Aim
To present an overview of the affect heuristic – the ease and speed with which people judge stimuli to be 'good' or 'bad'.

Main comments and findings
A review of research into the affect heuristic. What follows is a selection of key findings and points relating to the theory:

- The 'mere exposure effect' may be a factor in the affect heuristic: the authors cite research in which a favourable ('good') judgement was made of stimuli participants had been presented with several times over less familiar material.

- The affect heuristic may operate in very obvious ways. Research on this topic is cited by the authors: pictures of students accused of cheating who were smiling received less punishment than students accused of cheating who were not smiling. Smiling students were judged to be more trustworthy, good, honest, genuine, obedient, blameless, sincere, and admirable than the students who were not smiling.

- People are attracted to gambles that present a small loss against a bigger win rather than when the win alone is presented. A study used the following win/loss gamble: 7/36 win $9; 29/36 lose 5 cents, i.e. it had an attractive payoff ratio (which should appear as 'good' in terms of how people appraise it). Prior to adding this 5 cents loss angle, participants had rejected the idea of winning $9 on a bet: once the small loss was pitted against it, the acceptance of the bet was huge.

- Several empirical studies have demonstrated a strong relationship between imagery, affect, and decision-making. Many of these studies used a word-association technique. This method involves presenting participants with a word or very brief phrase and asking them to provide the first thought or image that comes to mind. One study asked participants to say what they felt about images of two American cities, San Diego and Denver, and to give their overall affective rating for each city. One participant showed a clear preference for San Diego, (e.g. 'Good beaches', 'Pretty town'), over Denver, (e.g. 'Crowded', 'Busy streets'). The results were highly predictive of expressed preferences for living in or visiting the preferred city. In one study they found that the image score predicted the location of actual vacations over the next 18 months.

- People are influenced by something called 'proportion dominance' which can cloud their judgement, causing them to use the affect heuristic. One of the authors of this research predicted (and found) that people would more strongly support an airport-safety measure expected to save 98% of 150 lives at risk than a measure expected to save all 150 lives. Saving 150 lives is good; however, it seems less powerful than saving 98% of lives because 98% is large in terms of percentages (even though 98% of 150 is clearly fewer than 150!). It is so close to the upper bound on the percentage scale that it may seem better than merely 150 as a number.

- The affect heuristic suggests that there is an inverse relationship between an activity's

185

perceived risk and perceived benefit and that this is linked to the strength of positive or negative affect associated with that activity. This implies that people base their judgments of an activity not only on what they think about it but also on what they feel about it. If they like an activity, they are moved to judge the risks as low and the benefits as high; if they dislike it, they tend to the opposite judgement—high risk and low benefit. This might explain why some people swim in a sea that has strong currents, go base-jumping or take psychoactive drugs (they have decided to perceive the benefits as outweighing the risks).

Conclusion
Decision-making may not be the result of logical and reflective reasoning; it may depend to a large extent on the affect heuristic.

Evaluation of Slovic et al. (2007)
Strengths
✓ The authors have put together a rather joyful and enthusiastic appreciation of the affect heuristic and this makes their article an extremely interesting, engaging and thought-provoking read.
✓ The research cited has real-world applicability, making it easy to relate to: having awareness of the affect heuristic could possibly help to prevent people making silly mistakes in the future.

Limitations
X There is an array and variety of research cited which is somewhat lacking in consistency and cohesion, making it difficult to draw meaningful conclusions.
X Some of the research cited appears overly simplistic and there is a lack of explanatory detail of procedure at times.

References
Slovic, P., Finucane, M. L., Peters, E., & MacGregor, D. G. (2007). The affect heuristic. *European Journal of Operational Research*, *177*(3), pp. 1333-1352.

****

KEY STUDY: *Lerner et al. (2015). Emotion and decision making.*

Background
A review of research into how emotion affects decision-making.

Aim
To present an overview of research on the topic of emotions acting as cognitive biases.

Main comments and findings
A review of research into emotion and decision-making. What follows are a selection of key findings and observations made by the authors:

- Most research on this topic has focused on the negative impact of emotions on decision- e.g. anger at injustice.

- The authors highlight a phenomenon called 'incidental emotion' – a process by which emotion experienced in one setting or from one cause is transferred to another setting or target. They cite a study in which participants read newspaper stories designed to induce positive or negative mood, and then estimated fatality frequencies for various potential causes of death, (e.g., heart disease). Participants who read negative stories offered pessimistic estimates of fatalities compared to participants who read positive stories, thus incidental emotion affected their judgement.

- Emotions may conserve cognitive energy by providing people with implicit perceptual skills for acting in specific ways: e.g. prior experience of feeling anger means that an individual can appraise the situation swiftly and not have to expend energy trying to work out which emotion they are feeling – and a subsequent response is immediate. One study showed that people who are predisposed to feeling fearful consistently made pessimistic judgements of future events whereas those predisposed to anger were optimistic about future events, possibly because anger is an emotion that is generally followed by definite action whereas fear often has no definite target or action that can be taken to reduce that fear.

- Emotions influence the depth of information processing related to decision-making with the suggestion that negative emotions should act as a warning signal, indicating threat and therefore should be processed more deeply and effortfully than positive emotions which signal that the environment is safe. Several studies have shown that people who felt positive were more influenced by heuristic cues, (e.g. appearance, likeability); they also relied more on stereotypes to judge people and situations.

- Emotions help us to operationalise social decisions: they are communication systems that help people navigate and coordinate social interactions by providing information about the motives and dispositions of others, ultimately allowing for the creation and maintenance of healthy and productive social relationships. One study investigating this idea found that people seem to use others' emotional displays to make inferences about their motives and, subsequently, their mental states.

Conclusion
Emotions play an integral role in decision-making, with both positive and negative outcomes.

Evaluation of Lerner et al. (2015)

Strengths
- ✓ The authors treat emotion as a positive influence on decision-making, which is a fresh perspective on the topic.
- ✓ The research cited derives from a wide range of sources and uses a variety of measures, which increases the validity of the findings via triangulation of data.

Limitations
- X Emotion is a notoriously tricky variable to operationalise and some of the cited research findings are a little vague as to how this was achieved.
- X A review article uses mainly secondary data over which there is no control and this lowers its reliability.

References

Lerner, J. S., Li, Y., Valdesolo, P., & Kassam, K. S. (2015). Emotion and decision making. *Annual Review of Psychology, 66,* pp. 799-823.

****

CRITICAL THINKING POINTS: EMOTION AND COGNITION

Is research into flashbulb memory overly reliant on the self-report method?

Flashbulb memory (FBM) is, according to early research, a memory that is quite distinct from everyday memories, being more vivid, accurate and long-lasting, and prompted by a shocking, emotionally charged event which is of some relevance to the person experiencing it. FBMs (like other types of memory) cannot be measured using brain-imaging technologies so the only method available to researchers is self-reports, as in the studies of Brown & Kulik (1977) and Neisser & Harsch (1992). These studies found conflicting evidence on the accuracy and longevity of FBMs, with Brown & Kulik claiming support for the idea that FBMs are more accurate than everyday memories, but Neisser & Harsch finding that FBMs are prone to modification, decay and unreliability over time. Both studies use the self-report method and so are vulnerable to the types of bias that can pose a threat to the validity of the findings. Social desirability bias may temper the way in which particular memories are presented (e.g. the participant may wish to present themselves in the best way possible); response bias may occur if the participant feels that a particular response is desirable (something which can happen when leading questions are used); or some participants may be convinced that they saw/heard/felt something that, in fact, did not happen at all (and with personal FBMs there is no way of checking this).

Does cultural misunderstanding invalidate some research into FBM?

Stoner et al. (2015) claimed that Japanese participants viewed the resignation of the Japanese Prime Minister in a more negative way than the Australian participants viewed their own Prime Minister's resignation. This finding may in fact perpetuate cultural stereotypes and may instead be based on misinterpretation of the Japanese participants' responses. Western, individualistic cultures place a lot of importance on the idea of maintaining a positive mindset, even in the face of negative events, whereas the Japanese tradition is to be more reflective and to consider the extent to which individual behaviours can damage the wider community, from the immediate family group to the whole nation. To label the Japanese response 'negative' may be an imposed etic as it casts the behaviour of different culture in the light of another culture – often one that may be more dominant.

The affect heuristic is a gift to advertisers and salespeople.

Slovic et al. (2007) identified a range of ways in which the affect heuristic affects decision-making. Their findings identify how, through the manipulation of emotions, people are persuaded to particular decisions and products sold to them. The finding that, shown photographs of smiling cheats, participants chose less harsh punishments over those chosen for non-smiling cheats has probable commercial value, as people tend to buy from those they find appealing. The research also discussed the apparent fact that gambles that present a small loss against a bigger win rather than one where the win alone is presented. This technique finds its parallel in the selling of goods, where instead of presenting a single price for a product customers are told that 'today the price is X lower than it was yesterday, so hurry because the price will rise again tomorrow.' So the customer thinks they will be 'saving' money at the 'bargain' price for a good that they may not even need and will cost more than they initially would have considered.

****

TOPIC 4 (EXTENSION): COGNITIVE PROCESSING IN A TECHNOLOGICAL (DIGITAL/MODERN) WORLD

KEY IDEA: How technologies (digital/modern) affect cognitive processes.

Content 1: The influence (positive and negative) of technologies on cognitive processes

A. Cognitive processing (Example: memory)

KEY STUDY: *Rosen et al. (2011). An empirical examination of the educational impact of text message-induced task switching in the classroom: Educational implications and strategies to enhance learning.*

Background
Examined the direct impact of text message interruptions on memory in a classroom environment and found the effects to be a slight, but significant, reduction in memory.

Aim
To examine the direct impact of text message interruptions on memory recall in a classroom environment.

Participants
185 college students (80% female; 20% male; age range 18-66 years; mean 25 years old). 83% of the sample was born between 1980 and 1989, and so belong to what is called the 'Net Generation'.

190

Procedure

Participants were told that they were going to view a 30-minute videotaped lecture relevant to their course and that during the session some of them would receive texts from the researchers to which they should respond as promptly as possible. They were informed that they would be tested on the material after the lecture. There were three conditions:

- The no-text condition (no texts were sent to participants in this condition).
- The 4-text condition (4 texts were sent to participants in this condition).
- The 8-text condition (8 texts were sent to participants in this condition).

Following the test after the lecture, participants were asked to list information about the text messages, including time received, whether a response was sent and the number of words in the response. They also noted any personal text messages they received during the lecture. Participants were also asked questions about their typical texting behaviours in the classroom and their attitudes about whether it was acceptable to text during class and whether texting during lectures harmed their ability to learn the material.

Results

Some of the participants did not receive all the text messages and some also received personal texts, so the groups were rearranged slightly:

- No/low texting – 0-7 texts received and sent
- Moderate texting – 8-15 texts received and sent
- High texting – 16 or more texts received and sent

75% of participants agreed that receiving and sending texts severely impairs learning when carried out during a lecture, but 40% agreed it was acceptable to text during a lecture. 18% said they never responded to a text in class; 67% stated that they would respond to a friend's text; 75% would respond to a text from a family member. The no/low texting group performed 10.6% better than the high texting group in their memory scores. The test score was significantly negatively correlated with the total number of words sent and received. Those participants who chose to wait more than 4-5 minutes to respond to a text message did substantially better than those who responded immediately.

Conclusion

Memory is affected by texting but not massively, in fact the participants who sent or received 16+ texts in half an hour did only slightly worse on the test than lower frequency texters. Waiting a few minutes before a text is opened or responded to appears to produce better performance, so it would seem wise for teachers and lecturers to use strategies that focus on when it is appropriate to take a break and when it is important to focus without distractions.

Evaluation of Rosen et al. (2011)

Strengths
✓ This was a well-designed field experiment that included attitudes to texting, and the researchers ensured that the relevant texts were received at crucial points in the videotape so that the results were easy to measure.
✓ There is a degree of ecological validity to this study as the participants were in a familiar situation carrying out behaviour that they were well used to performing.

Limitations
X The researchers did not control the number of texts being sent by other people which could confound their results as it introduces an extra variable that could have interfered with the IV.
X The use of an opportunity sample is not without bias because it only includes whoever happens to be present at the time: a random sample would achieve a less biased sample but it is more difficult and time-consuming to carry out.

Reference
Rosen, L. D., Lim, A. F., Carrier, L. M., & Cheever, N. A. (2011). An empirical examination of the educational impact of text message-induced task switching in the classroom: educational implications and strategies to enhance learning. *Psicología Educativa*, *17*(2), pp. 163-177.

****

KEY STUDY: *Hembrooke & Gay (2003). The laptop and the lecture: The effects of multitasking in learning environments.*

Background
Found that students who had their laptops open during a lecture remembered less of the content than a control group who kept them closed.

Aim
To examine the effects of multi-tasking in the classroom.

Participants
44 college students (22 female; 22 male) from a university in the North-East of the USA. The

researchers were interested to see the extent to which 'doodling' on the laptop (i.e. browsing unrelated websites, checking email) might interfere with learning in the classroom.

Procedure
Theis field experiment procedure took place during a lecture rather than in strict lab conditions. Half of the class were called out to another classroom, and while they were gone the other half of the class listened to the lecture and were encouraged to use their laptops as usual throughout. These students then left the lecture hall and the other half of the class then came back in and heard the same lecture – only this time they were told to close their laptops. Both groups of students were tested immediately following the lecture. Both groups of students were then given 20 questions, focusing on recognition and recall related to the contents of the lecture. Two months later the procedure was replicated but this time the students who had been in the closed laptop condition now participated in the open laptop condition and vice versa.

Results
Students in the open laptop condition performed significantly worse than those with the closed laptop when tested on their recall and recognition of the contents of the lecture. The longer the time spent on browsing, the worse the memory performance was. Brief distractions, of short duration, from the lecture did not impair memory performance or overall grade in the class at all.

Conclusion
Sustained multi-tasking in the classroom reduces memory for the content of the lesson.

Evaluation of Hembrooke and Gay (2003)
Strengths
- ✓ This is a field experiment (the students were not placed in artificial conditions and were doing what they would normally do), making it high in ecological validity.
- ✓ The inclusion of the replication study means that the researchers used the test-retest method for checking external reliability.

Limitations
- X The use of a snapshot design (a one-off study) means that extraneous variables may have interfered with the results: e.g. some students may have been feeling less engaged on the day of the study; some may have needed to check their email for personal reasons; the content of the lecture may have been less interesting for some than for others.
- X The use of a small sample of university students from Northeastern USA makes generalising

the findings difficult.

Reference

Hembrooke, H., & Gay, G. (2003). The laptop and the lecture: The effects of multitasking in learning environments. *Journal of Computing in Higher Education*, *15*(1), pp. 46-64.

****

KEY STUDY: *Sparrow et al. (2011). Google effects on memory: Cognitive consequences of having information at our fingertips.*

Background

Negative effect on memory of digital technology and using search engines.

Aim

To investigate the relationship between memory, technology and access to information.

Participants

Information about the sample of participants is not supplied in the original journal article.

Procedure

Participants were given a task in which they learned some new items of trivia that were unknown to them before the experiment. The independent variable consisted of two conditions: half of the participants were told that the information they had typed into the computer would be saved and that they would be able to access it at a later date. The other half of the participants were told that the information would be deleted. Each condition was further sub-divided: half of the participants in each condition were told that they would have to remember the information they had learned as they would need it at some later point.

A further experiment was then conducted with different participants in which a repeated measures design was used involving a third condition as well as the two conditions outlined above. The third condition involved the participants being told that the information they had saved would be in a folder. After participants typed in each trivia statement (30 in total) one of the following three messages appeared on the screen:

- Your entry has been saved.
- Your entry has been saved to folder X.
- Your entry has been erased.

Participants then completed a recognition task in which they were shown the 30 trivia statements, with half of them altered slightly. Participants were asked to make judgements about each statement: *Is this exactly what you read earlier? Has the statement been saved or deleted? Has the statement been saved to a folder; and if so, which one?*

Results
In the first version of the experiment (two conditions only; independent measures) participants who were told that they could access the information at a later date did not recall it as well as participants who were told that the information would be deleted. In the repeated measures experiment using three conditions, participants were found to have the best recall for statements that they were told had been deleted: they also had greater recall of the name of the folder in which the information was stored than of the information itself.

Conclusion
Reliance on technology such as internet search engines may lead to 'digital amnesia'- the state of being overly dependent on external sources to store and retrieve information. In other words, the 'Google effect' may be having a negative impact on memory.

Evaluation of Sparrow et al. (2011)
Strengths
✓ These findings seem to provide evidence for the idea that we are increasingly passing the responsibility of remembering information to the internet, which forms a kind of non-human 'collective memory'.
✓ The findings can be given a positive spin: we are evolving into beings whose memory is adapting to the opportunities created by the digital age.

Limitations
X The tasks used in this research were relatively simple and, more importantly, they did not have any real or personal meaning or relevance to the participants. In real life people may work harder to remember key information rather than simply relying on google.
X Not being given information about the sample used means that it is difficult to generalise the results: i.e. were the participants tech-savvy young people, older people or a mixed demographic?

Reference
Sparrow, B., Liu, J., & Wegner, D. M. (2011). Google effects on memory: cognitive consequences of having information at our fingertips. *Science*, 1207745. DOI: 10.11265.

KEY STUDY: *Blacker et al. (2014). Effects of action video game training on visual working memory.*

Background
Found that action video games cause improvements to the quantity and quality of information stored in visual working memory.

Aim
To investigate the extent to which action video games may improve the quantity/quality of information stored in the visual component of working memory (VWM).

Participants
This was a volunteer sample consisting of 34 male university students (mean 20 years).

Procedure
There were two conditions (randomly assigned) to the independent variable:

- The Action Game group: this group was given active and dynamic video games to play - e.g. Call of Duty, Black Ops games, Modern Warfare, etc. in a single player mode.
- The Control group: this group was given a non-action game - The Sims strategy game.

Participants in each group were asked to train for over 30 hours across a continuous stretch of 30 days. Prior to the training period the participants were assessed using a self-report (0-9 rating scale) that asked them how motivated they were to complete a VWM task. After training participants completed another self-report which asked them about how engaged they had been in the VWM task, by getting them to rate their level of enjoyment and absorption.

Results
The researchers found no significant differences in levels of self-reported motivation and engagement between the two groups on either the tasks or the VWM assessments. 15 out of 17 participants in the action group improved during training; all of the participants in the control group improved over the training period. The action game participants demonstrated significant improvement on one measure of VWM (a change control task), a small improvement on a colour wheel test and no improvement on a complex span task. Improvements were not seen in the control group's results.

Conclusion
Action video games may directly improve the VWM or improve it through the enhancement of

selective attention (which has a direct positive impact on the VWM).

Evaluation of Blacker et al. (2014)

Strengths

✓ The findings provide good evidence that the VWM may be responsive to training which is useful for educational contexts or other settings where improving cognitive skills is a key objective.

✓ By measuring motivation and enjoyment, equal in both groups, these were excluded as confounding variables that may have affected the improvement in VWM.

Limitations

X The sample is difficult to generalise from, being all male and small. (Females do also play video games, so it would be interesting to view their performance compared to males).

X There is no clear explanation of why improvement was seen on some VWM tests and not on others.

Reference

Blacker, K. J., Curby, K. M., Klobusicky, E., & Chein, J. M. (2014). Effects of action video game training on visual working memory. *Journal of Experimental Psychology: Human Perception and Performance*, *40*(5), pp. 1992-2004.

****

B . Reliability of cognitive processes (Example: memory)

The studies already used to explore the influence of digital technology on cognitive processes may be used to answer questions from this content point also.

See above for:
Rosen et al. (2011). *An empirical examination of the educational impact of text message-induced task switching in the classroom: Educational implications and strategies to enhance learning.*
Shows the effect of texting on memory for test material.

Sparrow et al. (2011). *Google effects on memory: Cognitive consequences of having information at our fingertips.* This study suggests that being able to use online search engines is decreasing memory ability.

Blacker et al. (2014). *Effects of action video game training on visual working memory.* Suggests that action video game training improved some aspects of working memory.

****

C. Emotion and cognition (Example: emotion associated with traumatic memories)

KEY STUDY: *Gerardi et al. (2008). Virtual reality exposure therapy using a virtual Iraq: case report.*

Links to
- **Abnormal Psychology.** Treatment of disorders – individual (cognitive) therapy for PTSD.

Background
Evaluated the effectiveness of virtual reality exposure therapy (VRET) for treatment of PTSD in an Iraq war veteran and found it to be effective.

Aim
To evaluate the effectiveness of virtual reality exposure therapy (VRE) using a Virtual Iraq programme for treatment of post-traumatic stress disorder (PTSD), which arises from cognitive processing of a traumatic event.

Participant
The participant was a 29-year old male who had reported the symptoms of PTSD 6 months after return from 10 years active service in Iraq. His PTSD manifested itself as traumatic memories that intruded upon other memories and thoughts: poor concentration; negative mood and irritability; sleep disturbance often resulting in 'cold sweats'; a strong startle response; hyper-vigilance.

Procedure
This was a case study in which the participant completed a series of questionnaires regarding his mood and cognition, including anxiety and depression inventories measured via a scale. The cognitive processing of one particular traumatic occurrence was identified as giving rise to the primary, most distressing and intrusive trauma memory. He also underwent weekly 90-minute VRE sessions (four sessions in total) in which he was exposed to two repetitions of his trauma memory, increasing in intensity with each session; and he reported his feelings and reactions after each session, including his Subjective Units of Distress (SUDS) ratings, between 1 and 100.

Results
The participant's *Clinician Administered PTSD Scale* (CAPS) score decreased significantly, by 56%, from a total score (106) in the extreme range of >80 to a total score (47) in the moderate/threshold range of 40 to 59. The PTSD Symptom Scale Self-Report (PSS-SR) score decreased significantly from a total of 35 to 10, which corresponded to the participant reporting a substantial decrease in the symptoms of his PTSD.

Conclusion
VRE may reduce the anxiety-related and distressing symptoms of PTSD that result from the cognitive processing of the event.

Evaluation of Gerardi et al. (2008)
Strengths
✓ Both subjective and objective measures of symptoms were used, and both clinician-reported differences and self-report changes were taken into account, which means that the internal validity of the case study is high.
✓ The findings have a direct application to therapeutic settings and could be used to develop testable theory to be applied in a variety of PTSD cases.

Limitations
X Using only one participant does mean that the findings can only be generalised to that participant, though as noted above they could be used to generate theory.
X There is no indication as to whether or not the improvement in PTSD symptoms persisted after the 4-week session of treatment ended.

Reference
Gerardi, M., Rothbaum, B. O., Ressler, K., Heekin, M., & Rizzo, A. (2008). Virtual reality exposure therapy using a virtual Iraq: case report. *Journal of Traumatic Stress, 21*(2), pp. 209-213.

****

KEY STUDY: *Morina et al. (2015). Can virtual reality exposure therapy gains be generalized to real-life? A meta-analysis of studies applying behavioral assessments.*

Links to
▪ **Abnormal Psychology.** Treatment of disorders – individual (cognitive) therapy for PTSD.

Background
Meta-analysis of VRET research with phobias and later follow-up, to check efficacy in real-life situations. Found VRET to have real-life application in changing emotion and memories, and therefore cognitive processing, associated with phobia.

Aim
To assess the extent to which virtual reality exposure therapy (VRE) gains can be observed in real-life situations.

Procedure
This is a meta-analysis that used the findings of 14 clinical trials using VRE in the treatment of specific phobias.

Main comments and findings

- VRE places individuals into virtual, computerised landscapes and environments, a result of which is that they perceive an interactive, 3-D world that can be directly controlled in a study.
  i.e. the phobic stimuli can be more easily modified and manipulated by therapists.

- Among the phobias investigated in the 14 studies included in the meta-analysis were: fear of spiders, fear of heights, fear of flying, fear of climbing stairs.

- The findings showed that phobic patients responded well to VRE treatment: their behavioural responses to the phobic stimulus showed clear improvement following VRE treatment.

- Some patients were on a waiting-list for VRE treatment and it was found that they did not improve as much as patients who were already undergoing VRE therapy.

- VRE was found to be as effective as other behavioural measures in the treatment of phobias.

- The findings are in line with previous meta-analyses on the efficacy of VRE for anxiety disorders.

Conclusion
VRE can produce significant change in cognitive processing in real-life situations, specifically in the treatment of certain phobias.

Evaluation of Morina et al. (2015)

Strengths

✓ As the findings agree with previous meta-analyses this gives them concurrent validity.

✓ The authors argue that patients are likely to find VRE more tolerable than other forms of therapy (e.g. systematic desensitisation) and that it is more cost-effective than psychotherapy.

Limitations

X The number of studies used in the meta-analysis is not large enough to draw any robust or meaningful conclusions.

X Some of the research used in the meta-analysis may be flawed due to the therapist not being sufficiently well trained or competent.

Reference

Morina, N., Ijntema, H., Meyerbröker, K., & Emmelkamp, P. M. (2015). Can virtual reality exposure therapy gains be generalized to real-life? A meta-analysis of studies applying behavioral assessments. *Behaviour Research and Therapy*, *74*, pp. 18-24.

****

KEY STUDY: *Freeman et al. (2017). Virtual reality in the assessment, understanding, and treatment of mental health disorders.*

Links to

▪ **Abnormal Psychology.** Treatment of disorders – individual (cognitive) therapy for all mental health disorders.

Background

Review of research into VRET as a replacement for more traditional therapy for all classes of mental disorders. Also, exploration of its use for better assessment and understanding of disorders.

Aim

To review the effectiveness of VRET over the first 20 years of its use in mental health settings.

Procedure

The researchers reviewed the findings of 285 studies in which VRET had been used to treat anxiety disorders (192), schizophrenia (44), substance-related disorders (22) and eating disorders (18).

Main comments and findings

- VRET has great potential to help people overcome mental health problems as it directly addresses the fact that those with mental disorders find it extremely difficult to interact with the world. VRET enables people to face the challenging situation or stimulus in a simulated environment and be guided and coached in how to respond to the fear-inducing situation appropriately.

- Most VRET treatments have focused on anxiety disorders and the outcomes of the studies considered in this review compare favourably with other face-to-face therapies: the simulated effects of being in a VR environment appear to carry across to the real world, along with the benefits of the therapy whilst in the VR world. These VRET treatments also seem to have long- term effects rather than simply being a quick, temporary fix.

- VRET has been used to assess the type of psychotic experiences which characterise schizophrenia, particularly paranoia and the particular characteristics of paranoia and what causes it. The most recent VRET research on schizophrenia has focused on delusions of persecution suffered by schizophrenic patients.

- VRET for use with people suffering from substance disorders has shown that a VR can elicit a strong craving for the drug, with most of the research in this field focusing on smoking. There are, as yet, no studies that show how VRET may help substance disorders.

- There is, similarly, little research to indicate how VRET might help those with eating disorders.

- One study using a VR world enabled anorexic patients to experience ownership of a healthy BMI (body mass index) and this led, in turn, to those patients experiencing less body dysmorphia (overestimating body size) for at least two hours afterwards.

Conclusion
VRET can aid the understanding of mental disorders, and simpler psychological treatments can be successfully administered in a VR environment.

Reference
Freeman, D., Reeve, S., Robinson, A., Ehlers, A., Clark, D., Spanlang, B., & Slater, M. (2017). Virtual reality in the assessment, understanding, and treatment of mental health disorders. *Psychological Medicine, 47*(14), pp. 2393-2400.

Content 3: Methods used to study the interaction between technologies and cognitive processes.

The studies already used to explore the influence of technologies on cognitive processes may be used to answer all questions from this topic.

A. Cognitive processing

See above for:
Rosen et al. (2011). *An empirical examination of the educational impact of text message-induced task switching in the classroom: Educational implications and strategies to enhance learning.*
Lab experiment conducted in a classroom during a lecture: IV = number of texts received and sent (3 groups, low, medium and high); DV = score on test based on lesson content. Participants were randomly assigned to conditions.

Blacker et al. (2014). *Effects of action video game training on visual working memory.*
Lab experiment. IV = whether participant trained on and played an action video game or a non-action video game; DV = performance on visual working memory tasks. Participants were randomly assigned to conditions.

B. Reliability of cognitive processes

See above for:
Hembrooke & Gay (2003). *The laptop and the lecture: The effects of multitasking in learning environments.*
Field experiment conducted at a university during a lecture: IV = whether or not a laptop was used during the lecture; DV = performance on a test. Participants were randomly assigned to conditions.

Sparrow et al. (2011). *Google effects on memory: Cognitive consequences of having information at our fingertips.*
Lab experiment into the effect on memory of technologies such as search engines. Participants were randomly assigned to conditions. IV1 = whether participants were told the information they had typed into the computer would be saved, or deleted. IV2 = whether participants were told they should remember the information for later recall, or whether they were told nothing. DV = participants' recall for trivia, both where to access it, and also the content details.

C. Emotion and cognition

See above for:
Gerardi et al. (2008). *Virtual reality exposure therapy using a virtual Iraq: case report.*
Case study of VRET therapy used to treat a 29 year-old Iraq war veteran PTSD sufferer.

Morina et al. (2015). *Can virtual reality exposure therapy gains be generalized to real-life? A meta- analysis of studies applying behavioral assessments.*
Meta-analysis of VRET research with phobias and later follow-up to check efficacy in real-life situations. 132 studies reduced to 14 key studies focusing on either fear of heights or fear of spiders.

****

CRITICAL THINKING POINTS: COGNITIVE PROCESSING IN A TECHNOLOGICAL WORLD

Will teaching have to change to incorporate students' interrupted attention in the classroom?
Teachers all over the developed world (and possibly beyond) are currently tearing their hair out over their students' seeming obsession and reliance on their mobile phones. One of the major complaints made by teachers – particularly when it comes to older teenagers or university students – is that 'they won't stop looking at their phones when I'm trying to teach!' The teacher feels – probably with some justification – that their fascinating lesson is being given only limited attention by the student and the teacher's ultimate concern is that the student will miss out on vital aspects of the lesson and not perform as well as they could do in exams. Research by Rosen et al. (2011) tackled this issue by allowing some students to text in a lesson while others were prevented from doing so. Ultimately the researchers had to conclude that the effects of texting on memory were relatively small: even when students were inundated with texts in the lesson their performance was only slightly worse than the non-texters. This suggests that students should be taught metacognitive strategies that focus on when they need to concentrate in a lesson.

Does some research on video games legitimise laziness?
The popular stereotype of a video gamer is of a socially isolated male who spends huge stretches of time in one chair (possibly kitted out for the purpose of gaming), surrounded by empty pizza boxes and energy drinks, hunched over a console with a glazed look in his bloodshot eyes in a face the colour of parchment. Not a positive image and one which is generally used to decry the overwhelming presence of video games in some people's lives, and which is often cited

as evidence of video games negatively affecting cognition. Such gamers must have welcomed research by Blacker et al. (2014) which concluded that action video games may directly improve visual working memory. The fact that the sample was too small to generalise from or to produce robust statistical evidence may be dismissed alongside the main findings linking better visual working memory to gaming. Findings such as this may be used to justify spending large amounts of a person's time on gaming rather than on other (possibly healthier) pursuits and may ultimately give addicted gamers a viable excuse for the long hours they spend gaming. However, if improved visual working memory is only going to be used for the gamer to become better at gaming then really, what is the point?
Isn't this simply feeding the beast?

Are researchers getting too excited about VRET?

Treating patients with mental disorders using a virtual reality environment does sound very exciting
– VREs are quite mesmerising as they can place people into any landscape or situation that may help to treat the disorder using methods which are not invasive (i.e. they do not require drugs or surgery) or traumatic (unlike, say, flooding). VRET allows patients to explore the roots or the manifestations of their disorder (particularly phobias), and it is possible that this new method could be used alongside older ones to treat phobias, e.g. systematic desensitisation. However, could it be the case the VRET is like a nice, big, shiny toy sitting in a department store window that researchers are pointing at and saying (metaphorically), 'I want that'? Research in this field may still be in its infancy but researchers, (e.g. Morina et al. 2015), do seem to be highly enthusiastic about the efficacy of VRET – which is a little odd given the lack of very robust empirical evidence. Prensky (2009) even goes so far as to suggest that VRET could be used to assist in the development of ethics and morality. Only time will tell if VRET becomes the go-to treatment for disorders such as phobias.

****

Sociocultural Approach

Ethics

Methods

The individual and the group

Cultural origins of behaviour and cognition

Cultural influences on individual behaviour

The influence of globalization on individual behaviour

Social identity theory

Culture and its influence on behaviour and cognition

Enculturation

The effect of the interaction of local and global influences on behaviour

Social cognitive theory

Cultural dimensions

Acculturation

Research methods used to study the influence of globalization on behaviour

Formation of stereotypes and their effects on behaviour

To what extent?

Contrast

Describe

Outline

Discuss

Evaluate

Explain

SOCIOCULTURAL APPROACH

Topic 1: The individual and the group.

Key Idea: Social and cultural contexts influence individual and group behaviour.

Content	Research	Use in Sociocultural Approach	Links to
Social identity theory	Classic **Tajfel et al. (1971)**	Minimal groups paradigm: he found that merely being put in a group is enough to instill loyalty to the group and some discrimination towards those outside the group. This formed the basis for Tajfel & Turner's (1979) social identity theory.	**Sociocultural approach:** Stereotypes. **Human relationships:** Group dynamics – prejudice and discrimination.
	Critique/Extension **Howarth (2002)**	She conducted focus group interviews of adolescents from Brixton and found that they had formed their own social identity in response to the stigmatizing identity of coming from Brixton.	**Human relationships:** Group dynamics – prejudice and discrimination.
	Recent **Pegg et al. (2018)**	Large survey that investigated the role of online social identity and alcohol use in teens. This found that higher levels of exposure to alcohol-related content on social networking sites was associated with higher levels of alcohol use, as the online social identity was maintained through an alignment of behaviour with other members of the online social group.	**Health:** Determinants of health – risk factors for addiction.

Further resources

Drury, J. (Feb 2016). Impact: from riots to crowd safety. *The Psychologist.*
https://thepsychologist.bps.org.uk/volume-29/february/riots-crowd-safety

Stott, C., Hoggett, J. & Pearson, G. (2012). Keeping the Peace: Social Identity, Procedural Justice and the Policing of Football Crowds,
British Journal of Criminology. 52(2), pp. 381-399.

Impact: from riots to crowd safety

SOCIOCULTURAL APPROACH

Topic 1: The individual and the group.

Key Idea: Social and cultural contexts influence individual and group behaviour.

Content	Research	Use in Sociocultural Approach	Links to
Social cognitive theory	Classic **Bandura, Ross & Ross (1961)**	Experiment that demonstrated that children who observed aggressive acts committed by adults in one setting would, through play, reproduce those acts in another setting when the adult role model was absent. This was especially likely if the adult role model was the same sex as the child.	**Development:** Influences on cognitive and social development – role of peers and play.
	Critique/Extension **Bandura (1986)**	Extended this early social learning approach to social cognitive theory: with behaviour, internal personal factors (biology and individual cognition) and environmental influences all interacting with one another. Key concepts of agency, self-efficacy and reciprocal determinism are central to the theory.	**Health:** Promoting Health – health promotion. SCT underpins some health promotion programmes.
	Recent **Joyce & Harwood (2012)**	Used social cognitive theory to explain how to improve intergroup interactions through vicarious contact via media with interactions between in-group and out-group.	**Human relationships:** Group dynamics – prejudice and discrimination.

Further resources

Youtube film. Albert Bandura gives a short introduction to his social cognitive theory. https://www.youtube.com/watch?v=S4N5J9jFW5U

Bandura. SCT.

SOCIOCULTURAL APPROACH

Topic 1: The individual and the group.

Key Idea: Social and cultural contexts influence individual and group behaviour.

Content	Research	Use in Sociocultural Approach	Links to
Stereotypes - A. formation of stereotypes	Classic **Hamilton & Gifford (1976)**	Illusory correlation is responsible for the acquisition of stereotypes.	**Development:** Developing an identity - gender identity and social roles.
	Critique/Extension **Smith and Alpert (2007)**	Illusory correlation is responsible for unconscious racial stereotypes in the police force.	**Abnormal Psychology:** Factors influencing diagnosis – the role of clinical biases in diagnosis.
	Recent **Meyer et al. (2016)**	Illusory correlation is more common in elderly people, especially when linked with fear.	
Stereotypes - B. effects of stereotypes	Classic **Steele and Aronson (1995)**	Stereotype threat takes place when an individual believes that they will be judged on the basis of any stereotypes which may exist about the groups to which they belong. This study showed that black Americans may under-perform on a verbal reasoning test not because they have lower ability than white Americans but because stereotype threat may affect their performance adversely. In other words, there appears to be no racial difference in verbal reasoning – but not in the presence of stereotype threat.	

Content	Research	Use in Sociocultural Approach	Links to
Stereotypes - B. effects of stereotypes (cont'd)	Critique/Extension **Spencer et al. (1999)**	Investigated stereotype threat in terms of its effect on women answering maths questions. Found that stereotype threat can negatively affect performance of females in maths when compared to males.	
	Recent **Shewach et al. (2019).**	Challenges the theory of stereotype threat, claiming that the focus has been on unrealistic experimental conditions rather than on 'high stakes settings' like real exam conditions. Therefore, the results lack validity.	

Further resources

TED talk on gender stereotypes by Justin Baldoni (2017). Why I'm done trying to be man enough. https://tinyurl.com/y84nsqc2

TEDx talk on unconscious bias by Yassmin Abdel-Magied (2014). What does my headscarf mean to you? https://tinyurl.com/o34ua9e

Youtube film on stereotypes by Prof. Susan Fiske. Social Psychology Videos: Stereotypes.
https://www.youtube.com/watch?v=6YfIM6HTJas

TED talk by Justin Baldoni

Susan Fiske on stereotyping

SOCIOCULTURAL APPROACH

Topic 2: Cultural origins of behaviour and cognition

Key Idea: Thinking and behaviour of individuals and groups varies cross-culturally

Content	Research	Use in Sociocultural Approach	Links to
Culture and its influence on behaviour and cognition. **A. Behaviour - conformity.**	Classic **Bond & Smith (1996)**	Conducted a meta-analysis of the results of 133 studies that had used Asch's line-judging task in 17 different countries. Found that people from more individualist cultures conformed less often than those from more collectivist cultures.	**Sociocultural approach:** Cultural dimensions.
	Critique/Extension **Takano & Sogon (2008)**	Investigated the rate of conformity of Japanese participants in a replication of Asch's classic conformity study. Found that the rate was similar to that found by Asch in his 1950s studies of US students.	**Sociocultural approach:** Cultural dimensions. Cultural groups
	Recent **DiYanni et al. (2015)**	Explored how culture and conformity interact when young children are engaging in imitation.	**Sociocultural approach:** Cultural groups. **Development:** Influences on cognitive and social development – role of peers and play.
B. Cognition – memory.	Classic **Rogoff & Waddell (1982)**	Comparison of memory processes between USA and Mayan 9 year-olds. Found that if recall tasks relied on 'chunking', then only the schooled USA children could succeed on the task. However, when using a 3D miniature diorama, differences in recall disappeared.	**Sociocultural approach:** Cultural groups.

Content	Research	Use in Sociocultural Approach	Links to
B. Cognition – memory (cont'd)	Critique/Extension **Wang (2008)**	Investigated autobiographical memory for childhood events in three culture groups: US, England and China. Found children from the US had the earliest memories, and from China the latest.	**Cognitive approach:** Emotion and cognition – the influence of emotion on cognitive processes (autobiographical memory).
	Recent **Kulkofsky et al. (2011)**	Investigated flashbulb memory cross-culturally and found that culture moderated the effects of personal importance, emotionality, surprise, and event rehearsal.	**Cognitive approach:** Emotion and cognition – the influence of emotion on cognitive processes (flashbulb memory).

Further resources
Radio 4 programme (1999). Memory and Culture.
http://www.bbc.co.uk/programmes/p00545jl

Radio 4. Memory and culture

Winerman, L. (2005). The culture of memory. *Monitor on Psychology.* APA https://www.apa.org/monitor/sep05/culture.aspx

The culture of memory

SOCIOCULTURAL APPROACH
Topic 2: Cultural origins of behaviour and cognition
Key Idea: Thinking and behaviour of individuals and groups varies cross-culturally

Content	Research	Use in Sociocultural Approach	Links to
Cultural dimensions	Classic **Hofstede (1980)**	Developed the theory that cultural dimensions shape the behaviour of whole cultures.	
	Critique/Extension **Levine and Norenzayan (1999)**	Study that investigated differences in the pace of life across large cities in a wide range of countries. Their research showed that individualistic cultures had a faster pace of living than more collectivist cultures.	
	Recent **Taras et al. (2016)**	Using a meta-analysis of data from 558 studies, the researchers conducted tests for each of the four dimensions that comprise Hofstede's original theory and concluded that country is not the same as culture, and that each country contains several different cultures that cross national boundaries.	**Sociocultural approach:** Cultural groups.

Further resources
Falle, R. (2007). East Meets West: an infographic portrait by Yang Liu.
http://bsix12.com/east-meets-west/

Geert Hofstede's comprehensive website.
http://www.hofstede-insights.com/

East meets West

SOCIOCULTURAL APPROACH

Topic 3: Cultural influences on individual behaviour.

Key Idea: Culture has an effect on behaviour.

Content	Research	Use in Sociocultural Approach	Links to
Enculturation	Classic **Fagot (1978)**	Enculturation of children into gender roles through differential treatment by parents.	**Sociocultural approach:** Cultural norms. **Development:** Developing an identity – gender identity and social roles are culturally mediated.
	Critique/Extension **Sroufe et al. (1993)**	Children who did not behave in a gender-stereotypical way were the least popular with their peers. These studies indicate that children establish social control in relation to gender roles very early, and it may well be that enculturation by peers is an important factor in gender development.	**Sociocultural approach:** Cultural groups. **Development:** Developing an identity – gender identity and social roles are 'policed' by peers.
	Recent **Basu et al. (2017)**	Comparative study into gender identity in two different collectivist cultures. Argues that we learn to be gendered and that the experience is different for boys and for girls. Parents play a key role in the development of gender roles in collectivist cultures.	**Sociocultural approach:** Cultural groups. **Development:** Developing an identity – gender identity and social roles are culturally mediated.

Further resources

Davis, N. (16 Feb 2018). A child's gender can be detected in their speech from age five, research says. *The Guardian.*
https://tinyurl.com/y7c7jwdt

TED talk by Alana Murabit (2015). What My Religion Really Says About Women. https://tinyurl.com/osrd58o

Guardian article on gender and speech

SOCIOCULTURAL APPROACH
Topic 3: Cultural influences on individual behaviour.
Key Idea: Culture has an effect on behaviour.

Content	Research	Use in Sociocultural Approach	Links to
Acculturation	Classic **Berry (2005 & 2006)**	There are large group and individual differences in how people go about their acculturation (described in terms of integration, assimilation, separation and marginalisation strategies), in how much stress they experience, and how well they adapt psychologically. The 2006 work is a survey into immigrant youth.	**Sociocultural Approach: Assimilation** **HL extension:** How globalization may influence behaviour and the effect of the interaction of local and global influences on behaviour.
	Critique/ Extension **Lueck & Wilson (2010)**	Investigated the variables that may predict acculturative stress in a nationally representative sample of Asian immigrants and Asian Americans.	
	Recent **Roley et al. (2014)**	Discovered correlations between acculturative stress, depression, likelihood for and seriousness of family conflict, and concluded that strong family relations moderated acculturative stress in Japanese adolescents living temporarily in the USA.	As above, plus **Abnormal Psychology:** Etiology of abnormal psychology - explanations for disorder(s).

Further resources
Almendraia, A. (22 May 2015). The stress of immigration can cause psychosis, according to new study. *The Huffington Post.*
http://www.huffingtonpost.co.uk/entry/immigration-psychosis_n_7347142

Huffington Post article on stress

TEDx talk on cultural homelessness by Sarah Lyons-Padilla. Cultural homelessness breeds extremists.
https://www.youtube.com/watch?v=HSGzZQrxrPE

Lyons-Padilla. Cultural homelessness

Youtube film, posted by *The Guardian* (18 May 2018). 'Refugees in Europe on their adopted homelands.'
https://www.youtube.com/watch?time_continue=84&v=2_7YBLfFFvc

The Guardian film on refugees

SOCIOCULTURAL APPROACH

Topic 4 (HL extension): The influence of globalization on individual behaviour.

Key Idea: Globalization (the growing interconnectedness of the world) has psychological effects on individuals.

Content	Research	Use in Sociocultural Approach	Links to
The effect of the interaction of local and global influences on behaviour – the individual and the group *and* cultural origins of behaviour and cognition.	Classic **Berry (2005 & 2006)**	There are large group and individual differences in how people go about their acculturation (described in terms of integration, assimilation, separation and marginalisation strategies), in how much stress they experience, and how well they adapt psychologically. The 2006 work is a survey into immigrant youth.	**Sociocultural Approach:** Cultural influences on individual attitudes, identity and behaviours – acculturation. **Assimilation**
	Critique/Extension **Lueck & Wilson (2010)**	Investigated the variables that may predict acculturative stress in a nationally representative sample of Asian immigrants and Asian Americans.	**Sociocultural Approach:** Cultural influences on individual attitudes, identity and behaviours – acculturation.
	Recent **Roley et al. (2014)**	Discovered correlations between acculturative stress, depression, likelihood for and seriousness of family conflict, and concluded that strong family relations moderated acculturative stress in Japanese adolescents living temporarily in the USA.	**Sociocultural Approach:** Cultural influences on individual attitudes, identity and behaviours – acculturation. **Abnormal Psychology:** Etiology of abnormal psychology - Explanations for disorders.

Content	Research	Use in Sociocultural Approach	Links to
The effect of the interaction of local and global influences on behaviour (cont'd) - cultural influences on individual attitudes, identity and behaviours.	Classic **Benet-Martinez & Haritatos (2002)**	How Bicultural Identity Integration (BII) affects how people manage their two cultural identities.	
	Critique/Extension **Bhugra and Mastrogianni (2004)**	Globalization increases the challenges of cross-cultural diagnosis and treatment of depression, as it influences both expressions of symptoms ('idioms of distress') and how care is given.	**Abnormal Psychology:** Factors influencing diagnosis - Validity and reliability of diagnosis *and* Treatment of disorders – the role of culture in treatment.
	Recent **Lyons-Padilla et al. (2015)**	Marginalisation in a globalized society leads to radicalisation. They related this to the concept of 'cultural homelessness.'	

Further resources

TED talk by Chimamanda Ngozi Adichie (2009). The danger of a single story.
https://tinyurl.com/mh9v5hl

TED talk by C.N.Adichie

TED talk by Taiye Selasi (2014). Don't ask where I'm from, ask where I'm a local. https://tinyurl.com/ppzky6a

TED talk by Taiye Selasi

219

SOCIOCULTURAL APPROACH

Topic 4 (HL extension): The influence of globalization on individual behaviour.

Key Idea: Globalization (the growing interconnectedness of the world) has psychological effects on individuals.

Content	Research	Use in Sociocultural Approach	Links to
Methods used to study the influence of globalization on behaviour – the individual and the group.	Example 1 **Lueck & Wilson (2010)**	Etic method - cross-cultural survey of 2095 Asian immigrants and Asian Americans.	**Quantitative methods:** survey using questionnaires.
	Example 2 **Benet-Martinez & Haritatos (2002)**	Experiment to investigate how individual differences in bicultural identity affect how cultural knowledge is used to interpret social events.	
Methods used to study the influence of globalization on behaviour - cultural origins of behaviour and cognition.	Example 1 **Bhugra and Mastrogianni (2003)**	Review and summary of studies focusing on transcultural aspects of depression.	**Quantitative methods:** meta-analysis
	Example 2 **Roley et al. (2016)**	Correlational study into acculturative stress, depression and family conflict.	
Methods used to study the influence of globalization on behaviour - cultural influences on individual behaviour.	Example 1 **Berry (2006)**	Etic method - large survey comparing international study of the acculturation and adaptation of immigrant youth from 13 different societies together with a sample of national youth.	**Quantitative methods:** survey using questionnaires.
	Example 2 **Lyons-Padilla et al. (2015)**	Survey of Muslims living in the USA that asked about their cultural identities and attitudes toward extremism. Found that immigrants who identify neither with their heritage culture nor their host culture feel marginalized, and insignificant. Experiences of discrimination make the situation worse and lead to greater support for radicalism.	**Quantitative methods:** survey using questionnaires.

Further resources

Lyons-Padilla, S. (13 June 2016). I've studied radicalization – and Islamophobia often plants the seed. *The Guardian.*
https://tinyurl.com/jvb5ule

Youtube film by Sarah Lyons-Padilla (2016). Belonging Nowhere: Marginalization and Radicalization Risk Among Muslim Immigrants.

https://www.youtube.com/watch?v=tY4jYLk3LUo

Lyons-Padilla.
Islamophobia

Surveys can be blunt tools for research

Cc image from pixabay.com

SOCIOCULTURAL APPROACH KEY STUDIES

TOPIC 1: THE INDIVIDUAL AND THE GROUP

Key Idea: Social and cultural contexts influence individual and group behaviour

Content 1: Social identity theory

KEY STUDY: *Tajfel et al. (1971). Social categorization and intergroup behaviour.*

Links to
- **Sociocultural approach.** The formation of stereotypes.
- **Human Relationships.** Group dynamics – social origin of prejudice and discrimination.

Brief summary
Minimal groups paradigm: they found that merely being put in a group at random is enough to instill loyalty to the group and some discrimination towards those outside the group. This formed the basis for Tajfel & Turner's (1979) social identity theory.

Aim
To investigate how social categorisation affects intergroup behaviour.

Participants
48 males aged 14-15 from the same state school in Bristol, UK. The boys were randomly allocated to 3 groups consisting of 16 boys per group.

Procedure
Once they had been randomly assigned to a group the boys were shown slides of paintings by the artists Klee and Kandinsky and told that their preference for one of these two artists would form the basis of their assignment to a group. The boys were not told which other boys were members of their group and there was no face-to-face contact with other group members once they had made their choice. The boys were then shown, individually, to a cubicle and asked to conduct the following task: assign money (virtual, not real) to members of either the boy's ingroup (based on their previously stated artist preference) or outgroup (preference for the other artist). The boys did not know each other's identity, only a code number which identified whether they were ingroup or outgroup. The researchers set up the trials in a randomised design which tested the boys on a range of measures, including whether they would opt for

maximum joint profit, maximum ingroup profit, or maximum difference between ingroup and outgroup.

Results
The boys made decisions which highlighted preference for the ingroup and discrimination towards the outgroup. They tended to favour the ingroup members with higher reward and to work in a way which maximised the difference between ingroup and outgroup, often at the expense of possible maximum joint profit. This favouritism was based solely on the mere *idea* of the other group rather than on any actual interaction between ingroup and outgroup members, and the difference between the groups was minimal, i.e. supposed preference for one artist over another.

Conclusion
Ingroup favouritism can be manipulated via the minimal groups paradigm in which participants use social categorisation to make decisions.

Evaluation of Tajfel et al. (1971)
Strengths
- ✓ This is a replicable experiment that uses a standardised procedure and quantitative data, which should ensure reliability.
- ✓ The boys were kept apart from each other with no face-to-face interaction allowed and anonymity was preserved thus they were responding to the idea of ingroups and outgroups without having any actual contact with group members, which limited possible sources of bias.

Limitations
- X The findings can only be generalised to boys aged 14-15 from Bristol.
- X The task used is highly artificial and does not reflect how people may respond to social categorisation in everyday life, therefore it lacks external validity.

Reference
Tajfel, H., Billig, M. G., Bundy, R. P., & Flament, C. (1971). Social categorization and intergroup behaviour. *European Journal of Social Psychology*, *1*(2), pp. 149-178.

****

KEY STUDY: *Howarth (2002). 'So, you're from Brixton?' The struggle for recognition and esteem in a stigmatized community.*

Links to
- **Human Relationships**. Group dynamics – prejudice and discrimination.

Brief summary
Howarth conducted focus group interviews of adolescents from Brixton and found that they had formed their own social identity in response to the stigmatizing identity of coming from Brixton.

Aim
An exploration of the ways in which other people's attitudes, based on prejudiced views, may contribute to an individual's social identity.

Participants
Forty-four 12-16 year-olds from Brixton (an area in South London) from an ethnically diverse demographic. Five interviews were also conducted with head teachers of Brixton secondary schools.

Procedure
The researcher ran a series of 8 focus group sessions, each with an average of 5 participants per session. The researcher began by introducing a topic, e.g. 'Tell me about your life in Brixton and how you think other people might feel about Brixton' and then the participants discussed the topic together with the researcher who recorded the session. Interviews with the head teachers were conducted so that the researcher could gain some insight into school students from Brixton and their cultural backgrounds.

Results
The researcher organised her qualitative findings under three main headings as follows:
- **Constructing social identities through representations:** there is often a shocked, negative or fearful attitude from others when finding out where the participants are from: e.g. references to weapons, drug use, etc. The participants felt that the media played a significant role in stereotyping and stigmatising them and that this could be seen in the body language of non- Brixton dwellers, such as a white woman holding on tightly to her handbag when two black Brixton teenagers were walking towards her.

- **The psychological violence of stigmatising representations:** the participants reported feeling that they see themselves through the eyes of strangers - as violent, deviant, aggressive - and that this has a massive impact on their self-identity and self-esteem with some participants reporting feelings of great shame and conflict about coming from Brixton, though others successfully fought against the stigma. Some of the participants have attempted to eradicate any traces of their Brixton identity, psychologically and metaphorically removing themselves from the area. Some participants experienced anger and depression and some succumbed to the self-fulfilling prophecy - i.e. 'they expect me to be hostile, so I'll be hostile'.

- **Social relationships and institutional cultures in empowerment:** the role of the family and school in the lives of Brixton teenagers was stressed, with the emphasis on both factors helping young people build self-esteem and a positive identity. However, not all parents are positive role models in this context. The headteachers reported that some parents actively block a school's efforts to integrate the students and so enable their children to become confident and well-rounded individuals, mainly due to some misguided attitudes towards child-rearing. The participants all felt that children can help their parents to shed prejudiced attitudes and gain a better insight into and understanding of the community in which they live.

Conclusion
Social identity can be hugely affected by the prejudiced attitudes of individuals and of society as a whole.

Evaluation of Howarth (2002)
Strengths
✓ The use of qualitative research methodology means that the data is rich, insightful and has huge explanatory power.
✓ Using focus groups, particularly when the participants are friendly with each other, allows for a relaxed atmosphere in which the participants are less likely to be guarded or artificial about what they say.

Limitations
X Using thematic analysis on the data is time-consuming, requiring many researcher hours.
X It is possible that the more dominant, confident members of a focus group can set the tone for the discussion, with more reserved members possibly not voicing their true feelings due to shyness or feeling overwhelmed.

Reference
Howarth, C. (2002). 'So, you're from Brixton?' The struggle for recognition and esteem in a stigmatized community. *Ethnicities*, *2*(2), pp. 237-260.

KEY STUDY: *Pegg et al. (2017). The role of online social identity in the relationship between alcohol-related content on social networking sites and adolescent alcohol use.*

Links to
- **Health.** Determinants of health – risk factors for addiction.

Brief summary
Large survey that investigated the role of online social identity and alcohol use in teens and found that higher levels of exposure to alcohol-related content on social networking sites (SNS) was associated with higher levels of alcohol use, as the online social identity was maintained through an alignment of behaviour with other members of the online social group.

Aim
To investigate how online social identity may be linked to alcohol use by teenagers, depending on how much online alcohol use they have been exposed to via social networking sites (SNS).

Participants
843 16-18 year-old students from 33 high schools in Australia who used SNS. The sample comprised 54.5% females and 45.5% males.

Procedure
The participants responded to questions which covered four distinct categories and answered using either a pre-determined rating scale or a numerical value. The categories were as follows:

- **Alcohol use:** how many times in the past 6 months the participant had drunk alcohol.
- **SNS alcohol exposure:** how often in the past 6 months the participant had seen posts from friends where alcohol was involved.
- **Online social identity:** degree of agreement to statements such as 'being a member of SNS is important to me'.
- **SNS intensity:** the number of hours per week that the participant used SNS.

Results
The researchers found that participants with a strong online social identity and intense use of SNS were more vulnerable to exposure to alcohol on SNS and were more likely to drink alcohol.

Conclusion
Adolescents with a strong OSI who use SNS a lot may align their behaviour to fit the perceived norms of the online community with which they identify.

Evaluation of Pegg et al. (2018)

Strengths

✓ The use of standardised questions and quantitative data mean that this study could be replicated in large numbers to test the robustness of the theory.

✓ The findings of this study could be used to inform drink-awareness programmes targeted at young people.

Limitations

X The research methodology is descriptive rather than enlightening: it can highlight *what* adolescents do in terms of alcohol and SNS but not *why* they do it.

X It is possible that some of the participants may have succumbed to social desirability bias in their responses, providing invalid data as to their actual alcohol use or use of SNS.

Reference

Pegg, K. J., O'Donnell, A. W., Lala, G., & Barber, B. L. (2017). The role of online social identity in the relationship between alcohol-related content on social networking sites and adolescent alcohol use. *Cyberpsychology, Behavior, and Social Networking, 21*, 50-55.

****

Content 2: Social Cognitive Theory

KEY STUDY: *Bandura, Ross & Ross (1961). Transmission of aggression through imitation of aggressive models.*

Links to

▪ **Development.** Influences on cognitive and social development – role of peers and play.

Brief summary

Experiment that demonstrated that children, observing aggressive acts committed by adults in one setting, would, through play, reproduce those acts in another setting when the adult role model was absent. This was especially likely if the adult role model was the same sex as the child.

Aim

To investigate the extent to which children will, after observing the aggressive behaviour of adult role models observed in one setting, then imitate that behaviour in another setting.

Participants

72 children (mean age 4 years), 36 males and 36 females, who attended Stanford University day nursery in the state of California, USA. Prior to the procedure, nursery staff had rated the children on their level of aggression to produce a matched pairs design. This design ensured that there were equal numbers of same-level aggressive children represented across the conditions.

Procedure

The procedure consisted of three distinct phases:

- **Phase 1:** each child was taken to an experimental room where they observed either an aggressive, non-aggressive or no model (see conditions below). Each session lasted around 10 minutes. The aggressive condition involved the model performing distinctively aggressive behaviours towards a Bobo doll (a large doll that swings on a weighted base) repeated 3 times (to measure direct imitation), e.g. punching, kicking, etc.

- **Phase 2:** the child was then taken to a room full of attractive toys. Then, shortly after this, they were told that the toys were meant for another child and that they had to leave the room.

- **Phase 3:** The child was then taken to a third room filled with aggressive and non-aggressive toys, including a Bobo doll, where they were left to play for 20 minutes while the researchers observed them from behind a one-way mirror. Measures were taken of physical and verbal aggression directly imitative of the aggressive condition and also more generalised non- imitative aggressive behaviour.

There were also 3 conditions to the experiment:

1. **Aggressive model** – The model behaved aggressively towards the bobo doll. 6 female participants 6 male participants.
2. **Non-aggressive model** – The model behaved in a non-aggressive way. 6 female participants 6 male participants.
3. **Control group** - No model was present. 12 female participants, 12 male participants

A same sex model or opposite sex model was used an equal number of times per condition.

Results

Children in the aggressive condition produced more directly imitative acts of aggression towards the Bobo doll, behaviours not seen in the non-aggressive or control conditions. There was more same-sex imitation of aggressive behaviour and boys overall showed more physical aggression than girls.

Conclusion
Aggression can be learned via a single exposure to the aggressive act and then imitated in another setting.

Evaluation of Bandura, Ross & Ross (1961)
Strengths
✓ The use of a matched pairs design means that this was a well-designed experiment that controlled for the confounding variable of individual differences in aggression.
✓ The findings of this study prompted a fierce debate (and a slew of other studies) on the role of TV violence and its effect on children, which has led to certain strictures being placed on what children should be exposed to via media channels.

Limitations
X The findings are subject to some issues of validity: children tend to learn aggressive behaviour across time, from role models they are familiar with, e.g. parents, rather than in artificial settings observing strangers. It is also possible that the children experienced demand characteristics and that they only attacked the Bobo doll because that is what they thought was required of them.
X The sample is too small and demographically specific for generalising from with any confidence.

Reference
Bandura, A., Ross, D., & Ross, S. A. (1961). Transmission of aggression through imitation of aggressive models. *The Journal of Abnormal and Social Psychology, 63*(3), pp. 575-582.

****

SOCIOCULTURAL APPROACH
Topic 1: The individual and the group.
Content: Social cognitive theory.
Key Idea: Social and cultural contexts influence individual and group behaviour.

KEY STUDY: *Bandura (1986). Social foundations of thought and action: A social cognitive theory.*

✓

✓ Links to
- **Health:** Promoting Health – health promotion. Social Cognitive Theory (SCT) underpins some health promotion programmes.

Background
Extended this early social learning approach to social cognitive theory: with behaviour, internal personal factors (biology and individual cognition) and environmental influences as all interacting with one another. Key concepts of agency, self-efficacy, vicarious reinforcement, motivation central to the theory.

Aim
To extend the original ideas of social learning (1961, 1977) into a fuller account of the ways in which human beings act as agents in their cognitions and social settings via self-efficacy and reciprocal determinism.

A summary of the main features of the theory
- SCT places learning within social contexts, stressing that individuals do not exist in a vacuum and that they are agents who act to determine their own outcomes. SCT operates along the lines of reinforcement i.e. how likely it is that an individual will repeat specific behaviours based on their feelings about the behaviour, their past experience, the specific environment and their expectation of success surrounding the behaviour. This demonstrates a definite progression on from Social Learning Theory, in which the individual was placed in a more passive role.

- Self-efficacy is a key element of SCT: the idea that an individual has the power and ability to organise and execute a given course of action to complete a task or solve a problem. Self-efficacy takes aspects of expectancy theory which involves the degree of motivation individuals have as to particular behaviours. *Outcome expectations* are beliefs that certain behaviours lead to specific outcomes e.g. revising for an exam will result in good grades. *Efficacy expectations* are beliefs about how successfully you can carry out the task e.g.

knowing that you will spend 8 hours a day revising, using a variety of strategies. If either outcome expectations or efficacy expectations are overly ambitious then the individual may lose their motivation to continue with the task e.g. if you don't get the highest possible mark in class tests then you may give up. Self-efficacy is rooted in beliefs that are aspirational to some extent but which will not impair an individual's continuing efforts to achieve them.

- Reciprocal determinism involves a triad of forces that interact to determine motivation for particular behaviours:

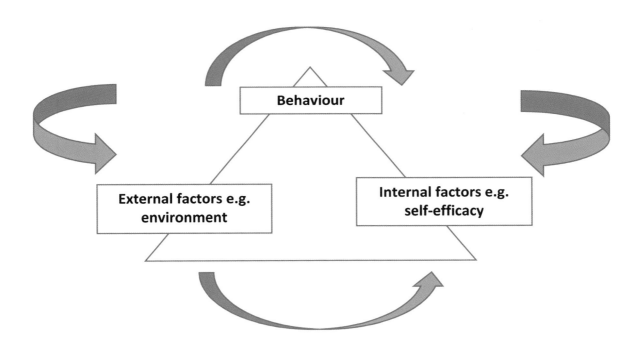

Behaviour (the outcome as performed by the individual), internal personal factors (which includes biological forces as well as thoughts, feelings and beliefs) and environmental factors (the physical location, other people, available facilities) all interact with none of these three elements being more dominant than the others. For example, desire to attend a particular university (behaviour) will be based on an individual's thoughts, beliefs and feelings about how likely this is (internal factors, including beliefs about our self-efficacy, which can be based on our natural talent for an academic subject) and external factors (access to a good school, teaching and revision resources).

Evaluation of Bandura (1986)

Strengths

✓ SCT has a broad application: it has been used particularly successfully in health programmes such as smoking-cessation strategies.

✓ SCT is a more holistic account of behaviour than its precursor, Social Learning Theory as it acknowledges the importance of a range of internal and external factors in behaviour.

Limitations

X Concepts such as self-efficacy may only have relevance for individualistic cultures: collectivist cultures may struggle to appreciate the idea that focusing on the self and self-achievement is a positive act: this limits the generalisability of the theory.

X The theory does not take individual differences into account e.g. an individual has the natural ability to do well as a musician, they have easy access to facilities and tuition but they ultimately reject the behaviour of playing music. There is not sufficient allowance made in the theory to explain why a lack of motivation may occur, even when all the factors are present to encourage it.

Reference

Bandura, A. (1986). *Social foundations of thought and action: a social cognitive theory*. Englewood Cliffs, NJ, US: Prentice-Hall.

****

KEY STUDY: *Joyce & Harwood (2014). Improving intergroup attitudes through televised vicarious intergroup contact.*

Links to

▪ **Human relationships.** Group dynamics – prejudice and discrimination.

Brief summary

Used social cognitive theory to explain how to improve intergroup interactions through a vicarious contact via media with interactions between in-group and out-group.

Aim

To investigate the extent to which attitudes towards an out-group member can be manipulated via emotional valence (the strength and quality of the emotional content).

Participants

147 students from the University of Arizona aged between 18-28 years old (mean age 20) who were all US citizens. The sample comprised 71% females and 29% males and was almost entirely white.

Procedure

The participants watched excerpts of a documentary which featured a US border control guard, Frank, who was living with a family of illegal immigrants for 30 days. There were 4 conditions to the experiment:

1. **Positive valence:** the footage featured only scenes of a positive nature between Frank and the family's teenage daughter: e.g. affection, empathy, co-operation.
2. **Negative valence:** the footage featured only scenes of a negative nature between Frank and the family's teenage daughter: e.g. conflict, aggression, disagreement.
3. **Mixed valence:** the footage featured 50% positive and 50% negative scenes.
4. **Control condition:** the participants watched scenes from 'Planet Earth', a nature documentary.

After watching the scenes, the participants filled in a series of questionnaires, scored via rating scales, on topics such as their attitude towards illegal immigrants and other marginalised groups such as the homeless, refugees, etc. They also answered questions relating to how much they identified with Frank and their attitude towards the family's daughter.

Results

The mean scores per condition are presented in the table: the higher the score, the more positive the attitude towards illegal immigrants.

Condition	Attitude towards illegal immigrants measured by a 7-point scale
Positive	3.81
Negative	2.88
Mixed	3.22
Control	2.63

The difference between the positive and negative results is significant and points to the idea that positive media portrayals can improve the attitudes of in-group members towards the out-group. The researchers also found that when a participant identified strongly with Frank, their rating of the out-group was less positive. They also found that the degree of liking for the immigrant family's daughter influenced the positive ratings of the out-group.

Conclusion

In order to improve intergroup attitudes, it is important for group members to see in-group and out-group members interacting positively.

Evaluation of Joyce & Harwood (2014)

Strengths

✓ This is a well-designed study with a good level of control, as the researchers ensured that in the positive and negative conditions they included 80% of positive/negative behaviours as appropriate per condition. They were also careful to ensure that the film in the control condition did not include any references to in-groups or out-groups, keeping the footage as neutral as possible.

✓ The findings of this study could be used to inform media gatekeepers on practical ways to encourage positive group relations: e.g. by depicting meaningful and positive intergroup interactions onscreen.

Limitations

X There could have been an array of extraneous variables influencing the ratings given by the participants. Examples would be: if Frank or the daughter reminded them of someone, or of any prior contact they had had with out-group members. This would affect the validity of the findings.

X Social desirability bias or other participant expectations may have influenced how participants responded: that is, the participants' ratings were possibly due to what they thought the researchers wanted them to say/do, rather than giving a true account of their attitudes.

Reference

Joyce, N., & Harwood, J. (2014). Improving intergroup attitudes through televised vicarious intergroup contact: Social cognitive processing of in-group and out-group information. *Communication Research*, *41*(5), pp. 627-643.

****

Content 3: Formation of stereotypes and their effects on behaviour

A. Formation of stereotypes

KEY STUDY: *Hamilton & Gifford (1976). Illusory correlation in interpersonal perception: A cognitive basis of stereotypic judgments.*

Links to

- **Development.** Developing an identity: gender identity and social roles.

Brief summary

Illusory correlation is responsible for the acquisition of stereotypes.

Aim

To investigate illusory correlation and group size as a mechanism for making judgements about attributes of group members.

Participants

40 students from a university in New York state, USA (20 males; 20 females).

Procedure

The participants were presented with two hypothetical groups: Group A consisted of 26 members and Group B consisted of 13 members. They then read a series of statements which each described a particular behaviour performed by either a member of A or B: e.g. *John, a member of A, visited a friend in hospital*. Behaviours were desirable or undesirable. Both A and B were assigned more positive than negative behaviours at a ratio of 9:4 (positive to negative) and two thirds of the statements overall were attributed to members of A. Thus, members of A were presented as performing more behaviours overall than B and positive behaviours were more frequent in both groups than negative behaviours.

The participants were then asked to provide ratings for the following measures:

1. Given a list of 20 attributes, and to assign each to either group A or B.
2. Given a particular example of a behaviour, and to say whether this behaviour was performed by a member of A or B.
3. Estimate how many negative behaviours can be attributed to either A or B.

Results

The mean scores for the ratings of how the participants attributed either desirable or undesirable attributes to each group is shown in the table below.

Attributes	Group A	Group B
Desirable (social behaviour)	6.7	6.0
Undesirable (social behaviour)	4.4	5.6
Desirable (intellectual behaviour)	7.2	6.3
Undesirable (intellectual behaviour)	4.4	5.0

Ratings for members of A were consistently higher than those for B; undesirable behaviours were attributed to members of B more than for members of A.

Conclusion

The results suggest people form an illusory correlation based on group size: the smaller group, B, appears more distinctive than A so that any undesirable behaviours (which are also less frequent and therefore more distinctive) are linked more often to the smaller group, B, than the majority, A. This has implications in terms of how minority groups are viewed by society.

Evaluation of Hamilton & Gifford (1976)

Strengths

✓ The procedure uses standardised measures which can be replicated relatively easily, making the results reliable.

✓ The findings shed some very interesting light on how easily negative attributes are assigned to a minority group, based simply on group size. The study could be used as the basis for prosocial programmes such as anti-bullying and tolerance campaigns.

Limitations

X The ways in which the participants rated the groups is artificial and does not fully reflect how people respond in real-life situations where they are exposed to an array of personal and social factors which may influence their response to an individual more than group membership would.

X The small sample size of students from one US university does not represent a wide-ranging demographic so the results are not generalisable beyond this limited group of participants.

Reference

Hamilton, D. L., & Gifford, R. K. (1976). Illusory correlation in interpersonal perception: A cognitive basis of stereotypic judgments. *Journal of Experimental Social Psychology*, *12*(4), pp. 392-407.

****

KEY STUDY: *Smith & Alpert (2007). Explaining police bias: A theory of social conditioning and illusory correlation.*

Links to

▪ **Abnormal Psychology:** Factors influencing diagnosis – the role of clinical biases in diagnosis.

Brief summary

Illusory correlation is responsible for unconscious racial stereotypes in the police force.

Aim
To consider the role of illusory correlation in the overestimation of negative behaviours of minority groups by the US police.

Procedure
A review article which considers a range of literature on the topic.

Main findings and comments

- There have been widely reported disparities in the way that the police treat civilians dependent on their ethnicity, with whites receiving less negative treatment than black or Hispanic civilians. For example, black and Hispanic people are more likely to be stopped and searched by the police and to be given a harsher penalty for a traffic offence than a white person.

- Police in the USA have a history of racial prejudice, with attitudes towards black people stretching back to the days of slavery and perpetuated over the years in brutal and prejudicial behaviour. The majority of US police officers are white and racism was regularly encouraged within police departments up to and including the late 1960s. As the authors themselves state, 'the society that produces America's small-town police officers also contains within it shared stereotypes about minority groups, ingrained perceptions, and beliefs that have been passed down by parents, teachers, political and social leaders, and the mass media' (p 1272).

- Some research points to the police not being properly trained in racial awareness and relying instead on 'folk wisdom', i.e. anecdotal, populist ideas based on scant evidence. This type of reasoning acts heuristically, allowing the police to make shortcuts in their thinking so that surface appearance such as skin colour begins to determine who is singled out for their attention, e.g. who is stopped and searched for weapons. Other research highlights the erroneous belief, held by the police, that ethnic minorities are more likely to be involved in drug-related crimes: an incorrect assumption in part fuelled by faulty media representation in the late 1980s. (Reagan's 'war against drugs' campaign is cited as a cause.)

- Research into conformity has shown that people who adhere to and follow the social norms of a group are most likely to develop stereotyped views based on factors such as race. Social identity theory also accounts for the idea of ingroup preference and for viewing the out-group as homogenous. The views of white police officers are therefore more likely to be reinforced that non-white citizens may have deviant tendencies when compared to their own ingroup.

- Due to the nature of their work, police officers may develop stereotyped views of ethnic minorities based on the fact that such cultural groups often live in the least affluent, most crime-ridden areas: areas that the police are often called to and which may involve violence, substance abuse, burglary, gun crime among a host of other anti-social behaviours. In this way the police may develop inbuilt illusory correlations linking crime and ethnicity.

Conclusion
American police may unwittingly operate a biased approach towards non-white citizens, one not necessarily motivated by racism but which is informed by representation of ethnic minority groups within the media and the cumulation of stereotyped views.

Evaluation of Smith & Alpert (2007)
Strengths
✓ This article takes a unique approach to a well-discussed problem by attempting to highlight the idea that the police are not (all) intentionally racist but that prejudice may occur at the level of the individual, based on misinformation and biased media representations.
✓ The authors accessed a wide range of literature on the topic from psychological research to official statistics to historical documents and anthropological reports which gives their article great depth and insight.

Limitations
X The topic may simply be too huge and difficult to sum up in one article: racism and prejudice within the US police force is a topic that is hugely complex and involves a multiplicity of factors which all need to be considered in order to reach any kind of meaningful conclusion.
X The article uses secondary data which means that the authors have had to rely on the accuracy and skill of other researchers and official record-keepers in collecting and maintaining data, which could lead to a lack of reliability.

Reference
Smith, M. R., & Alpert, G. P. (2007). Explaining police bias: A theory of social conditioning and illusory correlation. *Criminal Justice and Behavior*, *34*(10), pp. 1262-1283.

****

KEY STUDY: *Meyer et al (2015). Influences of Age and Emotion on Source Guessing: are older adults more likely to show fear-relevant illusory correlations?*

Brief summary
Illusory correlation is more common in elderly people, especially when linked with fear.

Aim
To investigate the extent to which age is a factor in the prevalence of illusory correlation linked to fear-inducing stimuli.

Participants
103 participants aged 60-95 years (69 females and 34 males) and 109 participants aged 18-31 years (80 females and 29 males). All participants lived in Germany.

Procedure
The participants were shown 16 pictures of fish and 16 pictures of snakes presented to each participant in a randomised order. The participants were asked to rate each image according to a 7- point scale (*harmless* to *threatening*). They were also asked to indicate whether or not they thought they had seen the image of the animal before. If the animals were identified as one which they had seen before, the participants were asked to say if they thought the animal was poisonous or not.

Results
Overall the participants identified snakes better than fish, particularly poisonous snakes. The older adults were better when it came to categorising information that fit into prior and well-established knowledge and concepts whereas the younger participants were more interested in unexpected or inconsistent information that did not fit with previous ideas. The older adults showed a stronger inclination to use illusory correlations in the way they treated information and were less keen to integrate new and unfamiliar information into the associations they made about the animals, particularly when it related to fear of snakes.

Conclusion
Older adults are more susceptible to illusory correlations associated with fear-inducing stimuli than younger adults, who are more open to new and contradictory ideas.

Evaluation of Meyer et al. (2015)

Strengths

✓ Although the procedure uses fear-relevant stimuli, the researchers followed ethical guidelines by informing the participants of this beforehand: one of the younger adults subsequently withdrew before beginning the procedure as they had a snake phobia.

✓ The results of this study replicate previous research on the topic so it has concurrent validity.

Limitations

X The procedure is artificial and does not reflect the ways in which people might encounter fear- inducing stimuli in real life. For example, a moving snake that is making hissing noises is arguably much more frightening than a still image.

X The choice of snakes as fear-inducing stimuli may not have any relevance for younger participants who may have seen more frightening animals via special effects films and games than the older group. The researchers could have used more appropriate fear-inducing stimuli for the younger group, such as images of knives or terrorist-related threats.

Reference

Meyer, M. M., Buchner, A., & Bell, R. (2015). Influences of Age and Emotion on Source Guessing: Are Older Adults More Likely to Show Fear-Relevant Illusory Correlations? *Journals of Gerontology Series B: Psychological Sciences and Social Sciences, 71*(5), pp. 831-840.

****

B. Effects of stereotypes on behaviour

KEY STUDY: *Steele & Aronson (1995). Stereotype threat and the intellectual test performance of African Americans.*

Brief summary

Stereotype threat takes place when an individual believes that they will be judged on the basis of any stereotypes which may exist about one or more of the social groups to which they belong. This expectation can negatively affect performance as seen in this study in which black Americans under-performed in a verbal reasoning compared to white Americans, possibly due to the researchers' manipulation of stereotype threat i.e. that black people are less verbally competent than white people.

Aim
To investigate stereotype threat in terms of its effect on black Americans and verbal reasoning.

Participants
114 black and white students from Stanford University, USA (no information given as to numbers of males and females).

Procedure
The participants were met by a male researcher who told them that they would be taking an aptitude test (the American Graduate Record Examinations verbal exam).

There were 2 conditions of the independent variable:

- In the **diagnostic condition (the stereotype threat condition)**, the participants were told that their performance on the test would be a good indicator of their underlying intellectual abilities and the emphasis on verbal reasoning was made clear.
- In the **non-diagnostic (no stereotype threat condition)**, the participants were told that the test was simply an exercise in looking at problem solving and no reference was made to verbal reasoning or ability.

Results
The results showed that black participants in the stereotype threat condition performed less well on the test than the white participants in the same condition. Participants in the no stereotype threat condition performed equally well, demonstrating that race did not appear to be a factor in verbal reasoning in this condition.

Conclusion
Black Americans may under-perform on a verbal reasoning test not because they have lower ability than white Americans but because stereotype threat may affect their performance adversely. In other words, there appears to be no racial difference in verbal reasoning – but not in the presence of stereotype threat.

Evaluation of Steele & Aronson (1995)
Strengths
- ✓ Knowing about the possible effects of stereotype threat on race could help teachers to be aware of this issue, which could in turn ensure that their lessons are inclusive and unbiased.
- ✓ Simply telling the participants about the nature of the test in the first condition appears to have been enough to trigger stereotype threat, demonstrating how powerful this phenomenon can be in the way it affects behaviour.

Limitations

X   The use of an independent groups design may result in unequal ability per condition i.e. it may have been that there were more verbally competent participants in the non-stereotype condition.

X   This is a socially sensitive topic so researchers must exercise care when reporting the results of their findings as they could be misinterpreted for political reasons.

Reference

Steele, C. M., & Aronson, J. (1995). Stereotype threat and the intellectual test performance of African Americans. *Journal of Personality and Social Psychology, 69*(5), p.797.

****

KEY STUDY: *Spencer et al. (1999). Stereotype threat and women's math performance.*

Brief summary

Stereotype threat takes place when an individual believes that they will be judged on the basis of any stereotypes which may exist about one or more of the social groups to which they belong. This expectation can negatively affect performance, as seen in this study in which females under-performed in maths compared to males, possibly due to the researchers' manipulation of stereotype threat i.e. women can't do maths.

Aim

To investigate stereotype threat in terms of its effect on women answering maths questions.

Participants

56 students from a university in Michigan, USA (28 males; 28 females). All of the participants were of equal ability in Maths, having completed a semester of calculus in which they had to have scored at least grade 'B'.

Procedure

Participants were tested in mixed gender groups of 3-6. They were told, 'We are developing some new tests that we are evaluating across a large group of University of Michigan students. Today you will be taking a math test.'

There were 2 conditions of the independent variable:

- In the **relevance** condition participants were told that the test had shown gender differences in the past—this was done deliberately to promote feelings of stereotype threat in the female participants as Maths is thought to be something that women underperform in compared to men.
- In the condition where the stereotype was to be **irrelevant**, participants were told that the test had never shown gender differences in the past.

Results

In the **relevance** condition (sensitive to gender differences), women significantly underperformed in relation to equally qualified men. In the **irrelevant** condition (no mention of gender differences affecting performance) there was no real difference in the performance of females compared to males.

Conclusion

Women may under-perform on a Maths test not because they have lower ability than men but because stereotype threat may affect their performance adversely. In other words, women are just as good at maths as men – but not in the presence of stereotype threat.

Evaluation of Spencer et al. (1999)

Strengths

- ✓ As the students were of roughly the same ability in Maths the difference in performance cannot be attributed to disparity in Maths which increases the validity of the findings.
- ✓ The standardised nature of the procedure e.g. the same Maths questions used in both conditions, the clear independent variable means that the study is replicable which increases the reliability of the findings.

Limitations

- X There is the possibility that demand characteristics may have affected the participants' performance e.g. some participants may have felt nervous as they were being tested at something they were supposed to be good at; some participants may have guessed the aim of the study (more likely in the **relevance** condition) which could have led to self-conscious, less natural behaviour.
- X Conducting research such as this may actually contribute to the reinforcement of stereotypes as the results could be interpreted as evidence of actual gender differences in Maths.

Reference

Spencer, S. J., Steele, C. M., & Quinn, D. M. (1999). Stereotype threat and women's math performance. *Journal of Experimental Social Psychology*, 35(1), pp. 4-28.

KEY STUDY: *Shewach et al. (2019). Stereotype threat effects in settings with features likely versus unlikely in operational test settings: A meta-analysis.*

Brief summary
Previous research has supported the idea of stereotype threat but this study challenges these findings as the researchers claim that the focus has been on unrealistic experimental conditions rather than on 'high stakes settings'. In other words, they have lacked validity.

Aim
To challenge the idea that stereotype threat negatively affects performance on specific tasks.

Procedure
The researchers conducted a meta-analysis of 212 studies of stereotype threat, yielding a total sample size of over 10,000 participants, the largest of its kind to date. The meta-analysis gathered data from research which looked at the effect of stereotype threat on cognitive ability. Some of this research consisted of lab experiments and some was taken from operational/real-life tests such as college admissions or job application tests.

Results
The results of the meta-analysis indicated that stereotype threat effect-size was 'small to negligible' on tests of cognitive ability in operational/real-life scenarios such as college admissions tests and employment testing.

Conclusion
Research conducted in high stakes situations such as taking a test for a place at college does not appear to trigger stereotype threat, so it may be the case that stereotype threat is only found in research involving manipulated lab conditions.

Evaluation of Shewach et al. (2019)
Strengths
- ✓ The use of a meta-analysis with such a large sample means that the results are robust and reliable.
- ✓ The researchers controlled for specific statistical errors, which they had identified in previous research, which further increases the reliability of the findings.

Limitations

X   The use of a meta-analysis is a 'cold', detached method for investigating human behaviour, as it does not take into account explanations for the behaviour: it can say *what* is happening but not *why*.

X   The research lacks ecological validity as it is based on the quantitative findings of previous research, which in turn may be artificial or contrived.

Reference

Shewach, O. R., Sackett, P. R., & Quint, S. (2019). Stereotype threat effects in settings with features likely versus unlikely in operational test settings: A meta-analysis. *Journal of Applied Psychology, 104*(12), pp. 1514-1534

****

CRITICAL THINKING POINTS: THE INDIVIDUAL AND THE GROUP

Are the variables involved in research on the individual and the group too complex to measure accurately?

Research using the Sociocultural Approach essentially involves the investigation of human behaviour in social contexts. This provides the researcher with opportunities to use a range of qualitative methods that generate rich, insightful data, such as observation, individual and focus group interviews. This type of data, however, is difficult to shape into anything approaching a consistent and objective form and this in turn leads to a level of subjectivity and interpretation, which is a world away from the objective and scientific methods of the biological and cognitive approaches.

Howarth's (2000) interviews with Brixton teenagers yielded some in-depth insight into the topic investigated but the data is difficult to sum up precisely and it may be prone to social desirability effects or researcher bias. Yet, the ways in which human beings behave in social contexts do not lend themselves to experimental methodology: they resist a 'cold', clinical approach in which variables are controlled and performance is measured quantitatively. Using a controlled observation such as Bandura, Ross & Ross (1961) with a standardised procedure and quantitative data goes some way towards addressing the idea that behaviour can be measured scientifically; but there are probably too many uncontrolled variables that could have influenced the results: e.g. the home life of each child; their mood on the day; their IQ, social skills and personality.

Could some results be based on pleasing the researcher and doing the 'right' thing?

Some of the studies in this section might have suffered from participant expectations:

participants thinking that a particular response was being sought by the researchers, which they then may have delivered in a bid to ensure the success of the study. It is possible that Tajfel's (1971) study was set up in a way that made the schoolboys conclude that they were supposed to show preference for their Klee/Kandinsky ingroup and so behaved accordingly. Children in this age group are used to being guided to the 'right' response by adults, so perhaps the boys were either consciously or unconsciously responding to this idea rather than using social categorisation in their choices. The motivation of participants in any study is, of course, unknown (possibly even to the participants themselves) but it is something that is worth considering, especially when the study's procedure is simple, and the aim of the researchers may not be too difficult to guess.

Theories of the individual and the group can be vague.

Social Identity Theory is based on the idea that people sort others into categories according to a range of usually superficial criteria: age, gender, and employment, for example. While this is at least anecdotally apparent it is a rather unformed and vague theory in itself, and, as the first point on this page emphasises, difficult to test and to measure. Bandura's (1986) Social Cognitive Theory seems to some extent to be based on common sense: we affect and are affected by our environment, by our own cognitions and by our biology and we will be motivated in a variety of ways to either carry out a behaviour or not. One way of looking at this somewhat unformed theory is to see its application to sectors such as health care programmes and the flourishing 'self-help' sector of publishing and media. Self-efficacy is, on its own, a fairly unscientific claim that a person can achieve a goal if they have the right mind-set, ability, attitude, approach, etc. This can then be applied in contexts such as smoking cessation strategies, assertiveness training, revision for exams, and other situations in which the concept of self-efficacy takes real and practical forms.

****

TOPIC 2: CULTURAL ORIGINS OF BEHAVIOUR AND COGNITION

Key Idea: Thinking and behaviour of individuals and groups varies cross-culturally

Content 1: Culture and its influence on behaviour and cognition

A. Behaviour: conformity

KEY STUDY: *Bond & Smith (1996). Culture and conformity: A meta-analysis of studies using Asch's (1952b, 1956) line judgment task.*

Links to
- **Sociocultural approach.** Cultural dimensions. Cultural groups.

Brief summary
Conducted a meta-analysis of the results of 133 studies that had used Asch's line-judging task in 17 different countries. Found that people from more individualist cultures conformed less often than those from more collectivist cultures.

Aim
To investigate conformity as a product of culture.

Procedure
A meta-analysis involving 133 studies from a total of 17 countries including Britain, USA, France, Japan, Fiji, Ghana, Hong Kong. The studies used were all replications of the Asch (1951) paradigm, a study of conformity which involves a naïve participant being asked to state which of three lines to the right of a card is the same length as one of the lines on the left of the card. For example:

Each participant was tested individually in a room with seven confederates (whom the participant thought were other participants like himself – the study only used males). The participant was always seated towards the end of the group so that he would be one of the last ones to give his judgement. The experimenter then asked each participant in turn to state which of the three lines on the right of the card was the same length as the target line on the left of the card. In

the *critical* trials the confederates always gave the same *wrong* answer. Asch found that the participants conformed and gave the same wrong answer as the confederates on 32% of the critical trials. Asch concluded that this was evidence of normative social influence: in order to be accepted and liked by the majority the participants had followed the group in giving the wrong answer to an easy task.

Bond & Smith conducted a statistical analysis of the results of cross-cultural studies using Asch (1951) and calculated the average effect size per country, with a higher effect size equalling a higher rate of conformity per country.

Results
The table below shows some of the results from Bond & Smith's meta-analysis (highest and lowest effect sizes are included as is the number of Asch replications conducted per country).

Country	Number of studies conducted	Effect size i.e. conformity rate
Fiji	2	2.48
Hong Kong	1	1.93
Japan	5	1.42
USA	79	0.90
Netherlands	1	0.74
France	2	0.56

The highest rates of conformity were seen in more collectivist countries, e.g. Fiji, Japan, and African countries, and the lowest rates of conformity were found in individualist countries, e.g. France, USA, Britain.

Conclusion
Conformity may be affected by whether an individual comes from a collectivist or an individualistic culture.

Evaluation of Bond & Smith (1996)
Strengths
✓ The use of a meta-analysis gives the researchers access to a mass of data from which they

can extract information showing main effects, trends or patterns in a time-efficient way.
✓ All of the studies in the meta-analysis used the same procedure as laid down by Asch which means that their results are directly comparable.

Limitations
X Even though the results of the studies were averaged to give an overall effect size there is a huge disparity in the number of studies conducted which could inflate or conflate the results. For example, the highest and the lowest rates of conformity came from countries in which only two Asch replications had been conducted which is less reliable than data from 79 studies (USA) as data using small samples are more vulnerable to anomalous, unrepresentative scores.

X A meta-analysis can only report on the statistical results of a collection of studies; it cannot offer explanations or provide insight as to why and how conformity might differ per culture.

Reference
Bond, R., & Smith, P. B. (1996). Culture and conformity: A meta-analysis of studies using Asch's (1952b, 1956) line judgment task. *Psychological Bulletin, 119*(1), pp. 111-137.

****

KEY STUDY: *Takano & Sogon (2008). Are Japanese more collectivistic than Americans? Examining conformity in in-groups and the reference-group effect.*

Links to
- **Sociocultural approach.** Cultural groups

Brief summary
Investigated the rate of conformity of Japanese participants in a replication of Asch's classic conformity study. Found that the rate was similar to that found by Asch in his 1950s studies of US students.

Aim
To investigate the rate of conformity of Japanese participants using the Asch (1951) paradigm.

Participants
297 university students from Japan. All of the students belonged to the same non-sporting college clubs.

Procedure

The participants were split into 40 groups, each comprising between seven and nine participants, with each group having just one naïve participant. The students then participated in Asch's classic conformity experiment involving identification of line length (for a more detailed description of Asch's study see the Bond & Smith [1996] study outline in this section).

Results

The participants gave the wrong (conforming) answer in 12 out of a total of 18 critical trials, with a conformity rate of 25.2%. 14 participants did not conform in any of the critical trials, and 3 conformed in all 12 critical trials.

Conclusion

The Japanese do not appear to be any more conformist than any other culture, including the USA, even though their culture is agreed to be more collectivist than many. This contradicts the findings of Bond and Smith (1996).

Evaluation of Takano & Sogon (2008)

Strengths

- ✓ The results of this study almost exactly agree with previous research which showed that strict replications of Asch (1956) resulted in 25% conformity rate which supports the view that ideas regarding cultural conformity may be outdated or invalid.
- ✓ All of the students were members of non-sports clubs which have a much less vertical hierarchy than sports clubs; vertical discipline might result in a non-typically high rate of normative conformity which could confound the results.

Limitations

- X It is possible that some of the participants might have been familiar with the Asch study, as it is one of the best known in social psychology. This would produce demand characteristics that could make the results lack validity.
- X As with Asch's original procedure, there was no interaction between group members, which is not a true reflection of how an individual is influenced by the majority in real life. This means that the study lacks external validity.

Reference

Takano, Y., & Sogon, S. (2008). Are Japanese more collectivistic than Americans? Examining conformity in in-groups and the reference-group effect. *Journal of Cross-Cultural Psychology, 39*(3), pp. 237-250.

****

KEY STUDY: *DiYanni et al. (2015). The role of consensus and culture in children's imitation of inefficient actions.*

Links to

- **Sociocultural approach.** Cultural groups
- **Development:** Influences on cognitive and social development – role of peers and play.

Brief summary

Explored how culture and conformity interact when young children are engaging in imitation.

Aim

To investigate the role of culture in conforming to an adult role model.

Participants

87 children aged 3 to 5 years old (mean age 4 years 8 months) from the North-Eastern USA. 44 of the children were first-generation Chinese-American (they were born in the USA but their parents were not) and 43 of the children were second-generation Caucasian American (both they and their parents were born in the USA).

Procedure

The participants were randomly allocated to one of two groups: the **consensus** condition and the **single model** condition and experienced each condition as follows:

- **Consensus condition:** the children were shown a video of an adult who said that she needed to use a tool to crush a cookie for use as pie topping. She had two tools in front of her to help her do this: one of the tools was the *functionally affordant* tool - it was suitable for the task due to its shape and strength; the other was the *non-affordant* tool - it was not suitable for the task due to its shape (it had soft pom-poms all over its base). The model then hit a cookie twice in a row using the *affordant* then the *non-affordant* tools. She then held up the *non-affordant* tool and stated that this was the tool she needed. Throughout this entire procedure two other adult models (who maintained neutral expressions) were shown watching the female model.

- **Single model condition:** the procedure was identical to the consensus condition but in this condition the model had three cookies in front of her and she used the *affordant* and *non-affordant* tools on each cookie, saying every time that she was choosing the *non-affordant* tool for the task. The model was alone in this condition; there were no other adults observing her.

As soon as the video was over the experimenter presented the *affordant* and the *non-affordant* tools to each child and asked them which one they would need if they wanted to crush a cookie. The child could then use the tool they had chosen to try to crush the cookie themselves. They were then asked why they had chosen that particular tool.

Results
The table below shows the percentage scores for imitation of the model per condition for both groups.

Condition	Chinese-American % imitation of model	Caucasian American % imitation of model
Consensus	68.2	33.3
Single model	31.8	36.4

It can be seen from these results that the Chinese-American children imitated the adult's choice of the wrong tool for the task more than the Caucasian-American children with a statistically significant difference between the *consensus* scores. This may be due to Chinese households emphasising collectivist values (such as the preservation of harmony, group norms and the need to agree and co-operate) more than individualistic values.

Conclusion
Chinese-American children appear to conform to the majority more than Caucasian-American children.

Evaluation of DiYanni et al (2015)
Strengths
✓ The study used both quantitative and qualitative data in the form of percentage scores and explanations regarding why the particular tool was chosen which means that the results per group can be compared, and there is some explanatory element to the choices the children made.
✓ The researchers used multiple observers of the procedure, achieving a high score in agreement on inter-rater reliability.

Limitations
X It is possible that the higher score for the consensus condition among the Chinese-Americans could be the result of a more hierarchical home life, that is Chinese parents may be more likely to instill a sense of respect for adults than American parents. This could mean that the Chinese- American children's scores were based on politeness rather than

conformity.

X It is possible that due to the age of the children they simply did not know what to do in the experiment and may therefore have imitated the adult's behaviour in the absence of any other information, which would make the results less valid.

Reference

DiYanni, C. J., Corriveau, K. H., Kurkul, K., Nasrini, J., & Nini, D. (2015). The role of consensus and culture in children's imitation of inefficient actions. *Journal of Experimental Child Psychology*, *137*, pp. 99-110.

****

B. Cognition: memory

KEY STUDY: *Rogoff & Waddell (1982). Memory for information organized in a scene by children from two cultures.*

Links to
- **Sociocultural approach.** Cultural groups

Brief summary
Previous research of cross-cultural memory performance has suggested that non-Western children perform poorly, but this may be due to the artificial nature of the tasks. This study highlights that when the context given is meaningful, then memory performance between Western and non- Western children is not significantly different.

Aim
To investigate cross-cultural performance on a memory task.

Participants
30 children aged 8-11 years old (mean age of 9), 15 boys and 15 girls who came from a Mayan community in Guatemala and 30 children aged 8-10 years (mean age 9) from Salt Lake City, USA. All children attended school.

Procedure
The participants were individually presented with a 3-D scene depicting buildings, roads, mountains (a volcano in the case of the Mayan children), trees, housing, a lake and a beach. Each child was then shown 80 separate items spread out on a table next to the scene. They then watched as a researcher chose 20 of the items and placed them within the scene; they were told to take note of where each item was. After a short break of 4 minutes, (during which

time the researcher removed all the items and placed them back on the table with the rest of the items), the child was invited back into the room and asked to place the chosen items in the positions the researcher had previously selected for them. This procedure was repeated a second time using a different set of 20 items from among the 80 on the table.

Results
Children from both cultures performed equally well on the task: there was no difference in the performance of Mayans when compared to that of the American children. Previous research had shown that Mayan children performed poorly at standard memory tests (i.e. items presented in list form). The researchers noted that all 30 of the American children used rehearsal but only one of the Mayan children did, suggesting a more structured approach to memorising information from the American children and a more context-based, relaxed approach from the Mayan children.

Conclusion
Children from different cultures appear to have equally good memories for context-based information.

Evaluation of Rogoff & Wadell (1982)
Strengths
- ✓ The findings of this study contradict previous research into memory and culture which challenges lazy generalisations being made about someone based purely on their ethnicity.
- ✓ Using a 3-D model is a more meaningful way of testing memory: it has more ecological validity than a standard list-type test as it reflects the ways in which children are used to seeing the world and operating within it.

Limitations
- X The sample is too small to draw any strong conclusions: to test the reliability of the results the study should be replicated with much larger samples from a range of countries.
- X Although the task has higher ecological validity than a list-type task, it was still carried out in lab conditions which could make some children feel self-conscious and produce demand characteristics.

Reference
Rogoff, B., & Waddell, K. J. (1982). Memory for information organized in a scene by children from two cultures. *Child Development*, pp. 1224-1228.

****

KEY STUDY: *Wang (2008). Being American, being Asian: the bicultural self and autobiographical memory in Asian Americans.*

Links to
- **Sociocultural approach.** Cultural groups

Brief summary
Investigated autobiographical memory for childhood events in three culture groups: US, England and China, chosen because they differ in the degree in which they value individuality and an autonomous self. Found children from the US had the earliest memories, and from China the latest.

Aim
To investigate autobiographical memory for childhood events in three culture groups plus the influence of gender

Participants
101 participants from the USA, 104 participants from England and 97 participants from China, all of whom were college students. 210 females and 92 males made up the sample.

Procedure
The participants, who were organised in small groups, were asked by a researcher to recall as many childhood events as possible from when they were five years old. Then each participant was asked to recall the date when it occurred, how old they were at the time (to the nearest month). After this, they were asked to use a five-point scale to rate each memory in terms of its frequency as a talking point in their family; how important it was to them; how clear, detailed, emotional and positive/negative it was and where it came from (others or the self).

Results
Participants from the USA recalled the highest number of memories from childhood, with those from England coming second and Chinese participants recalling the fewest childhood memories. Moreover, the Chinese participants recalled memories from a later age than did the American and English participants. The best recalled memories were those that had been rehearsed to some extent and were of moderate personal relevance. Most of the memories came from the individual rather than others. There was a significant effect of gender, with females recalling more memories from childhood than males.

Conclusion
Chinese people may be less prone to recalling vivid events from childhood than American or

English people due to cultural influences: Americans are more likely to see their childhood from an individualistic perspective, whereas Chinese are more likely to view their early childhood in a way which sees the individual in relation to the groups to which they belong, such as their family.

Evaluation of Wang et al. (2008)

Strengths

✓ The study used free recall by participants in a non-manipulated way, which is more likely to be conducive to participants feeling relaxed enough to recall childhood events in a non-pressurised environment, generating valid data.

✓ Asking the participants to recall childhood events within the same five-year time frame means that the researchers were then able to compare the frequency, number and quality of the memories across the 3 cultural groups, so that emerging patterns could be clearly identified.

Limitations

X Individual differences may have confounded the results: some of the participants may have had more eventful childhood experiences that would have been more vivid and therefore easier to recall.

X Only one collectivist culture (China) was represented in the sample, whereas two individualist cultures were represented. This means that the findings are biased towards the individualistic cultures and may even suffer from an imposed etic, that is, a culturally-specific idea is wrongly imposed on another culture, e.g. autobiographical memory is experienced in ways which are only meaningful when given an individualistic perspective.

Reference

Wang, Q. (2008). Being American, being Asian: the bicultural self and autobiographical memory in Asian Americans. *Cognition*, *107*(2), pp. 743-751

****

KEY STUDY: *Kulkofsky et al. (2011). Cultural variation in the correlates of flashbulb memories: An investigation in five countries.*

Links to
- **Sociocultural approach.** Cultural groups
- **Cognitive approach.** Emotion and cognition – the influence of emotion on cognitive processes (flashbulb memory).

Brief summary
Investigated flashbulb memory cross-culturally and found that culture moderated the effects of personal importance, emotionality, surprise, and event rehearsal.

Aim
To investigate the ways in which culture influences flashbulb memory (FBM).

Participants
274 adults from a primarily middle-class demographic but from different cultural groups: 61 Chinese; 65 German; 48 Turkish; 50 British; 50 American. The participants were aged between 32 and 65 years old.

Procedure
The participants were given five minutes to free-recall as many public events occurring within their own lifetime as they could. They were then given a questionnaire about each separate memory including questions relating to the date of the event, where they were at the time, who they were with, what they were doing, etc. This generated a score from 0-5 per memory per participant (5 indicating a lot of detail and information about the event). The participants were then asked to provide a 0-7 rating for each memory in terms of issues, for example, how important it was for them or for the world, how personal their connection to it was, how often they had talked about the event over the years.

Results
The table below outlines the mean number of event scores per cultural group.

Culture	Events recalled
British	14.76
American	12.26
German	9.06
Turkish	6.50
Chinese	5.99

Overall the Chinese participants recalled fewer events that were deemed to be personally important or emotionally intense and they also reported less rehearsal of these events compared to the other nationalities.

Conclusion

Collectivist cultures such as China may place less emphasis on the significance of FBMs than individualist cultures in which personal experience is given a higher profile and significance.

Evaluation of Kulkofsky et al. (2011)

Strengths

✓ Taking qualitative data in the form of verbalised recall for events gives the study some depth and insight; plus, the translation of this into quantitative data means that the results could be easily compared and analysed.

✓ The Chinese participants showed an ability equal to the other participants to recall events of public significance, which supports the idea that it is only personal events that demonstrate a culturally-influenced difference in FBM.

Limitations

X The fewer emotionally intense and personal memories recalled by the Chinese participants may have been due to a modesty bias rather than a cultural neglect of personally significant memories: the Chinese may have under-played the number of memories recalled because they did not wish to appear boastful or competitive.

X The participants were given only five minutes to recall the memories which may have been too much time pressure for some of the participants, resulting in them possibly going 'blank' or not being able to access relevant FBM-type events.

Reference

Kulkofsky, S., Wang, Q., Conway, M. A., Hou, Y., Aydin, C., Mueller-Johnson, K., & Williams, H. (2011). Cultural variation in the correlates of flashbulb memories: An investigation in five countries. *Memory*, *19*(3), pp. 233-240.

****

Content 2: Cultural Dimensions

KEY STUDY: *Hofstede (1980). Culture's Consequences: International differences in work-related values.*

Brief summary
Developed the theory that cultural dimensions shape the behaviour of whole cultures.

Aim
To investigate four dimensions that affect behaviour (including cognition) across cultures in an attempt to define the values that define those countries.

Participants
Over 60,000 employees of IBM from over 50 countries surveyed between 1967-1978.

Procedure
The IBM employees were given questionnaires to complete which focused on a range of issues relating to their attitudes towards topics such as how they viewed power inequalities; whether or not they were comfortable with uncertainty; how important group membership was to them.

Results
The responses by participants were arranged according to categories, four of which (from findings obtained between 1971 and 1973 which initially featured in the first report Hofstede included in his 1980 book) are explained in the table on the next page.

Cultural Dimension	Explanation
Individualism vs. Collectivism	Individualism is based more on a focus on the self with looser bonds between the self and family and other groups; collectivism may involve responsibility for extended family and a greater sense of 'we' rather than the 'I' of individualism.
Power Distance	The extent to which someone is resigned to the idea that there is inequality in society and that some will always have power whereas others will have none. Member of some cultures will be more likely to feel equal to those of higher status whereas other cultures respond with a greater degree of respect towards hierarchical structures.
Uncertainty Avoidance	This involves the idea that some cultures will be happier with the idea that the future is not certain, that an element of surprise about the future is not necessarily negative. Some cultures prefer a more certain and settled idea of the future than others.
Masculinity vs. Femininity	Masculine values are linked to material success and rewards, having a competitive and assertive approach. Feminine values are more in line with cooperation, care and modesty.

Conclusion

Cultural dimensions can be applied to understand and explain the cultural norms specific to a particular country.

Evaluation of Hofstede (1980)

Strengths

✓ This is an ambitious study using a huge cross-cultural sample making it generalisable to a range of cultures and with some reflexivity built in (i.e. Hofstede is aware of the need to keep revisiting the research and modifying it in order to keep the findings relevant).

✓ The findings on Hofstede's website are presented graphically so that it is easy to compare several countries at once on each dimension.

Limitations

X One country does not necessarily represent one type of culture: the USA for example is composed of a range of cultural groups that make the findings somewhat over-generalised.

X The participants may have succumbed to social desirability bias in their responses, perhaps being influenced by the ways in which their culture dictates what their attitudes should be rather than what they really were.

Reference

Hofstede, G., 1980. Culture's Consequences: international differences in work-related values. Beverly Hills, CA: Sage.

****

KEY STUDY: *Levine & Norenzayan (1999). The pace of life in 31 countries.*

Brief summary

Study that investigated differences in the pace of life across large cities in a wide range of countries. Their research showed that individualistic cultures had a faster pace of living than more collectivist cultures.

Aim

To investigate the influence of culture on pace of life in large cities. The researchers formulated four hypotheses which are important to mention here:

1. Cities with a higher level of affluence and wealth will have a faster pace of life.
2. The hotter the city, the slower the pace of life will be.
3. Individualistic cultures will be faster than collectivist cultures.
4. The larger the city, the faster the pace of life.

Participants

Residents and visitors out and about in cities from a range of 31 countries across the world, both individualist (e.g. USA) and collectivist (e.g. Japan).

Procedure

The researchers, for the sake of practicality, recruited a bank of data collectors to enable them to sample the pace of life in each country: students travelling abroad or returning home and other psychologists in the field of cross-cultural research were given three specific categories under which to observe and collect their data. These categories were:

1. Walking speed of pedestrians.
2. Speed of service at the post office.
3. Accuracy of clocks in banks, selected at random.

Results

The fastest pace of life was observed in Switzerland, with countries in Western Europe and Japan also having high scores. The countries with scores from the middle of the list included the

USA, Eastern European countries and more recently industrialised Asian countries. The slowest pace of life was seen in Latin American counties, the Middle East and non-industrialised Asian countries. Therefore, the four hypotheses were supported by the results, for example the hotter countries were slower, and economic vitality and affluence predicted pace of life, with the wealthier countries being faster.

Conclusion
The individualist/collectivist cultural dimension does appear to be a good predictor as to pace of life in cities.

Evaluation of Levine & Norenzayan (1999)
Strengths
✓ This is an ambitious study, using researchers across the globe to collect a huge amount of data, which increases the reliability of the quantitative data.
✓ The study is high in ecological validity as it was conducted in the real world, using naturalistic observation done covertly.

Limitations
X The nature of the methodology means that there are numerous extraneous variables which could have interfered with the results: e.g. people may walk slowly if they are tired or have a disability; some post officer workers might simply wish to finish their work day on time and so may hurry more towards the end of their shift.
X Analysing such a huge mass of data is time-consuming and some details may get overlooked or possibly misinterpreted due to the many different researchers used in the procedure.

Reference
Levine, R. V., & Norenzayan, A. (1999). The pace of life in 31 countries. *Journal of Cross-cultural Psychology, 30*(2), pp. 178-205

****

KEY STUDY: *Taras et al. (2016). Does country equate with culture? Beyond geography in the search for cultural boundaries.*

Links to
▪ **Sociocultural approach.** Cultural groups

Brief summary
Using a meta-analysis of data from 558 studies, the researchers conducted tests for each of the

four dimensions that comprise Hofstede's original theory. These dimensions are Individualism/ Collectivism; Power Distance; Uncertainty Avoidance and Masculinity/Femininity. Taras et al. (2016) concluded that country is not the same as culture, and that each country contains several different cultures that cross national boundaries.

Aim
To evaluate the extent to which the terms 'culture' and 'country' can be used interchangeably.

Procedure
A meta-analysis of 558 studies from a total of 32 countries that had used Hofstede's cultural dimensions as a framework for defining country and culture in a way which is interchangeable.

Main findings and comments
- The authors suggest that the terms 'country' and 'culture' are frequently used to express the same thing – a set of values, beliefs and behaviours that define a nation. They question whether this is possible as there may be better ways of defining culture than by simply using the term 'country' as a proxy (a substituted term) for 'culture'. They suggest that there may be more suitable factors that could be used to define culture, such as socio-economic status, aspects of lifestyle and beliefs, for example.

- Using 'country' as a proxy for 'culture' only works, in the views of the authors, if said country ḋargely homogenous, with little variation in values, norms and behaviours; and if it is very different from other countries, so that it can easily stand alone to represent 'culture' as well as 'country' as a distinct entity.

- One of the main changes in how we live is that people do not stay put the way that they used to: travel across borders is relatively easy; people migrate long-term to other countries; technology means instant connection to people thousands of miles away; we live in an increasingly global community which does, inevitably, impact upon culture.

- Some research has attempted to 'cluster' cultures within and across country boundaries but thishas often resulted in a confused set of results. The authors suggest that the answer to this conundrum is not to attempt to segment countries but to look for smaller numbers of the population that share cultural values and behaviours in a more homogeneous way but who are separate and different from each other: e.g. section A in this part of the country/world is homogeneous and is distinct from section B which is homogeneous along differentlines.

- The authors point out that Hofstede himself (Hofstede, 1980, 2011) highlighted correlations between his cultural dimensions and specific characteristics such as age, gender, occupation, socioeconomic status and freedom which may be one way of finding 'clusters' of cultural dimensions that are meaningful and which cross borders. The authors note that previous research in this field has assumed that culture is stable, so by changing the parameters (i.e. by not using 'country' as a proxy for 'culture') it may be possible to see the changing, dynamic nature of culture and to appreciate that it is not the sole province of 'country' but of other factors as well.

- After conducting a statistical meta-analysis of the studies, the authors report that using 'country' as a proxy for 'culture' is not fit for purpose. Correlations between each of the four cultural dimensions (as defined by Hofstede) and country did not show any significant result: stronger links were found among the dimensions and gender, age, occupation etc.

- There are real similarities between people from one country and those from another country: the same values can be found between countries thousands of miles apart. The authors propose that factors such as socioeconomic status, equality, freedom, age, occupation and historic era are better markers of culture than the blanket use of 'country'.

Conclusion
Cultural dimensions may be too restrictive in linking 'country' inextricably to 'culture'.

Evaluation of Taras et al. (2016)
Strengths
✓ The use of a meta-analysis gives the researchers access to a mass of data from which they can extract information showing main effects, trends or patterns in a time-efficient way. 558 studies will have provided ample quantitative data, making the findings robust and reliable.
✓ The authors provide new insight into considering culture, providing a relevant way of addressing the realities of life in the 21st century and the increasing ways in which culture is being re- defined as a result of globalization.

Limitations
X The authors themselves point out that the studies they used did not use samples of participants that showed much variability which, to some extent, limits the generalisability of the findings.
X The sampled studies could not use race as a variable by which culture could be measured or defined due to the lack of representation within the studies sampled, limiting the validity of the findings as race/ethnicity must surely be a strong factor in cultural identity which

crosses many national borders.

References

Hofstede, G. (2011). Dimensionalizing cultures: The Hofstede model in context. *Online readings in psychology and culture, 2*(1), Article 8, pp 1-26.

Taras, V., Steel, P., & Kirkman, B. L. (2016). Does country equate with culture? Beyond geography in the search for cultural boundaries. *Management International Review, 56*(4), pp. 455-487.

****

CRITICAL THINKING POINTS: CULTURAL ORIGINS OF BEHAVIOUR AND COGNITION

Does using replications of the Asch paradigm generate too many demand characteristics?
Research on the possible effects of culture on conformity has tended to use either direct replications of the Asch paradigm (Takano & Sogon, 2008) or meta-analyses of cross-cultural replications (Bond & Smith, 1996). One of the main limitations of using this procedure is that it may be subject to an array of demand characteristics, the first of which is that the participants were asked to perform an unusual and highly artificial task - that of matching line lengths. The fact that the task was artificial means that the participants may have felt self-conscious during the procedure and may therefore have not behaved as they would in a more natural setting. The second possible demand characteristic revolves around the task being so easy and unambiguous. It is possible that participants gave the same wrong answer as the confederates simply because the answer given was so obviously wrong that the participants may have wondered, 'What do they know that I don't? Is this a trick?' and may thus have followed the wrong response more out of wariness than conformity. Another demand characteristic may have occurred because Asch's study is very well-known in the psychological literature: modern replications such as Takano & Sogon's from 2008 may have used participants who were already aware of the study, which could then lead to an invalid response.

Perhaps culture has too many variables within it to be able to define it conclusively?
Culture is used as a blanket term to describe an array of variables from the way in which food is cooked and eaten to the deeply held values of a group of people. One of the problems with trying to define and categorise culture (as Hofstede has attempted to do with his research on cultural dimensions) is that it is so wide-ranging, subject to change and to fluctuation that it is difficult to know where to begin when trying to summarise or define it. One of the main drawbacks in trying to agree about what constitutes culture is that an etic approach, where

several cultures are compared, may produce a version of culture which has some bias and which assumes that some values (on appropriate gendered behaviour, for example) are held in the same regard as the culture from which the researcher hails. An emic approach would provide a more enlightened account of each culture; but this too has problems as it is time-consuming, may involve misinterpretation if the researcher is not from the culture he or she is researching and may ultimately be futile if it is based on researching one particular family grouping or geographical location. As Taras et al. (2016) argue in their article, 'country' is not synonymous with 'culture.'

Is some of the methodology involved in culture and cognition problematic?
Both Wang et al. (2008) and Kulkofsky et al. (2011) asked participants to recall personal memories from childhood, giving them only a short amount of time (only 5 minutes in Kulkofsky's study) in which to do so. The nature of this research, in which the researcher should aim for the participant feeling relaxed and comfortable, may make it counterproductive of meaningful results to put a time- limit on the recollecting. It is possible that some of the participants may have felt rushed or pressured, which is an ethical issue, and might also mean that they produce memories that are overly vague, half-complete or even false. It might have been a better idea to either give participants more time during the procedure or to ask them to write down and keep a log of relevant memories as and when they occurred to them within a specific time frame, e.g. one month, after which time the log is given to the researchers.

Memories vary cross-culturally
Adaptation and combination of two cc. images from pixabay.com

TOPIC 3: CULTURAL INFLUENCES ON INDIVIDUAL BEHAVIOUR

Key Idea: Culture has an effect on behaviour.

Content 1: Enculturation.

KEY STUDY: *Fagot (1978). The influence of sex of child on parental reactions to toddler children.*

Links to
- **Sociocultural approach.** Norms.
- **Development.** Developing an identity – gender identity and social roles are culturally mediated.

Background
Enculturation of children into gender roles through differential treatment by parents.

Aim
To investigate if parents treat children differently depending on the gender of the child.

Participants
24 families who each had only one child aged between 20-24 months old; 12 families had one son, the other 12 families had one daughter. The parents were all 20-30 years old, with both parents living at home, and all parents were white and middle-class.

Procedure
This was an overt naturalistic observation: the researchers observed the families in their own homes over a five-week period, involving five separate one-hour observation periods. The behaviours the researchers were observing were categorised into 46 separate child behaviours and 19 separate parental reactions, ranging from positive to neutral to negative. The parents were told
that the research was centred on child behaviour but not that the focus was specifically on gender. The parents were also asked to rate the 46 child behaviours as more appropriate for a boy or a girl or equally for the two after the 5-week observation period was complete.

Results
The researchers found that gender-specific behaviours were given higher approval from parents than cross-gender behaviour. For example, girls met with a negative parental reaction

when they engaged in behaviour that was overly active or which involved fine motor skills, such as manipulating an object. When girls asked for help this was considered a positive behaviour; boys asking for help was viewed negatively. There was no positive correlation found between the observed parental reactions and their responses to the questionnaire. The researchers also noted that the parents did not seem to be aware that they were perpetuating and reinforcing gender stereotypes: when interviewed about their children, the parents of the girls often expressed the opinion that their daughters were competent and capable.

Conclusion

The process of enculturation in terms of reinforcing gender roles and behaviour may operate at a level that parents are simply unaware of but which may be entrenched in the culture.

Evaluation of Fagot (1978)

Strengths

✓ The use of two observers means that the findings have high inter-rater reliability with agreement scores of 93% for child behaviours and 83% for the parent behaviours.

✓ The observations took place over a series of weeks, which means that they provide stronger evidence and more robust and rich data than a single snapshot study. Using a five-week period would also mean that the participants would be less likely to feel self-conscious or uncomfortable in the presence of the observers as they would become more familiar over time.

Limitations

X This research was conducted in the 1970s; ideas about gender have changed massively since then, which makes the findings somewhat lacking in temporal validity.

X The parents may have succumbed to the observer effect, behaving in ways that were not representative of their natural behaviour, such as pandering to stereotypes due to feelings of self- consciousness based on ideas as to what is 'correct' behaviour in context.

Reference

Fagot, B.I. (1978). The influence of sex of child on parental reactions to toddler children. *Child Development, 49* (2), pp. 459-465.

****

KEY STUDY: *Sroufe et al. (1993). The significance of gender boundaries in preadolescence: Contemporary correlates and antecedents of boundary violation and maintenance.*

Links to
- **Sociocultural approach.** Norms.
- **Development.** Developing an identity – gender identity and social roles are 'policed' by peers.

Brief summary
Children who did not behave in a gender-stereotypical way were the least popular with their peers. These studies indicate that children establish a kind of social control in relation to gender roles very early, and it may well be that enculturation by peers is an important factor in gender development.

Aim
To investigate if gender-stereotyped roles are influenced by enculturation by peers.

Participants
48 children who came from households where poverty was an issue and who tended to have young, single mothers with below-average high school completion rates, from Minnesota, USA. 80% were white; 14% were black; 6% were Native American or Hispanic. The children were allocated to one of three groups of 16 (equal numbers of males and females per group). Each group of 16 took part in a 4-week summer camp held on the university campus, at the rate of one group per year. (Each group had a mean age of 10 years at the time of taking part in the camp.)

Procedure
The participants attended the camp 5 days a week for 4.5 hours per day, and during this time they took part in sporting activities, arts, circle time, singing and went on several day trips. The researchers made 317 observations on average per child and they recorded a total of 138 hours of video of each group of 16 with each child appearing more than once on the recording. Event sampling was used, and more than one observer coded the behaviours observed. The type of behaviours that the researchers were interested in were based on gender and included categories such as *no interest shown in the opposite gender; watching opposite members casually or with more intent; relaxed interactions*. They were also particularly interested in what they termed *'Gender Boundary Violating Behaviour'* such as 'hovering' near an opposite gender group for too long; a single child joining an opposite gender group; flirting and behaving in a

provocative way towards the opposite gender. On the last day of camp the children completed an exit poll, rating the popularity of each child at the camp.

Results

The researchers found that gender boundaries were rarely breached and that they appear to represent a valid social norm for children of this age (10 years). Most of the children associated with their own gender, with very little cross-gender interaction observed. This was particularly true for boys who tended to impose harsher sanctions for gender boundary violation. Children who violated gender boundaries were viewed as less popular and more socially incompetent than those who stuck to same-gender activities.

Conclusion

Understanding the rules of gender boundaries appears to determine the extent to which a child is seen as socially competent and it may be one of the products of enculturation.

Evaluation of Sroufe et al. (1993)

Strengths

✓ The use of naturalistic observation means that the findings are high in ecological validity.
✓ The observers used a strict coding method, with several checks being made on the videotaped observations particularly, which means that the research is high in inter-rater reliability.

Limitations

X There are some ethical dilemmas with this study: filming under-16s is fraught with particularly sensitive issues and may have invaded their privacy; rating other children in terms of popularity may also perpetuate stereotypical views on a range of issues; the researchers would have had to ensure that the parents understood the aims and procedure of the research before giving their consent.

X The use of naturalistic observation can produce findings that may be subjective or a result of misinterpretation. For example, 'hovering' may not actually be what the child was doing at the time – they may simply have been waiting for someone, daydreaming or deciding what to do next.

Reference

Sroufe, L. A., Bennett, C., Englund, M., Urban, J., & Shulman, S. (1993). The significance of gender boundaries in preadolescence: Contemporary correlates and antecedents of boundary violation and maintenance. *Child Development, 64*(2), pp. 455-466.

****

KEY STUDY: *Basu et al. (2017). Learning to be gendered: gender socialization in early adolescence among urban poor in Delhi, India, and Shanghai, China.*

Links to
- **Sociocultural approach.** Norms.
- **Development.** Developing an identity – gender identity and social roles are 'policed' by peers.

Background
Comparative study into gender identity in two different collectivist cultures. Argues that we learn to be gendered and the experience is difference for boys and for girls. Parents play a key role in the development of gender roles in collectivist cultures.

Aim
To investigate enculturation in adolescents regarding attitudes towards gender-appropriate behaviour.

Participants
Adolescents aged 11-13 years and their parents. One sample was obtained from a slum area in Delhi, India (16 males, 15 females); the other sample was from a low-income, disadvantaged area
of Shanghai, China (17 males, 17 females). The parents of the adolescents comprised a separate sample (24 from Delhi, 34 from Shanghai). Delhi parents were younger (25-44 years) than the Shanghai parents (35-54 years). 40% of the Delhi parents had no formal education whereas 75% of the Shanghai parents had at least some level of formal education.

Procedure
Narrative interviews of one hour each were conducted with the children and their parents separately. The topic being discussed was 'gender socialisation' with discussions exploring ideas as to how each gender should dress, behave, prepare for adulthood, and so on.

Results
The researchers used thematic analysis which generated a range of themes and norms, some of which were:

- Girls, particularly in Delhi, should be covered up, not wear jeans, just long skirts and should behave in a 'ladylike' way otherwise they would be punished. Boys could wear what they liked and were encouraged to be brave and tough.

- In Shanghai the parents put a lot of emphasis on 'proper' demeanour for girls such as sitting with an upright posture, being calm, gentle and quiet: not behaving like this would bring dishonour on her family. Although boys were not faced with such strictures, they were expected to be polite and considerate towards girls.

- Delhi parents were more focused on girls preparing for life as a wife and mother, whereas the Shanghai parents had expectations of career success for both boys and girls.

- There were huge restrictions in both countries regarding male-female interaction, with most families expressly forbidding it and threatening punishment for even the mildest of interactions, such as looking at a member of the opposite sex.

- Mothers emerged as the most influential and dominant figure in the gender socialisation process, with other significant adults (such as teachers and older siblings) also playing a role. Children from both countries reported that punishments, such as beatings and shaming in front of friends, were used without hesitation for perceived or actual rule violations, particularly those regarding male-female interactions.

Conclusion
Some cultures appear to reinforce traditional gender norms which the researchers felt may have a negative impact on children, e.g. the use of corporal punishment (beatings) for perceived norm violations. The researchers conclude that some cultures adhere to deeply entrenched gender norms which appear to be unequal, e.g. boys being given more freedom than girls.

Evaluation of Basu et al. (2017)
Strengths
- ✓ The use of narrative interviews means that this research collected a good amount of qualitative data that is rich, thick and insightful
- ✓ Conducting the research in India and China was a good decision on the part of the researchers, as these countries are becoming more industrialised and as a result, modernised, so it is interesting to see what influence such modernisation has had on traditional values.

Limitations
X Narrative interviews are extremely time-consuming to analyse and do not always provide data which is useful to the researcher given their unstructured format.

X   The sample size is very small for both countries (who each have large, multi-cultural populations) and in the case of Delhi particularly, represents an uneducated demographic. More affluent areas of the two cities may well have reported less traditional attitudes towards gender socialisation.

Reference

Basu, S., Zuo, X., Lou, C., Acharya, R., & Lundgren, R. (2017). Learning to be gendered: gender socialization in early adolescence among urban poor in Delhi, India, and Shanghai, China. *Journal of Adolescent Health, 61*(4), S24-S29.

****

Content 2: Acculturation

KEY STUDY: *Berry (2005). Acculturation: living successfully in two cultures.*

Links to
- **Sociocultural approach.** Assimilation/assimilate
- **Sociocultural approach HL extension.** How globalization may influence behaviour and the effect of the interaction of local and global influences on behaviour.

Brief summary
There are large group and individual differences in how people (in both groups in contact) go about their acculturation (described in terms of integration, assimilation, separation and marginalisation strategies), in how much stress they experience, and how well they adapt psychologically. The 2006 work (see below) is a survey into immigrant youth.

Aim
To consider the process of acculturation in terms of the best strategies to use so that members of both cultures benefit mutually.

Procedure
An article in which the focus is acculturation strategies that could be used by the non-dominant group (those who have moved to the dominant culture from their culture of origin) for best mutual benefit.

Main findings and comments of 2005 article
Acculturation is a process that can lead to changes in the behaviours, attitudes, views and lifestyles of both the dominant and the non-dominant cultures. The process is not one-way;

both cultures stand to gain or lose aspects of their original culture in the process: e.g. colonisation of one country by another tends to result in some aspects of the colonised culture being lost or modified, but it may also involve the dominant culture gaining something beneficial. For example, the British colonisation of India in the 19th century could be said to have had at least one beneficial result for both parties: the prevalence and huge popularity of Indian food in the UK.

STRATEGY	DEFINITION
Assimilation	This involves an individual immersing him/herself in the dominant culture, with little regard for the culture of origin. Someone using this strategy would wish to be involved in all aspects of the dominant culture: e.g. social groups, work environment, possibly a change of religion.
Separation	This is the opposite strategy to assimilation: it involves the rejection of the dominant culture, a total lack of involvement or interest in it while the culture of origin is preserved, and its traditions adhered to.
Integration	This works as a sort of 'half-way house' between assimilation and separation: involvement with the dominant culture but not at the expense of the culture of origin; an individual maintains a strong cultural identity, but they are also open to embracing the dominant culture. This is thought to be the most successful strategy to avoid *acculturative stress*, a state of anxiety that develops when two cultures clash or when an individual feels conflicted as to their group membership.
Marginalisation	This is a highly negative state for an individual to be in. It is likely that refugees experience marginalisation as it involves having to lose the culture of origin, e.g. fleeing the home country due to war, famine, natural disaster, etc. The individual is likely to feel a sense of being isolated and culture-less, having lost their own culture and having little motivation to immerse themselves in the dominant culture.

Berry (2005) identified four strategies that the incoming, non-dominant group may use in the acculturation process:

Conclusion
For acculturation to be successful the individuals involved must adapt (e.g. their attitudes,

behaviours, expectations, habits) and that adaptation may be the result of a combination of personality traits: e.g. optimism, sociability; life events, e.g. finding work; social support, e.g. having a network of friends.

Evaluation of Berry (2005)

Strengths

✓ The research makes sense: moving to an entirely new culture is fraught with potential stress so it would seem that the best solution is, as Berry suggests, integration as it involves the preservation of original culture as well as the embracing of aspects of the new culture.

✓ This is a holistic approach to behaviour as it acknowledges the roles played by a variety of factors in the acculturation process: e.g. personality, social context, education, friends and family.

Limitations

X The research does not account for people who have a mixed cultural heritage, for example those with parents from two different cultures who have moved into a dominant culture.

X Having only four strategies for acculturation is possibly rather limiting and may not include all aspects and degrees of acculturative approaches.

Reference

Berry, J. W. (2005). Acculturation: Living successfully in two cultures. *International Journal of Intercultural Relations, 29*(6), pp. 697-712.

****

KEY STUDY: *Berry et al. (2006). Immigrant youth in cultural transition: Acculturation, identity, and adaptation across national contexts*

Links to

- **Sociocultural approach.** Assimilation/assimilate

Brief summary

These are some of the main findings from an international study of the acculturation and adaptation of immigrant youth settled in 13 societiesmas well as a sample of national youth. The study investigated how immigrant youth deal with the process of acculturation; how well they adapt and the possible relationships between the two.

Aim

To investigate attitudes towards acculturation in immigrant youths.

Participants

7,997 adolescent immigrants who were either first generation (born in original country) or second generation (born in country to which their parents emigrated), aged 13-18 (mean age 15 years), 52% female, 48% male. 26 cultural backgrounds were represented in the sample, taken from cities in 13 countries around the world including New Zealand, Australia, Canada, Finland, Israel and Portugal.

Procedure

The participants were given a questionnaire, measured via a 5-point rating scale of 'most disagree with' to 'most agree with' statements. The questions were grouped into categories to measure the degree of acculturation, including questions about their attitudes towards their own and the dominant culture; how much peer contact they had within their own and the dominant
culture; attitudes towards family values; if they had experienced discrimination; how well adapted they were psychologically and socially.

Results

36% of the participants demonstrated integration in their responses; similar results have been found with surveys of immigrant adults. One worrying result is that the third largest group to emerge from the data showed a 'confused' sense of cultural identity, akin to marginalisation. The strongest sense of belonging to the original culture emerged from those who lived in ethnically homogeneous neighbourhoods. Girls tended to report that they experienced acculturative stress via depression and anxiety whereas boys dealt with acculturative stress using aggression and confrontation.

Conclusion

Acculturation is not experienced in the same way by all immigrants and there may be further work to be done to encourage integration on both sides.

Evaluation of Berry et al. (2006)
Strengths

✓ This is a huge sample generating robust quantitative data, which makes it easy to compare and to draw conclusions from.
✓ The findings could be used to formulate interventions and strategies for isolated and marginalised immigrants who may well suffer psychological harm without some positive acculturative experiences.

Limitations

X The use of a questionnaire does not allow for qualitative data which could add insight and depth to the findings, shedding light on why as well as what immigrants feel and think.

X   It is possible that some participants may have found the questionnaire overly long and so
they may not have given valid responses to all of the questions.

Reference

Berry, J. W., Phinney, J. S., Sam, D. L., & Vedder, P. E. (2006). *Immigrant Youth in Cultural
Transition: acculturation, identity, and adaptation across national contexts*. Lawrence Erlbaum
Associates.

****

KEY STUDY: *Lueck & Wilson (2010). Acculturative stress in Asian immigrants: The impact of social and linguistic factors.*

Links to

- **Sociocultural approach HL extension.** How globalization may influence behaviour and the
effect of the interaction of local and global influences on behaviour.

Brief summary

Investigated the variables that may predict acculturative stress in a nationally representative
sample of Asian immigrants and Asian Americans.

Aim

To investigate which aspects of language and social contexts can predict acculturative stress in
Asian immigrants who have settled in the USA.

Participants

2095 Asian immigrants, 1271 of whom had been at least 18 years old when they came to the
USA. The sample consisted of 600 Chinese, 508 Filipino, 520 Vietnamese and 467 from other
countries in Asia.

Procedure

The participants responded to a questionnaire which focused on issues such as how proficient
they were in their native language and in English; if they felt guilty about leaving family behind
to move to the USA; prejudicial or discriminatory treatment they had experienced from others;
fear about
being deported; their socio-economic status; relationships within their family; their social
networks and how 'at home' they felt in the USA.

Results

70% of the participants reported having experienced acculturative stress. All variables that the researchers asked the participants about were significantly associated with acculturative stress apart from socio-economic status, gender, social networks and age at time of migration. A key finding was that the ability to speak both English and their native language to a proficient level was negatively correlated with acculturative stress (i.e. the more able in language, the less acculturative stress was reported).

Having strong and cohesive family links also helped ease acculturative stress, but high levels of experience of discrimination increased the stress. Overall the strongest effect was for language proficiency: native language and English skills and, particularly, being bilingual. Loss of the native language contributed significantly to acculturative stress.

Conclusion

Language plays a key role in the process of integration, both the maintenance of the native language as well as the proficient acquisition of the new language.

Evaluation of Lueck & Wilson (2010)

Strengths

- ✓ The sample is representative of the population of Asian immigrants to the USA so the study can be generalised to Asian immigrants to the USA.
- ✓ Previous research on this topic has emphasised the need for migrants to the USA to learn English; this is the first piece of research to highlight the need for bilingualism and the preservation of the native language to ease integration and avoid acculturative stress.

Limitations

- X The participants were interviewed at the time of being recruited but their main responses were via the questionnaire using rating scales and closed questions which limits the explanatory power of their responses.
- X The study lacks ecological validity as it is given in the form of responses to a questionnaire which is an artificial way of gaining insight into real experiences and which may suffer from response bias (i.e. some questions may have led the participants to think that a particular answer was preferred).

Reference

Lueck, K., & Wilson, M. (2010). Acculturative stress in Asian immigrants: the impact of social and linguistic factors. *International Journal of Intercultural Relations, 34*(1), pp. 47-57.

****

KEY STUDY: *Roley et al. (2014). Family cohesion moderates the relationship between acculturative stress and depression in Japanese adolescent temporary residents.*

Links to

- **Sociocultural Approach HL extension:** How globalization may influence behaviour and the effect of the interaction of local and global influences on behaviour.
- **Abnormal Psychology:** Etiology of abnormal psychology - explanations for disorder(s).

Brief summary

Discovered correlations between acculturative stress, depression, likelihood for and seriousness of family conflict, and concluded that strong family relations moderated acculturative stress in Japanese adolescents living temporarily in the USA.

Aim

To investigate the extent to which family cohesion can mediate acculturative stress and depression in acculturating Japanese adolescents.

Participants

26 Japanese adolescents with a mean age of 14 years, 65% female and 35% male who were temporarily residing in the USA, most of whom had been living there for less than 3 years. The second sample comprised 76 parents of children, in grades 1-12, who were attending a Japanese language school in the same area of the USA.

Procedure

The participants were given questionnaires which were then put through correlational analyses so that correlations between the following variables could be calculated: acculturative stress; depressive symptoms; likelihood for family conflict; seriousness of family conflict.

Results

The adolescents' responses revealed significant correlations between acculturative stress and depression, family conflict and seriousness of that conflict. The parent sample showed that acculturative stress was significantly correlated with depressive symptoms. The findings also highlighted the greater risk for depression in adolescents who experience acculturative stress with little parental support; therefore parental support may mediate the negative effects of acculturative stress.

Conclusion

The negative effects of acculturative stress, including depression, can be lessened if an adolescent has supportive parents and a home life where there is minimum conflict.

Evaluation of Roley et al. (2014)

Strengths

✓ Correlations provide data in the form of graphs and correlation coefficients (a statistical calculation) which show the strength and direction of correlations. This gives the researcher a clear way of establishing relationships between variables.

✓ The findings of this research could be applied to intervention strategies or programmes which seek to help temporary – or permanent – immigrants cope with acculturative stress.

Limitations

X Correlations can only show relationships between variables, they cannot show cause-and-effect nor can they explain why the relationship exists.

X The participants were only temporary migrants; knowing that they were returning to Japan at some point may have mitigated the effects of acculturative stress and depression, but this was not measured by the researchers.

Reference

Roley, M. E., Kawakami, R., Baker, J., Hurtado, G., Chin, A., & Hovey, J. D. (2014). Family cohesion moderates the relationship between acculturative stress and depression in Japanese adolescent temporary residents. *Journal of Immigrant and Minority Health, 16*(6), pp. 1299-1302.

****

CRITICAL THINKING POINTS: CULTURAL INFLUENCES ON INDIVIDUAL BEHAVIOUR

Does some research into this topic actually perpetuate stereotypes?

Research by Basu et al. (2017) and Fagot et al. (1978) focuses on the ways in which perceptions of gender influence parenting. Both studies conclude that parents operate different standards when it comes to deciding how to treat daughters and sons, with daughters tending to be viewed as being more needy, dependent and requiring more protection than sons. Basu et al. (2017) highlighted the greater constraints that daughters are put under, with more compliance expected of them with regards to their demeanour, the ways in which they present themselves and their acceptance of traditional roles of wife and mother. Fagot et al. (1978) found that parents tended to express disapproval when their daughters exhibited robust physical behaviour but this disapproval was not extended to sons. It could be argued that, by reporting on attitudes such as these, stereotypical ideas as to what constitutes 'correct' gendered behaviour are reinforced. These findings could also be used to justify the repression of girls to suit an agenda that is based on maintaining highly traditional gender roles in societies in which girls are denied education and free expression.

Shouldn't all research into acculturation be emic?

Research into acculturation seeks to explain the experience of immigrants acclimatising (or not) to the culture into which they have taken up residence. To properly understand what it means to leave one's homeland and move to a new country/culture can only really be achieved by someone who has gone through or is going through that very experience. Taking an 'outsider's' perspective may provide a researcher with an objective view of the experience, but it is ultimately lacking in the one element that would really give the research some credibility and insight: that of the immigrant themselves. It may not be possible for researchers to present a completely unbiased account of the experience of immigrants due to the nature of enculturation (i.e. we are all products of our own cultural upbringing) and it may also not be possible for immigrants who participate in acculturation research to feel 100% natural in their responses, thus threatening the validity of the findings from both ends of the research process.

There is a pressing need for meaningful research to be done into acculturation.

*We live in a world where the sight of refugees fleeing their homeland is almost an everyday news item: footage of people leaving their native country in highly hazardous conditions, often risking (and losing) their lives, to seek refuge in foreign countries. The settling of these refugees in new countries where they face huge challenges such as not speaking the language, contending
with a different climate, food, housing, job prospects, lack of support network, financial hardship can all serve to produce what Berry (2005) terms 'marginalisation'. Berry's research into the experience of immigrants and acculturation is extremely valuable given the high numbers of displaced peoples in the world today. His assertion that integration is the key to a positive transition to the new culture is one from which both the immigrants and the resident community could benefit, with both cultures being enriched by the experience. Finding practical ways of achieving integration is something that needs to be addressed by governments and policy makers across the world.*

****

TOPIC 4 (EXTENSION): THE INFLUENCE OF GLOBALIZATION ON INDIVIDUAL BEHAVIOUR.

Key Idea: Globalization (the growing interconnectedness of the world) has psychological effects on individuals.

Content 1: The effect of the interaction of local and global influences on behaviour

Content 2: Methods used to study the influence of globalization on behaviour

Studies used to investigate acculturation and acculturative stress (see above) may be used for both of these content sections, plus the key studies described in detail below. In the detailed studies below, see the *Brief summary* and *Procedure* sections for the research method, which has been written in bold to help with answering questions on *Content 2: Methods used to study the influence of globalization.*

Berry (2006). Immigrant youth in cultural transition: Acculturation, identity, and adaptation across national contexts.
Etic method - large **survey** comparing international study of the acculturation and adaptation of immigrant youth from 13 different societies together with a sample of national youth.

Lueck & Wilson (2010). Acculturative stress in Asian immigrants: The impact of social and linguistic factors.
Etic method - cross-cultural **survey** of 2095 Asian immigrants and Asian Americans.

Roley et al (2016). Family cohesion moderates the relationship between acculturative stress and depression in Japanese adolescent temporary residents.
Correlational study into acculturative stress, depression and family conflict.

****

KEY STUDY: *Benet-Martinez & Haritatos (2002). Negotiating biculturalism: cultural frame switching in biculturals with oppositional versus compatible cultural identities.*

Brief Summary

Experiment to investigate how individual differences in bicultural identity affect how cultural knowledge is used to interpret social events.

Aim

To investigate variation within, rather than between cultures using the experience of participants with a mixed cultural identity.

Participants

65 first-generation Chinese-Americans (39 female; 26 male; a mean age of 20 years) who attended a West Coast university in the USA. All of the participants had been born in China; all of them had lived there for at least 5 years; all of them were now resident in the USA where they had lived for at least 5 years. This was a self-selecting sample who were paid $12 for their participation in the study.

Procedure

Participants were randomly allocated to one of two conditions:

The American 'priming' condition involved the participants being presented with a series of images that captured aspects of American culture: e.g. the Statue of Liberty, Mickey Mouse, Mount Rushmore.

The Chinese 'priming' condition involved the participants being presented with a series of images that captured aspects of Chinese culture: e.g. the Great Wall of China, a Chinese dragon, the Summer Palace at Beijing.

The participants were then shown an animation of a fish swimming alone in front of a group of other fish. They were asked to respond to a rating scale which measured their interpretation of the fish's behaviour. A rating of 1 indicated agreement with the idea that the fish was responding to group pressure, i.e. that the other fish were bullying or teasing it; a rating of 9 (highest possible) indicated that the participant strongly agreed with the idea that the fish was being independent and had chosen to stand apart from the group, possibly because it had taken on a leadership role. They then filled in a questionnaire that asked them about aspects of their cultural heritage and their bicultural identity.

Results

Participants who had a strong bicultural identity – when primed using American images - and who had integrated well into American life made more internal attributions about the fish's behaviour: i.e. they were more likely to agree that the fish was being independent, in line with individualistic cultural values. The reverse was true for participants with a low bicultural identity:

they made more external attributions, suggesting the fish was being bullied, even when they were primed with American images.

Conclusion

Bicultural identity differs within cultures and may resist the processes of acculturation which involve integration.

Evaluation of Benet-Martinez & Haritatos (2012)

Strengths

✓ Previous research in this field has focused on between-cultures' differences, so this research could be said to have broken new ground by highlighting individual differences within cultures.

✓ The participants all had some similarity in their backgrounds, e.g. living at least 5 years in both countries, so any differences between them should therefore derive from factors involved in integration rather than on having had no experience of one of the cultures.

Limitations

X The participants were self-selecting which imposes a bias on the sample as it tends to be a similar personality type that volunteers to take part in research. The fact that they were paid may also have produced a demand characteristic, as it may have rendered some of their responses artificial if they perhaps felt they were 'supposed' to behave a certain way.

X The length of time lived in each country varied within the sample, with the highest mean coming from the years lived in China (12) compared to the years lived in the USA (8), so this may have produced more of a pro-China mindset in some of the participants.

Reference

Benet-Martínez, V., Leu, J., Lee, F., & Morris, M. W. (2002). Negotiating biculturalism: Cultural frame switching in biculturals with oppositional versus compatible cultural identities. *Journal of Cross-cultural Psychology*, *33*(5), pp. 492-516.

****

KEY STUDY: *Bhugra & Mastrogianni (2004). Globalization and mental disorders: overview with relation to depression.*

Links to
- **Abnormal Psychology.** Sociocultural etiology of depression.

Brief Summary
Meta-analysis of studies focusing on transcultural aspects of depression .

Aim
To investigate how globalization may play a role in depression: from diagnosis through to treatment.

Procedure
This was a **meta-analysis** of research: the findings of at least 91 pieces of research from the 1980s through to the 2000s was analysed with the researchers looking for examples of the ways in which globalization may impact on mental health and contribute to depression and the ways in which depression is treated.

Main findings and comments
- Depression is a disorder that is not culture-specific: people in all cultures experience depression, though it is strongly associated with life in emerging economies with their attendant poverty, ill health, lack of opportunity and lack of food contributing greatly to depression and anxiety, particularly so for women, who tend to report depression twice as often as do men.

- Symptoms may be expressed in culturally specific ways and it may not be appropriate to use Westernised forms of diagnosis such as the DSM (Diagnostics and Statistics manual which classifies mental disorders) for all cultures. However, the march of globalization means that a more universal approach to diagnosing depression may, in fact, take precedence in some cultures and with that the increased use of drug treatments for depression.

- Acculturative stress may be at the heart of some depression-led behaviour, e.g. young Indian women living in London in the late 1990s were involved in self-harm which was linked to the conflict they experienced due to a clash of their Indian culture and the culture of their adopted country (the UK).

- People who have relied on fewer medical or clinical methods for treating their depression, e.g. the use of healers, seeking support from a family and friends network, may begin to regard this treatment as outdated and so may seek modern treatments instead.

Conclusion

Globalization may mean that more people become depressed as they reject traditional treatments and choose modern solutions, which may have a detrimental effect as these modern methods may not suit the cultural profile of an individual.

Evaluation of Bhugra & Mastrogianni (2004)

Strengths

- ✓ At least 20 countries were included in the research analysed with city and village life being part of the overall sample which means that the data is robust and the research is reliable.
- ✓ The findings could be used to inform doctors and clinicians on how to address cross-cultural differences in the diagnosis and treatment of depression as it is short-sighted to assume that 'one size fits all'.

Limitations

- X The research may actually suffer from the fact that it embraces such a diverse sample of cultures because it is difficult to form an overall, clear and objective conclusion. Using such a sample can create 'white noise' (different extraneous variables) within the data, making it difficult to analyse.
- X Some of the findings are overly simplistic. For example, the studies that identify poverty and hunger as sources of depression and anxiety: this does seem to beg the question, 'When are poverty and hunger anything but depressing for those experiencing them?'

Reference

Bhugra, D., & Mastrogianni, A. (2004). Globalization and mental disorders: overview with relation to depression. *The British Journal of Psychiatry*, *184*(1), pp. 10-20.

****

KEY STUDY: *Lyons-Padilla et al. (2015). Belonging nowhere: marginalization and radicalization risk among Muslim immigrants.*

Brief Summary
Survey of Muslims living in the USA.

Aim
To investigate attitudes relating to acculturation and biculturalism in first and second generation Pakistani immigrants.

Participants
198 Muslims living in the USA (107 female; 78 male; 13 gender not specified; mean age of 27 years). 92 of the sample were first-generation immigrants; 105 were second-generation Americans. 105 participants in the sample originally came from Pakistan.

Procedure
Questionnaires, with answers measured via a rating scale. The questions were focused on aspects of acculturation such as assimilation, separation, integration, marginalisation, discrimination and how they felt about radical Islamic groups.

Results
Participants who reported most feelings of marginalisation also reported discrimination more and higher instances of feelings of having lost something significant. These findings predicted more support for radical Islamic fundamentalism and support for groups such as ISIS. High levels of reported separation were also linked to support for radical Islamist groups. Integration was identified as a predictable indicator of less discrimination.

Conclusion
Marginalised individuals may turn against their adopted country if they feel that it has no cultural or spiritual relevance for them. As the researchers state, '*Policymakers clearly need to be able to identify risk factors for the radicalization of established immigrants and to understand
the psychological processes that attract at-risk individuals to violent extremist groups, with an eye toward creating effective prevention-oriented interventions*' (p6).

Evaluation of Lyons-Padilla et al. (2015)
Strengths
✓ Using a range of questionnaires means that the researchers were able to triangulate their

data (check one set of findings against each of the others) which increases internal validity.

✓ The findings have a very direct relevance and could be used to implement interventions and strategies to prevent the danger of disaffected people joining radical groups.

Limitations

X The mean age of the participants was 27 so it may be that some of the more extreme responses were the result of participants 'acting out' - i.e. conforming to macho stereotypes in order to present themselves in a certain way. Their actual behaviour and feelings may not then have been fully and honestly reported.

X Radicalisation is not limited to the USA so these findings may not be as relevant when applied to other countries that have experienced Islam-related terror attacks, such as France.

Reference

Lyons-Padilla, S., Gelfand, M. J., Mirahmadi, H., Farooq, M., & van Egmond, M. (2015). Belonging nowhere: marginalization and radicalization risk among Muslim immigrants. *Behavioral Science & Policy, 1*(2), pp. 1-12.

****

CRITICAL THINKING POINTS: THE INFLUENCE OF GLOBALIZATION ON INDIVIDUAL BEHAVIOUR

Globalization: a good thing or a bad thing?

The march of globalization does not seem to show any signs of abating. With the increasingly sophisticated world in which we live, where technology can create connections and reveal lifestyles, events, behaviours that would previously have remained unknown and hidden, it seems only a matter of time before the world does indeed become the 'global village' predicted by Marshall McLuhan in his book, 'The Gutenberg Galaxy'. From an economic/business standpoint it could be argued that globalization is a good thing as it allows commerce to flow freely with easier communication networks and links between suppliers and customers, thus benefiting communities through increased wealth. It could also be argued that some hidebound attitudes, e.g. about the role of women, about race and ethnicity can be challenged and replaced with more enlightened views that ultimately benefit everyone. Globalization does, however, come at a cost, with one of the risks being cultural imperialism causing traditional values to be discarded in favour of those of a dominant culture. It could even be argued that globalization creates a 'vanilla' culture where cultural values have merged in a way that leads to a lack of distinct features and character, robbing both the dominant and the indigenous cultures of what made them unique.

Does some research in this field create a self-fulfilling prophecy?
Research by Lyons-Padilla et al. (2015) used a group of young Pakistani immigrants to the USA as their sample, asking them questions regarding acculturation and their attitudes towards radical Islamic groups. It could be argued that by drawing attention to issues such as discrimination and marginalisation that the researchers were laying the groundwork for a self-fulfilling prophecy to emerge: e.g. 'This is something that I might experience (discrimination, marginalisation) so why should I feel positive about this culture I've moved to when it clearly does not value me?' Such attitudes may well give rise to hostility towards the dominant culture and the seeking of new meaning and significance via membership of radical groups.

Are some topics too difficult to apply to globalization?
Bhugra & Mastrogianni (2004) attempted to review the ways in which globalization may play a role in depression, from diagnosis through to treatment. One of the problems in attempting to understand the etiology and treatment of depression on a world-wide scale is that, although it is a statistically frequent disorder, with around 25% of adults suffering from depressive symptoms at any one time, it is a disorder which is not experienced in exactly the same way across cultures and across individuals. Some cultures may not even acknowledge that depression exists as a mental
*disorder, preferring to see it as a physical or spiritual ailment that should be treated via methods other than those prescribed by Western ideals,such as drugs. Globalization may account for some depressed patients rejecting traditional diagnoses and treatments of depression, but it does not follow that **all** depressed patients around the world will follow suit – and anyway this would be extremely difficult to track and to measure.*

Reference
McLuhan, M. (1963). *The Gutenberg Galaxy.* Toronto: University of Toronto.

****

We hope you will continue to find this book helpful over the years. For further psychology resources and ideas for using the content in this book, please see our blog at https://psychologysorted.blog/ and our Facebook page https://www.facebook.com/Psychology-Sorted-369513393598737/

These studies are all only suggestions. The best way to teach psychology is design your own course, and use as many varied and interesting up-to-date resources as possible. The best way to study psychology is to find out why you are interested in it, and what in particular grabs your attention, and follow that trail. Good luck and happy studying!

Laura and Claire

All roads lead to psychology
Image adapted from one by Gerd Altmann on pixabay.com

BIBLIOGRAPHY AND AUTHOR INDEX

SECOND EDITION

Pages

Ajzen, I. (1971). Attitudinal vs. Normative messages: an investigation of the differential effects of persuasive communications on behavior. *Sociometry*, pp. 263-280
126, 127, 160-162

Alba, J. W., & Hasher, L. (1983). Is memory schematic? *Psychological Bulletin, 93*(2), pp. 203-231
125, 129, 150-151, 173

Atkinson, R. C., & Shiffrin, R. M. (1968). Human memory: a proposed system and its control processes in K. W. Spence, & J. T. Spence (Eds.), *The Psychology of Learning and Motivation: advances in research and theory*, Vol. 2, pp. 89-195. New York: Academic Press
124, 139-141, 142

Baddeley, A. D., & Hitch, G. (1974). Working memory. In *Psychology of Learning and Motivation, Vol. 8,* pp. 47-48. New York: Academic Press
124, 143-145, 146

Bandura, A. (1986). *Social foundations of thought and action: a social cognitive theory*. Englewood Cliffs, NJ, US: Prentice-Hall.
209, 231-233

Bandura, A., Ross, D., & Ross, S. A. (1961). Transmission of aggression through imitation of aggressive models. *The Journal of Abnormal and Social Psychology, 63*(3), pp. 575-582
209, 228-230, 246

Barr, C. S., Newman, T. K., Shannon, C., Parker, C., Dvoskin, R. L., Becker, M. L., ... & Suomi, S. J. (2004). Rearing condition and rh5-HTTLPR interact to influence limbic-hypothalamic-pituitary- adrenal axis response to stress in infant macaques. *Biological Psychiatry, 55*(7), pp. 733-738
20, 23, 103-105, 117, 121, 122.

Bartlett, F. C., & Burt, C. (1933). Remembering: A study in experimental and social psychology. *British Journal of Educational Psychology, 3*(2), pp. 187-192
125, 128, 148-150, 173

Basu, S., Zuo, X., Lou, C., Acharya, R., & Lundgren, R. (2017). Learning to be gendered: gender socialization in early adolescence among urban poor in Delhi, India, and Shanghai, China. *Journal of Adolescent Health, 61*(4), S24-S29
215, 272-274, 281

Pages

Beesley, S. J., Hopkins, R. O., Holt-Lunstad, J., Wilson, E. L., Butler, J., Kuttler, K. G. & Hirshberg, E. L. (2018). Acute Physiologic Stress and Subsequent Anxiety Among Family Members of ICU Patients. *Critical Care Medicine*, *46*(2), pp.229-235 — **12,** 65-66

Benet-Martínez, V., Leu, J., Lee, F.,& Morris, M. W.(2002).Negotiating biculturalism: Cultural frame switching in biculturals with oppositional versus compatible cultural identities. *Journal of Cross-Cultural Psychology*, *33*(5), pp.492-516 — **219, 220,** 284-285

Bennett, C. M., & Miller, M. B. (2010). How reliable are the results from functional magnetic resonance imaging? *Annals of the New York Academy of Sciences*, *1191*(1), pp. 133-155 — **4,** 29-30, 60

Berry, J. W., Phinney, J. S., Sam, D. L., & Vedder, P. E. (2006). *Immigrant Youth in Cultural Transition: acculturation, identity, and adaptation across national contexts*. Lawrence Erlbaum Associates. — **216, 218, 220,** 276-278, 283

Berry, J. W. (2005). Acculturation: Living successfully in two cultures. *International Journal of Intercultural Relations*, *29*(6), pp. 697-712 — **216, 218,** 282

Bhugra, D., & Mastrogianni, A. (2004). Globalization and mental disorders: overview with relation to depression. *The British Journal of Psychiatry*, *184*(1), pp. 10-20 — **219, 220,** 286-287, 290.

Blacker, K. J., Curby, K. M., Klobusicky, E., & Chein, J. M. (2014). Effects of action video game training on visual working memory. *Journal of Experimental Psychology: Human Perception and Performance*, *40*(5), pp. 1992-2004 — **133, 136,** 196-197, 198, 203, 205

Bond, R., & Smith, P. B. (1996). Culture and conformity: A meta-analysis of studies using Asch's (1952b, 1956) line judgment task. *Psychological Bulletin*, *119*(1), pp. 111-137 — **212,** 248-250, 251, 266

British Psychological Society (2012). *Guidelines for Psychologists Working with Animals.* BPS: Leicester, UK — **22, 23, 24,** 114-115, 117, 119, 121

	Pages
Brown, R., & Kulik, J. (1977). Flashbulb memories. *Cognition, 5*(1), pp. 73-99	**131,** 178-179, 189
Caspi, A., Sugden, K., Moffitt, T. E., Taylor, A., Craig, I. W., Harrington, H., ... & Poulton, R. (2003). Influence of life stress on depression: moderation by a polymorphism in the 5-HTT gene. *Science, 301*(5631), pp. 386-389	**15,** 79-80, 95
Chan, S., & Harris, J. (2011). Moral enhancement and pro-social behaviour. *Journal of Medical Ethics, 37* (3), pp.130-131	**11,** 54-55
Christakis, N. A., & Fowler, J. H. (2014). Friendship and natural selection. *Proceedings of the National Academy of Sciences, 111*(Supplement 3), pp. 10796-10801	**17,** 89-90,
Conner, M., & Heywood-Everett, S. (1998). Addressing mental health problems with the theory of planned behaviour. *Psychology, Health & Medicine, 3*(1), pp. 87-95	**126,** 163-164
Conner, M., McEachan, R., Jackson, C., McMillan, B., Woolridge, M., & Lawton, R. (2013). Moderating effect of socioeconomic status on the relationship between health cognitions and behaviors. *Annals of Behavioral Medicine, 46*(1), pp. 19-30	**126,** 165-166
Conroy-Beam, D., & Buss, D. M. (2016). Do mate preferences influence actual mating decisions? Evidence from computer simulations and three studies of mated couples. *Journal of Personality and Social Psychology, 111*(1), pp. 53-66	**18,** 94-95
Corkin, S., Amaral, D. G., González, R. G., Johnson, K. A., & Hyman, B. T. (1997). HM's medial temporal lobe lesion: findings from magnetic resonance imaging. *Journal of Neuroscience, 17*(10), 3964-3979	**7,** 40-42, **124,** 139, 141,
Crockett, M. J., Clark, L., Hauser, M. D., & Robbins, T. W. (2010). Serotonin selectively influences moral judgment and behavior through effects on harm aversion. *Proceedings of the National Academy of Sciences, 107*(40), pp. 17433-17438	**10,** 11, 52-53, 54, 55, 60
Cox, J. R., & Griggs, R. A. (1982). The effects of experience on performance in Wason's selection task. *Memory & Cognition, 10*(5), pp. 496-502	**159-160**
Dixson, B.J.W. (2016). Waist-to-hip ratio, in T.K. Shackelford, V.A. Weekes-Shackelford (eds.), *Encyclopedia of Evolutionary Psychological Science*. Springer: Switzerland	**18,** 92-93

	Pages
DiYanni, C. J., Corriveau, K. H., Kurkul, K., Nasrini, J., & Nini, D. (2015). The role of consensus and culture in children's imitation of inefficient actions. *Journal of Experimental Child Psychology, 137*, pp. 99-110	**212,** 252-254
Evans, J. S. B. (2003). In two minds: dual-process accounts of reasoning. *Trends in Cognitive Sciences, 7* (10), pp. 454-459	**126,** 158-160
Fagot, B.I. (1978). The influence of sex of child on parental reactions to toddler children. *Child Development, 49* (2), pp. 459-465	**215,** 268-269, 281,
Fernald, L. C., & Gunnar, M. R. (2009). Poverty-alleviation program participation and salivary cortisol in very low-income children. *Social Science & Medicine, 68*(12), pp. 2180-2189	**12,** 61-62, 78
Fisher, H., Aron, A., Mashek, D. J., Strong, G., Li, H., & Brown, L. L. (2005). Reward, motivation, and emotion systems associated with early-stage intense romantic love. *Journal of Neurophysiology, 94*(1), pp. 327-337.	2, **4, 5, 9,** 27-28, 60
Freeman D., Reeve, S., Robinson, A., Ehlers, A., Clark, D., Spanlang, B., & Slater, M. (2017). Virtual reality in the assessment, understanding, and treatment of mental health disorders. *Psychological Medicine, 47*(14), pp. 2393-2400	**134,** 201-202
Gerardi, M., Rothbaum, B. O., Ressler, K., Heekin, M., & Rizzo, A. (2008). Virtual reality exposure therapy using a virtual Iraq: case report. *Journal of Traumatic Stress, 21*(2), pp. 209-213	**134, 137,** 198-199, 204
Glanzer, M., & Cunitz, A. R. (1966). Two storage mechanisms in free recall. *Journal of Verbal Learning and Verbal Behavior, 5*(4), pp. 351-360	**124,** 141-143
Gotgay, G., Giedd, J., Lusk, L., Hayashi, K., Greenstein, D., Vaituzis, A., Nugent III, T., Herman, D., Clasen, L., Toga, A., Rapoport, J., Thompson, P. (2004). Dynamic Mapping of Human Cortical Development During Childhood Through Early Adulthood. *Proceedings of the National Academy of Sciences, 101*(21), pp. 8174-8179	**7,** 38-40
Guo, J., Kyle Simmons, W., Herscovitch, P., Martin, A. & Hall, K.D. (2014). Striatal dopamine D2-like receptor correlation patterns with human obesity and opportunistic eating behavior. *Molecular Psychiatry, 19* (10), pp. 1078-1084	**10,** 47-49
Hamilton, D. L., & Gifford, R. K. (1976). Illusory correlation in interpersonal perception: A cognitive basis of stereotypic judgments. *Journal of Experimental Social Psychology, 12*(4), pp. 392-407	**14,** 235-237

Pages

Hare, R. M., Schlatter, S., Rhodes, G., & Simmons, L. W. (2017). Putative sex-specific human pheromones do not affect gender perception, attractiveness ratings or unfaithfulness judgements of opposite sex faces. *Royal Society Open Science*, *4*(3), 160831 — **13,** 76-77, 78

Hembrooke, H., & Gay, G. (2003). The laptop and the lecture: The effects of multitasking in learning environments. *Journal of Computing in Higher Education*, *15*(1), pp. 46-64 — **133, 136,** 192-194, 203

Hofstede, G. (2011). Dimensionalizing cultures: The Hofstede model in context. *Online readings in psychology and culture*, *2*(1), Article 8, pp 1-26. — 217

Hofstede, G., 1980. *Culture's Consequences: international differences in work-related values.* Beverly Hills, CA: Sage — **214,** 260-262, 264, 265, 266

Howarth, C. (2002). So, you're from Brixton?' The struggle for recognition and esteem in a stigmatized community. *Ethnicities*, *2*(2), pp. 237-260 — **208,** 225-226

Inoue, Y., Takahashi, T., Burriss, R. P., Arai, S., Hasegawa, T., Yamagishi, T., & Kiyonari, T. (2017). Testosterone promotes either dominance or submissiveness in the Ultimatum Game depending on players' social rank. *Scientific Reports*, *7*, pp. 1-9 — **12,** 68-70, 78

Jackson, S. E., Kirschbaum, C., & Steptoe, A. (2017). Hair cortisol and adiposity in a population- based sample of 2,527 men and women aged 54 to 87 years. *Obesity*, *25*(3), pp. 539-544 — **20,** 107-108, 121

Joyce, N., & Harwood, J. (2014). Improving intergroup attitudes through televised vicarious intergroup contact: Social cognitive processing of in-group and out-group information. *Communication Research*, *41*(5), pp. 627-643 — **209,** 233--235

Kulkofsky, S., Wang, Q., Conway, M. A., Hou, Y., Aydin, C., Mueller-Johnson, K., & Williams, H. (2011). Cultural variation in the correlates of flashbulb memories: An investigation in five countries. *Memory*, *19*(3), pp. 233-240 — **213,** 258-259, 267

Lashley, K.S. (1930). Basic neural mechanisms in behavior. *Psychology Review*, 37, pp. 1–24 — **5,** 35

Pages

Lassi, G., & Tucci, V. (2017). Gene-environment interaction influences attachment-like style in mice. *Genes, Brain and Behavior, 16*(6), pp. 612-618 — **21,** 112-113

Lerner, J. S., Li, Y., Valdesolo, P., & Kassam, K. S. (2015). Emotion and decision making. *Annual Review of Psychology, 66*, pp. 799-823 — **132,** 187-188

Levine, R. V., & Norenzayan, A. (1999). The pace of life in 31 countries. *Journal of Cross-cultural Psychology, 30*(2), pp. 178-205 — **214,** 262-263

Loftus, E. F., & Palmer, J. C. (1974). Reconstruction of Automobile Destruction: an example of the interaction between language and memory. *Journal of Verbal Learning and Verbal Behavior, 13*(5), pp. 585-589 — **128,** 129, 168-169, 176,

Luby, J., Belden, A., Botteron, K., Marrus, N., Harms, M. P., Babb, C., ... & Barch, D. (2013). The effects of poverty on childhood brain development: the mediating effect of caregiving and stressful life events. *JAMA pediatrics, 167*(12), pp.1135-1142 — **8,** 43-44, 97, 101

Lueck, K., & Wilson, M. (2010). Acculturative stress in Asian immigrants: the impact of social and linguistic factors. *International Journal of Intercultural Relations, 34*(1), pp. 47-57 — **216, 218, 220,** 278-279, 283

Lynskey, M. T., Agrawal, A., & Heath, A. C. (2010). Genetically informative research on adolescent substance use: methods, findings, and challenges. *Journal of the American Academy of Child & Adolescent Psychiatry, 49*(12), pp. 1202-1214 — **17,** 87-88

Lyons-Padilla, S., Gelfand, M. J., Mirahmadi, H., Farooq, M., & van Egmond, M. (2015). Belonging nowhere: marginalization and radicalization risk among Muslim immigrants. *Behavioral Science & Policy, 1*(2), pp. 1-12 — 217, **219, 220,** 221, 288-289, 290

Maguire, E. A., Gadian, D. G., Johnsrude, I. S., Good, C. D., Ashburner, J., Frackowiak, R. S., & Frith, C.D. (2000). Navigation-related structural change in the hippocampi of taxi drivers. *Proceedings of the National Academy of Sciences, 97*(8), pp. 4398-4403 — **4, 5, 7,** 33-34, 40

McGue, M., Elkins, I., & Iacono, W. G. (2000). Genetic and environmental influences on adolescent substance use and abuse. *American Journal of Medical Genetics Part A, 96*(5), pp. 671-677 — **17,** 85-87

	Pages
McLuhan, M. (1963). *The Gutenberg Galaxy.* Toronto: University of Toronto	290
Meyer, M. M., Buchner, A., & Bell, R. (2015). Influences of Age and Emotion on Source Guessing: are older adults more likely to show fear-relevant illusory correlations? *Journals of Gerontology Series B: Psychological Sciences and Social Sciences, 71*(5), pp. 831-840	**210,** 240-241
Miller, G. E., Chen, E., & Zhou, E. S. (2007). If it goes up, must it come down? Chronic stress and the hypothalamic-pituitary-adrenocortical axis in humans. *Psychological Bulletin, 133*(1), pp. 25-45	**12,** 63-65
Milner, B., Corkin, S., & Teuber, H. L. (1968). Further analysis of the hippocampal amnesic syndrome: 14-year follow-up study of HM. *Neuropsychologia, 6*(3), pp. 215-234	**7,** 40-42, **124,** 139, 141
Morina, N., Ijntema, H., Meyerbröker, K., & Emmelkamp, P. M. (2015). Can virtual reality exposure therapy gains be generalized to real-life? A meta-analysis of studies applying behavioral assessments. *Behaviour Research and Therapy, 74,* pp. 18-24	**134, 137,** 199-201, 204, 205
Murphy, T., Dias, G. P., & Thuret, S. (2014). Effects of diet on brain plasticity in animal and human studies: mind the gap. *Neural Plasticity,* Article ID 563160	**19,** 101-102
National Institute of Health (2010). *Human Connectome Project.* University of Southern California, at http://www.humanconnectomeproject.org/	**5,** 35
Nave, G., Nadler, A., Zava, D., & Camerer, C. (2017). Single-dose testosterone administration impairs cognitive reflection in men. *Psychological Science, 28*(10), pp. 1398-1407	**13,** 70-71
Neisser, U., & Harsch, N. (1992). Phantom flashbulbs: False recollections of hearing the news about Challenger. In E. Winograd & U. Neisser (Eds.), *Emory symposia in cognition, 4. Affect and accuracy in recall: studies of 'flashbulb' memories* (pp. 9-31). New York: Cambridge University Press	**131,** 179-181, 189
Nithiantharajah, J. & Hannan, A. J. (2006). Enriched environments, experience-dependent plasticity and disorders of the nervous system. *Nature Reviews Neuroscience, 7*(9), pp. 697-709	**21,** 110-112
Pavkov, T. W., Lewis, D. A., & Lyons, J. S. (1989). Psychiatric diagnoses and racial bias: an empirical investigation. *Professional Psychology: Research and Practice, 20*(6), pp. 364-368	**126, 130,** 156-157, 174, 177

Pages

Pegg, K. J., O'Donnell, A. W., Lala, G., & Barber, B. L. (2017). The role of online social identity in the relationship between alcohol-related content on social networking sites and adolescent alcohol use. *Cyberpsychology, Behavior, and Social Networking, 21*, 50-55 — **208,** 227-228

Prensky, M. (2009). H. sapiens digital: From digital immigrants and digital natives to digital wisdom. *Innovate: Journal of Online Education, 5*(3), p.1 — 205

Risch, N., Herrell, R., Lehner, T., Liang, K. Y., Eaves, L., Hoh, J., ... & Merikangas, K. R. (2009). Interaction between the serotonin transporter gene (5-HTTLPR), stressful life events, and risk of depression: a meta-analysis. *Jama, 301*(23), pp. 2462-2471 — **15,** 81-82

Robbins, T. W., Anderson, E. J., Barker, D. R., Bradley, A. C., Fearnyhough, C., Henson, R., ... & Baddeley, A. D. (1996). Working memory in chess. *Memory & Cognition, 24*(1), pp. 83-93 — **124,** 145-146

Rogoff, B., & Waddell, K. J. (1982). Memory for information organized in a scene by children from two cultures. *Child Development*, pp. 1224-1228 — **212,** 254-255

Roley, M. E., Kawakami, R., Baker, J., Hurtado, G., Chin, A., & Hovey, J. D. (2014). Family cohesion moderates the relationship between acculturative stress and depression in Japanese adolescent temporary residents. *Journal of Immigrant and Minority Health, 16*(6), pp. 1299-1302 — **216, 218, 220,** 280--281, 283

Romach, M.K., Glue, P., Kampman, K. et al. (1999). Attenuation of the Euphoric Effects of Cocaine by the Dopamine D1/D5 Antagonist Ecopipam (SCH 39166). *Archives of General Psychiatry, 56*(12), pp. 1101–1106. Doi:10.1001/archpsyc.56.12.1101 — **10,** 50-51

Rosen, L. D., Lim, A. F., Carrier, L. M., & Cheever, N. A. (2011). An empirical examination of the educational impact of text message-induced task switching in the classroom: educational implications and strategies to enhance learning. *Psicología Educativa, 17*(2), pp. 163-177 — **133, 136,** 190-192, 197, 203, 204

Rosenzweig, M. R., Diamond, M. C., Bennett, E. L., Lindner, B., & Lyon, L. (1972). Effects of environmental enrichment and impoverishment on rat cerebral cortex. *Developmental Neurobiology, 3*(1), pp. 47-64 — **19, 22,** 97-98, 114

Scheinost, D., Sinha, R., Cross, S. N., Kwon, S. H., Sze, G., Constable, R. T., & Ment, L. R. (2016). Does prenatal stress alter the developing connectome? *Pediatric Research, 81*(1-2), pp. 214-226 — **24,** 119-120, 121

	Pages
Schmaal, L., Veltman, D. J., van Erp, T. G., Sämann, P. G., Frodl, T., Jahanshad, N., ... & Vernooij, M.W. (2016). Subcortical brain alterations in major depressive disorder: findings from the ENIGMA Major Depressive Disorder working group. *Molecular psychiatry, 21*(6), p. 806	**5,** 37-38
Schneider, W., & Niklas, F. (2017). Intelligence and verbal short-term memory/ working memory: Their interrelationships from childhood to young adulthood and their impact on academic achievement. *Journal of Intelligence, 5*(2), pp. 26-45	**124,** 147-148
Shewach, O. R., Sackett, P. R., & Quint, S. (2019). Stereotype threat effects in settings with features likely versus unlikely in operational test settings: A meta-analysis. *Journal of Applied Psychology, 104*(12), pp. 1514-1534	**211,** 245-246
Shively, C. A., Register, T. C., & Clarkson, T. B. (2009). Social stress, visceral obesity, and coronary artery atherosclerosis: product of a primate adaptation. *American Journal of Primatology, 71*(9), pp. 742-751	**20,** 105-107, 108, 121
Singh, D. (1993). Adaptive significance of female physical attractiveness: role of waist-to-hip ratio. *Journal of Personality and Social Psychology, 65*(2), pp. 293-307	**18,** 90-91, 92, 93, 96
Slovic, P., Finucane, M. L., Peters, E., & MacGregor, D. G. (2007). The affect heuristic. *European Journal of Operational Research, 177*(3), pp. 1333-1352	**132,** 184-186, 189
Smith, M. R., & Alpert, G. P. (2007). Explaining police bias: A theory of social conditioning and illusory correlation. *Criminal Justice and Behavior, 34*(10), pp. 1262-1283	**210,** 237-239
Sparrow, B., Liu, J., & Wegner, D. M. (2011). Google effects on memory: cognitive consequences of having information at our fingertips. *Science,* 1207745. DOI: 10.11265	**133, 137,** 194-195, 197, 203
Spencer, S. J., Steele, C. M., & Quinn, D. M. (1999). Stereotype threat and women's math performance. *Journal of Experimental Social Psychology, 35*(1), pp. 4-28.	**211,** 243-244
Sroufe, L. A., Bennett, C., Englund, M., Urban, J., & Shulman, S. (1993). The significance of gender boundaries in preadolescence: Contemporary correlates and antecedents of boundary violation and maintenance. *Child Development, 64*(2), pp. 455-466	**215,** 270-271

	Pages
Stanton, M. A., Heintz, M. R., Lonsdorf, E. V., Santymire, R. M., Lipende, I., & Murray, C. M. (2015). Maternal 302ehaviour and physiological stress levels in wild chimpanzees (Pan troglodytes schweinfurthii). *International Journal of Primatology, 36*(3), pp. 473-488	**23,** 117-118
Steele, C. M., & Aronson, J. (1995). Stereotype threat and the intellectual test performance of African Americans. *Journal of Personality and Social Psychology, 69*(5), p.797	**210,** 241-243
Stone, C. B., Luminet, O., & Takahashi, M. (2015). Remembering Public, Political Events: A Cross- Cultural and-Sectional Examination of Australian and Japanese Public Memories. *Applied Cognitive Psychology, 29*(2), pp. 280-290	**131,** 181-182
Streeter, C. C., Whitfield, T. H., Owen, L., Rein, T., Karri, S. K., Yakhkind, A., ... & Jensen, J. E. (2010). Effects of yoga versus walking on mood, anxiety, and brain GABA levels: a randomized controlled MRS study. *The Journal of Alternative and Complementary Medicine, 16*(11), 1145-1152	**11,** 58-59
Sundali, J., & Croson, R. (2006). Biases in casino betting: The hot hand and the gambler's fallacy. *Judgment and Decision Making, 1*(1), pp. 1-12	**130,** 174-176
Tajfel, H., Billig, M. G., Bundy, R. P., & Flament, C. (1971). Social categorization and intergroup behaviour. *European Journal of Social Psychology, 1*(2), pp. 149-178	**208,** 223-224
Takano, Y., & Sogon, S. (2008). Are Japanese more collectivistic than Americans? Examining conformity in in-groups and the reference-group effect. *Journal of Cross-Cultural Psychology, 39*(3), pp. 237-250	**212,** 250-251, 266
Taras, V., Steel, P., & Kirkman, B. L. (2016). Does country equate with culture? Beyond geography in the search for cultural boundaries. *Management International Review, 56*(4), pp. 455-487	**214,** 263-266, 267
Thimm, J. C. (2017). Relationships between early maladaptive schemas, mindfulness, self- compassion, and psychological distress. *International Journal of Psychology and Psychological Therapy, 17*, pp. 1-15	**125, 129,** 152-153, 173
Thomas, C., & Baker, C. I. (2013). Teaching an adult brain new tricks: a critical review of evidence for training-dependent structural plasticity in humans. *NeuroImage, 73*, pp. 225-236	**4,** 31-33

Pages

Tiedens, L. Z., & Linton, S. (2001). Judgment under emotional certainty and uncertainty: the effects of specific emotions on information processing. *Journal of Personality and Social Psychology, 81*(6), pp. 973-988 — **132,** 183-184

Tobi, E. W., Slieker, R. C., Luijk, R., Dekkers, K. F., Stein, A. D., Xu, K. M., ... & Biobank-based Integrative Omics Studies Consortium (2018). DNA methylation as a mediator of the association between prenatal adversity and risk factors for metabolic disease in adulthood. *Science Advances, 4*(1), eaao4364 — **16,** 84-85

Tremblay, P., Dick, A. S., & Small, S. L. (2013). Functional and structural aging of the speech sensorimotor neural system: functional magnetic resonance imaging evidence. *Neurobiology of aging, 34*(8), pp. 1935-1951 — **5,** 35-36

Tversky, A., & Kahneman, D. (1974). Judgement under Uncertainty: heuristics and biases. *Science, 185*(4157), pp. 1124-1131 — **126, 130,** 154-156, 174

Volkow, N. D., Fowler, J. S., Wang, G. J., & Swanson, J. M. (2004). Dopamine in drug abuse and addiction: results from imaging studies and treatment implications. *Molecular psychiatry, 9*(6), pp. — **9,** 45-47

Vredeveldt, A., Groen, R. N., Ampt, J. E., & Koppen, P. J. (2017). When discussion between eyewitnesses helps memory. *Legal and Criminological Psychology, 22*(2), pp. 242-259 — **128,** 171-173

Wang, Q. (2008). Being American, being Asian: the bicultural self and autobiographical memory in Asian Americans. *Cognition, 107*(2), pp. 743-751 — **213,** 256-257, 267

Wason, P. (1966). Reasoning, in B.M. Foss (ed.), *New Horizons in Psychology.* Harmondsworth: Penguin — 158-160

Weaver, I. C., Cervoni, N., Champagne, F. A., et al. (2004). Epigenetic programming by maternal behavior. *Nature Neuroscience, 7*(8), pp. 847-854 — **20, 23,** 109-110, 119

Wedekind, C., Seebeck, T., Bettens, F., & Paepke, A. J. (June 1995). MHC-dependent mate preferences in humans. *Proceedings of the Royal Society, London: Biology, 260* (1359), pp. 245-249 — **14,** 74-75

Wexler, B. E. (2010). Neuroplasticity, cultural evolution and cultural difference. *World Cultural Psychiatry Research Review, 5*, pp. 11-22 — **19,** 99-100

Pages

Xu, F., Wu, Q., Xie, L., Gong, W., Zhang, J., Zheng, P., ... & Fang, L. (2015). Macaques exhibit a naturally occurring depression similar to humans. *Scientific Reports, 5, Article 9220*, pp. 1-10 — **22,** 115-116

Yehuda, R., Daskalakis, N. P., Bierer, L. M., Bader, H. N., Klengel, T., Holsboer, F., & Binder, E. B. (2016). Holocaust exposure induced intergenerational effects on FKBP5 methylation. *Biological Psychiatry, 80*(5), pp. 372-380 — **15,** 82-83

Young, S. N. (2013). The effect of raising and lowering tryptophan levels on human mood and social behaviour. *Philosophical Transactions of the Royal Society B: Biological Sciences, 368*(1615), 20110375 — **11,** 56-58

Yuille, J. C., & Cutshall, J. L. (1986). A case study of eyewitness memory of a crime. *Journal of Applied Psychology, 71*(2), pp. 291-301 — **128,** 169-171

Zak, P. J., Kurzban, R., Ahmadi, S., Swerdloff, R. S., Park, J., Efremidze, L., ... & Matzner, W. (2009). Testosterone administration decreases generosity in the ultimatum game. *PloS One, 4*(12), e8330. — **12,** 67-68

Zhou, W., Yang, X., Chen, K., Cai, P., He, S., & Jiang, Y. (2014). Chemosensory communication of gender through two human steroids in a sexually dimorphic manner. Current Biology, 24(10), pp. 1091-1095. — **14,** 72-73

Printed in Poland
by Amazon Fulfillment
Poland Sp. z o.o., Wrocław

61402591R00182